I0890954

Developing Global Business Communication in Asia

This book is an essential guide for anyone who wishes to develop successful business communication. It provides authentic and memorable workplace scenarios where learners become English communicators when solving authentic problems doing business together.

The book aims to help learners:

- Use authentic workplace materials to solve problems using English
- Understand how language can be used as a lingua franca effectively when communicating
- Understand how intertextuality between shared spoken and written texts drives communication
- Improve communicative performance in spoken and written texts
- Become familiar with the communication realities of workplaces that are becoming increasingly technology driven and globalised

This book will help learners become better equipped with communication strategies through its real life applicable and skills-based examples and will be a useful reference in the digital age.

Jane Lockwood is currently Adjunct Associate Professor in the Department of English at Hong Kong Polytechnic University after working in educational management and academic teaching and research at the University of Education and City University of Hong Kong. She completed her doctorate studies at Hong Kong University where she investigated the impact of business communication on in-house courses in Hong Kong workplaces. She has published widely on business English in the workplace with specific reference to the business processing outsourcing industry (BPO) in Asia, and on how business English communication is being impacted by technology. Her primary interest is in turning theoretical findings into practical educational usage. She has co-published a coursebook, *Contact US*; developed the business performance language assessment scale (BUPLAS) framework for the BPO industry in Asia and developed business English curricula for a wide range of businesses and universities.

Neil Elias is currently CEO of Future Perfect business English specialists. For the past 35 years Neil has been based in Asia-Pacific, generally in the financial services and offshore outsourcing industries. With a background in information technology and consulting, he became the first Asian Regional IT Director for an Australian insurance group with responsibility for six countries including PRC and Thailand. Returning to consulting, he set up a Japanese operation for a US/Indian technology company before being headhunted to set up and manage a Philippines operation for a large US-based financial group. In 2006, he was again selected to start up a Philippines operation centre for a European IT Group, Logica, as well as serving as director of Future Perfect, a business training company in the Philippines. He left Logica when it was taken over in 2012, and took on the CEO role at Future Perfect. Neil served on the Board of Trustees of the Business Processing Association of the Philippines and on the board of the European Chamber of Commerce.

Developing Global Business Communication in Asia

A Business Simulated Case Study Approach

Jane Lockwood and Neil Elias

Routledge
Taylor & Francis Group
LONDON AND NEW YORK

First published 2021
by Routledge
2 Park Square, Milton Park, Abingdon, Oxon OX14 4RN

and by Routledge
52 Vanderbilt Avenue, New York, NY 10017

Routledge is an imprint of the Taylor & Francis Group, an informa business

British Library Cataloguing-in-Publication Data
A catalogue record for this book is available from the British Library

Library of Congress Cataloging-in-Publication Data
A catalog record for this book has been requested

ISBN: 978-0-367-35652-1 (hbk)
ISBN: 978-0-367-35653-8 (pbk)
ISBN: 978-0-429-34096-3 (ebk)

Typeset in ITC Galliard
by Apex CoVantage, LLC

Access the Support Material: www.routledge.com/9780367356538

Contents

Acknowledgements

The authors would like to acknowledge the two entities below for the quality and depth of their work in both research and practice which helped shape our approach in this book.

- Future Perfect Business English Limited: Hong Kong, Manila, Bengaluru
- Research Centre for Professional Communication in English (RCPCE), Department of English, Hong Kong Polytechnic University

We would also like to thank Nick, Dan and Tom for their advice and assistance in ensuring the business scenarios reflected the real world of advertising and information technology.

Introduction

1. Introduction

Business English applied linguists have complained for decades that business English coursebooks have been market-led rather than research-led; after all, business English is a big lucrative business in itself. *Developing Global Business Communication in Asia* is based on an authentic case study and is research-led; it has been written to meet the needs of undergraduate and postgraduate courses in business English communication in Asia. This means that the reading and listening texts, and the spoken and written activities are authentic and reflect what the research is saying is critical in the development of business English skills for Asian students. Many of the existing coursebooks on the commercial market typically use only face-to-face contexts, they involve only Western companies and they generally assume Western language and cultural norms. This coursebook challenges those assumptions and provides a more nuanced and research-led approach for Asian students who want to understand and develop their English communication for global business.

Over the last two decades, research and practice increasingly show that Asian global businesses use English in a very pragmatic way, relying mostly on their use of 'English as a lingua franca'. It is now the case that more second language speakers use English with other second language speakers for business; this huge and continued shift now means that Asian students need nuanced English language and intercultural competencies as they develop their skills using Business English as a Lingua Franca (BELF) with L1 and L2 speakers. The traditional notion that good English language and intercultural skills in the workplace aspire to Western English-speaking norms is fast being replaced by BELF norms where second language speakers interact with each other. Not only do we now live in a world where English is the lingua franca for business, but also where virtual business encounters have become the norm, and where intercultural understanding goes well beyond ethnicity and a knowledge about how to deal with Americans. These new norms are explored and practised in this book.

Key features of the coursebook

Developing Global Business Communication in Asia provides language and cultural guidance on how global workplaces in Asia operate when using English as a lingua franca. It comprehensively looks at the kind of spoken and written business texts that are now commonly produced in such workplaces enabled by technology in business transactions.

This coursebook is based on a ***global business simulated case study*** where a young Singaporean company called CommunicAsian carries out a big project for a UK-based telecom company called GlobeNet which has an office and personnel based in Hong Kong.

The key features of the coursebook:

- Simulates an authentic ***business case study*** using a series of scenarios set in Asia, but working globally with a UK client
- Based on ***current research*** into business communication needs in ***Asian workplaces*** when working ***globally***
- Explores ***intercultural and linguistic norms*** in Asian business exchanges; i.e. understanding ***Western and Eastern cultural norms***, and how they can effectively interface; understanding ***professional cultures*** e.g. IT engineers versus administrative support staff; and ***corporate management cultures*** e.g. public versus private enterprises
- Highlights the importance of ***intertextuality*** in spoken and written texts in a ***global business context*** where spoken and written texts are constantly networked and referenced to what has already been said and what needs to come next in email, chat and voice exchanges at work
- Takes a second language (L2), as well as a first language (L1) perspective on what makes for successful business interactions by exploring the role of English communication in L1 and L2 business interactions in an Asian business context, where ***Business English is used as a Lingua Franca (BELF)***
- Develops understanding and skills in the use of ***language accommodation strategies*** where students learn to adjust their communication with different types of L1 and L2 speakers using BELF

- Develops understanding and skills in the use of ***cultural adaptability strategies*** where students learn to adjust their cultural responses to different national, professional and business cultures
- Explores the benefits of using ***'plain English'*** in global business contexts, assisting in language accommodation
- Develops integrated ***language proficiency skills*** (reading, writing, listening and speaking) in the communication skills effective for business exchange in this case study
- Emphasises successful ***language performance*** as the result of making **good and informed language choices** rather than presenting prescriptive and generic models as templates applied to every business situation
- Develops ***critical thinking dispositions*** and skills through ***problem-based tasks*** in a real-world Asian-based case study
- Develops ***soft skills for work*** as an integrated approach to business English communications development
- Situates ***technology*** as playing a major role in ***virtual business English communication***, in both spoken and written modes
- Develops specific ***virtual spoken communication strategies*** when working remotely with team members scattered globally
- Assumes that participants will be ***working in teams*** to produce collaborative business texts

These ***key features*** are further explored in the next section where the specific language and pedagogical course approaches are explained.

2. Course approach – the language and the pedagogical approaches

General comments on what principles underpin our approaches

We believe the important skills and understanding required for effective communication embedded in *Developing Global Business Communication in Asia* include:

(i) **Cultural and linguistic diversity and a 'global mindset'**. This coursebook promotes an understanding of the ***cultural complexity*** of working globally, not only in terms of where work colleagues come from but also the organisational culture and expectations of the case study companies and the different professional cultures employed within their ranks. Students learn to appreciate diversity in cultural and linguistic identities and practices at work. These all impact communication. Developing a 'global mindset' where these variables are understood and communicated around is a key aim of this coursebook.

(ii) **Technological impact on global business communication**. *Developing Global Business Communication in Asia* builds on the practical suggestions coming out of some referenced recent studies in the coursebook. In particular these include the unique business challenges of communicating globally using the latest technology. Students will learn tips and techniques for communicating virtually in English where project managers and teams are often working remotely.

(iii) **Use of accommodation and adaptability strategies**. *Developing Global Business Communication in Asia* promotes an understanding of when, and how, to use a range of accommodation and adaptability strategies. You may be communicating in the morning with your Thai counterpart whose English may not be very good; and in the afternoon with your UK counterpart in London. How is this done to ensure clarity, professionalism and desired outcome? The scenarios reflect this complexity and provide practice in interacting with internal and external professionals where their English ability may be better or worse, and whether or not they share a national, professional and/or corporate culture. Being able to use a range of ***accommodation and adaptability strategies*** in these situations, both linguistically and culturally, is key to good global business communication in English.

(iv) **Integrated language proficiency skills in listening, speaking, reading and writing**. In order to make the appropriate language choices in speaking and writing, whatever the situation, students need to understand the explicit and implicit nuances of what has been said or written.

(v) As well, we have to appreciate that no business text can exist, nor can it be produced, in isolation; business communication in spoken and written texts is reliant on what situation(s)/communication(s) has preceded it and what is likely to follow it; this is called '***intertextuality***'. The case study approach, using the life cycle of a long-term project therefore provides plenty of opportunity to improve overall language proficiency and the practical use of 'intertextuality' in an authentic business setting.

In summary, therefore, the belief behind *Developing Global Business Communication in Asia* is that Asian business professionals not only use Business English as a Lingua Franca (BELF) for instrumental purposes (i.e. to get things done), but also to build relationships. In doing so, the book promotes and supports the development of different English-speaking identities of business professionals using different varieties of English, different cultural assumptions, and different strategies at work. Our coursebook protagonists are not, in the main, American or British nationals, but mostly Asian nationalities working in an Asian-based corporation and working across many countries with diverse cultures and languages. The authors seek to give voice and agency to Asian L2 English communicators of business English and see them as absolutely equal to their L1 counterparts. Hence, the coursebook has relevance to L1 business communicators particularly in regard to accommodation, adaptability and the new challenges of communicating with virtual teams globally.

Let's now explore what this means in terms of our specific language and pedagogical approaches.

The language approach

Developing Global Business Communication in Asia assumes a CEFR (Common European Framework of Reference) language proficiency ***level of B2***. This means students have a good intermediate level of English. However, we expect students will not only be challenged to improve their overall level of proficiency, but will also, and just as importantly, improve their language accommodation and cultural adaptability strategies for using BELF.

This course avoids the 'prescriptive' approach to the learning and producing of business text types that are traditionally aligned to Western English-speaking cultures such as America. This is because we are witnessing something much more dynamic in the twenty-first century where we adapt and adjust our communication according to the context, purpose and audience of who we are communicating with. Halliday (see Halliday & Mattheissen, 2014) said language is a 'system of choices' and, therefore, communication is a system of choices. It is not rule-based nor a mere list of expressions that are fit for purpose in every situation.

There are many ways of communicating professionally in a business context depending on the specific situation and the purpose of the exchange, and depending on those we are interacting with. Think for example about the following questions: Are we writing an email to our Vietnamese supplier in English to find out the new delivery date? Or are we writing to head office in New York to tell them the shipment will be late again? Our audience for our professional communication, whether it be spoken or written, may be a L1 speaker or not; it may be another Asian colleague who speaks English as a second language who may be a better or worse speaker than you; it may be face-to-face or it may be virtual. Finally, our message may be of high importance or not; it may be sensitive or not – these all impact the language choices you make. This course aims to support students, as business communicators, to think about and select language that is fit for purpose. ***Language and communication is a system of choices not a list of isolated expressions.***

Because the authentic business case study uses commonly occurring business words and expressions, a comprehensive dictionary of words and expressions has been compiled in Appendix 1. Such words/expressions have been **bolded** in the unit texts and students can use the dictionary to understand the meanings.

Important ***functional use of language*** used in context is constantly promoted and highlighted in this course. Being able to persuade, confront, defuse upset, explain, instruct and express ambiguity are examples of functional language used commonly in business spoken and written exchanges. This means lexico-grammatical choices within the appraisal system (see Rose & Martin, 2012) where modality, conditionality, the use of adverbs and adjectives and choices within the tense system all carry specific and contextualised meanings.

However, as teachers and students of business English, the constant reference to our audience as L2 speakers, means we modify our choices to ensure comprehensibility. This is where the use of accommodation strategies and Plain English may provide better choices. This coursebook addresses these types of choices and provides practice in using business English with such an expanded repertoire in L 1 and L 2 successful business exchanges. These include, for example, the way we paraphrase and standardise our language to ensure it is understood; the way we might slow down our speech and repeat our messages; and the way we might echo the limited repertoire of English of the people we talk to so as to maximise the possibility of understanding.

Much is being written about multi-modality in English communication, and where technology and visuals are so readily available, effective business communication strategies using webchat, software translation and visual representations of the message are all new resources at our disposal.

The pedagogical approach

This coursebook assumes beliefs about language outlined in the discussion above. The general pedagogical approach is student-centred, where the students, rather than the teacher, are doing most of the speaking and writing. At the start of each unit, clear ***learning targets*** are set out to ensure that students can clearly see what will be covered in the tasks and activities. At the end of each unit, students are invited to ***self-assess and reflect*** on those targets, thus raising awareness of the strengths and opportunities for learning in the subsequent units.

The course broadly uses a communicative language teaching (CLT) approach ensuring that students are actively engaged in using functional spoken and written language texts in a range of situations. This coursebook also reflects the pedagogical "learning and teaching" cycle approach (see Rose & Martin, 2012) where key spoken and written texts are explicitly modelled and deconstructed for the students (in the Activity 2 of each unit) so they understand how and why certain choices are made in texts before they are scaffolded in the output tasks (in the Activity 3 of each unit).

The authentic spoken and written texts used in the Activity 2 tasks (e.g. report writing, presentations, negotiations in face-to-face and remote meetings) are typically modelled and then deconstructed so that students see how they work in both generic structure and lexico-grammatical choices. This sets them up for success in the tasks in Activity 3 of each unit.

Teachers and students work with the following types of input and output integrated skills tasks such as:

- **Problem-solving roleplays**: these include paired and group work as collaborative teams; individual/team presentations; informal networking tasks; assertiveness and conflict resolution tasks (e.g. at meetings and negotiations; authentic face-to-face and virtual listening and speaking tasks). The trainer and students can take on certain roles within the scenarios to provide authenticity in the real-life simulations.
- **Business text modelling and deconstruction**: these include use of authentic listening and reading texts for response in the tasks in Activity 2s. Writing models include a range of reports (e.g. proposal and monthly reporting, emails where giving information, instruction and explanation is provided). In speaking, interviews, meetings and presentations are all modelled for the students.
- **Business writing output**: working from spoken and written models provided and outlined above, students then produce their own texts to match audience expectations and ensure understanding; these are completed in response to the tasks set in the Activity 3s. These tasks are scaffolded by the teachers and peers.

The linguistic and pedagogical approaches in this course mirror what have been found to be 'best practices' in current language teaching developed over the last two to three decades. However, these approaches are now blended together here to incorporate the rising importance of BELF. In recent years attention to the effective use of language accommodation and cultural adaptability strategies have come to the fore. The old emphasis on just climbing up the proficiency ladder to native speaker competence is broadened, in this course, to ensure language accommodation and cultural adaptability strategies engage our BELF business interlocutors.

3. The aim and outcomes of *Developing Global Business Communication in Asia* are as follows:

The aim is to provide a series of authentic and memorable workplace scenarios based in an Asian-based company working globally and with a UK telecommunications company. Through being active participants, in this case study students become professional communicators when solving problems as they do face-to-face and virtual business together in English.

The specific student *outcomes* are to:

- Understand how language and culture can be used effectively as a 'lingua franca' to accommodate first and second language speakers of English in a global business context
- Understand how 'intertextuality' between shared spoken and written texts drives and builds meaningful communication
- Improve English communicative performance and enhance proficiency in spoken and written texts, and in listening and reading in a real-world business setting
- Improve accommodation strategies for language and adaptability strategies for intercultural responses in a global business context
- Become familiar with the communication realities of global workplaces that are becoming increasingly technology driven where English is the 'lingua franca' being used with new media
- Understand and improve communication skills when working virtually with business teams and individuals

Each of the 10 units is introduced by a series of ***learning targets***.

4. Course description and structure

This 70-hour coursebook is based around a fictitious Singaporean-based public relations company, CommunicAsian. The case study tracks the life of a project that CommunicAsian carries out for GlobeNet, a telecommunications company based in the UK but with regional offices in Hong Kong.

Whilst the course covers the common text types found in a business context (e.g. reports, emails, meetings and presentations), this is a ***knowledge*** and ***skills-based course***. The aim is to give students realistic and up-to-date business problems to solve at an Asian-based workplace. They will do this by using and developing the English skills they will need in a twenty-first century globalised workplace that works virtually most of the time and employs the latest technologies.

The ***coursebook*** includes:

- The **coursebook** comprising 10 units, each providing 7 hours of work. Each unit is ordered in the same way throughout and includes knowledge and language input readings, the story so far..., activities and tasks, authentic listenings, relevant academic readings (Appendix 3) and a dictionary of global business vocabulary and common expressions highlighted in the texts (Appendix 1).
- **Listening texts and recordings** – The listening transcripts form Appendix 2 and can be accessed as an e-resource.

Each unit is organised into four broad activities as follows:

- **Activity 1**: **(Input – teacher led) (1.5 hours).** The twenty-first century workplace readings: these provide knowledge input with group discussion tasks to be completed in or out of class. The business 'Story so far ...' provides the professional and personal contexts for skills development and provides an engaging human interest story line using the characters in the coursebook.
    - **The two readings**. At the beginning of each unit the readings orient the students to the business and communication issues and tasks covered in that unit; both pertinent to aspects of global business communication. The business and language orientation of these readings are also relevant to the learning targets of each unit. For those postgraduate students who may be using this course to improve both their knowledge and skills of global business communication, the academic studies on business communication will be of particular interest. Teachers and trainers may also find this

background introductory information adds depth to their own teaching of business communication skills.

This activity has been designed so that students can do it as a 'flipped classroom' before each contact lesson; these texts can be read and thought about before they come to class. Students may find the business vocabulary and expressions challenging and therefore the book has a comprehensive dictionary (Appendix 1) of all the **bolded** words and expressions found in the coursebook's spoken and written texts. This will enable the students to complete the reading and listening activities autonomously. Used as a classroom activity, there is plenty of scope for stimulating discussion around the texts and topics covered.

- **'The story so far ...'**. This is an engaging narrative involving the main protagonists and events within the business project carried out between GlobeNet and CommunicAsian. The story so far contributes to building a deeper knowledge of the businesses and the people in this case study; it also contains some unexpected twists and turns to keep students engaged.

- **Activity 2: (Input – teacher led) (2 hours).** Each activity contains a number of different tasks. The tasks mostly deal with understanding key reading and listening texts which serve as language models for the students. In the Activity 2s the spoken and written texts are explicitly deconstructed and modelled for the students so that they understand the generic structures and the key linguistic features, including a rich range of business vocabulary and expressions. These input texts and tasks then inform and allow students to build the output tasks in the next activity.
- **Activity 3: (Output – student led) (3 hours).** In the output tasks students are expected to construct and practise a range of business texts. Spoken and written skills development tasks (e.g. roleplays; report writing; email exchanges etc) mirror what is happening in the business and build on the models and language work completed in Activity 2. In the units there are 'email exchanges' tasks between the main characters designed to build up expertise in understanding and practising the importance of intertextuality in writing. In the output tasks students may work individually, in pairs or in groups depending on their sites of learning.
- **Activity 4: (Reflective self-assessment) (0.5 hour).** The task is exactly the same in each unit where students are invited to reflect on how well they performed in the unit, noting their own strengths and weaknesses. This can be done as a classroom activity where students share their reflections with others in the class; alternatively, they can do this for homework.

5. How to use *Developing Global Business Communication in Asia*

Notes to teachers

This course focuses on the key spoken business skills of meetings, presentations and casual conversation, and the key written skills of email, webchat exchanges, report and proposal writing for global business. These skills are applied to both ***internal and external audiences*** in ***virtual as well as face-to-face (in the case of the spoken skills) contexts.***

There are 10 units in this course and each unit is based on 7 hours of classroom time, roughly divided between reading and writing, listening and speaking and a final self-reflection. There are four activity types in each unit and each activity comprises a series of tasks to be completed by the students.

Although this course is organised around the broad narrative of the CommunicAsian project with GlobeNet, and each unit is sequenced to reflect the narrative, the tasks do not need to be done in set order. For example, teachers may use the course to weight the skills development towards speaking and listening and leave out some of the reading and writing tasks.

Each activity can be used flexibly by the teacher depending on your students and the amount of time available for classroom work. It is recommended that for:

Activity 1: Readings and 'The story so far …'. Students may complete the background readings and 'The story so far…' in each unit before they come to class. In this way, teachers use this activity as a 'flipped' classroom approach where students do some of the readings before they come to class. This is enabled by a dictionary specially compiled with all the key (bolded) business words and expressions in the readings (Appendix 1). These readings set the scene and support the topics and Activities 2 and 3. Suggestions for further readings are referenced at the end of Activity 1 and a full reference list has been compiled as Appendix 3.These appendices allow the teachers to tailor the course to the needs of the student group; for example postgraduate students at university and trainers may have an interest in the theoretical tenets of the learning, whereas undergraduate students may simply want to enhance their communication skills to ensure better job prospects.

Activity 2: Input: Understanding and modelling spoken and written texts. In these teacher-led tasks, the authentic and project-related reading and listening texts provide explicit input on understanding how these texts (e.g. business presentations and report proposals) are organised together with their specific linguistic features. This is done by explicitly modelling and deconstructing these texts and draws on the language learning pedagogy described (see Teaching and Learning Cycle, Rose & Martin, 2012). This knowledge about how texts work lays the foundation for students to produce their own speaking and writing texts in Activity 3.

The transcripts of the listening texts are in Appendix 2 and the recordings can be accessed as an e-resource. If teachers do not use the e-resource they can ask the students to take different roles as a class reading activity. However, best practice in listening skills development discourages students reading the transcript before listening to it, so students should cover the transcript as they listen to it either as an e-resource or a class performance exercise.

Activity 3: Output: Spoken and written skills development tasks. In these student-led tasks, students produce a series of business texts as part of the simulated case study requirements. They are scaffolded in their construction of these texts by their teachers who provide constant feedback and support. Students are encouraged to work collaboratively in groups on these output tasks and are encouraged to provide peer feedback and assessment. Teachers can refer back to the models provided in the Activity 2 where students are struggling in order to remind them about what the texts look like and how they are organised. As students get ready to complete the written tasks (e.g. email exchange threads) individually, in pairs or as groups, teachers should be posing key open-ended questions. These questions can trigger their intertextual knowledge of what has happened before as well as what should happen next. For example, challenging questions such as:

What do we know about how Tony and Vivek view each other?

How do you think the recipient(s) feel(s) about this topic? Why?

What does Vivek really want to achieve by copying Dawn into this message?

What's Dawn's real purpose in this email message she is about to write?

How long do you think this email should be? Why?

Teachers may use different strategies to enable peer and teacher feedback such as 'gallery posting' their output written texts around the classroom, where all students wander around reading and annotating each others'. During this process teachers should keenly observe what students appear to find challenging in the text production, and use these observations to summarise the challenges and evaluate the success of their output.

Whilst it is good to highlight the success of student spoken and written output texts, even selecting two or three as particularly good, means teachers do not need to provide 'model answers' to all these tasks. Success will be variable according to how students understood the text modelling and deconstruction in the Activity 2, how well they draw on their intertextual knowledge, how well they interpret the purpose, how well they pull together the content and how well they organise their texts and make appropriate language choices. These are all very important business English communication skills.

Activity 4: Self-evaluation. The task remains the same in Activity 4 where students are encouraged to reflect on their own knowledge and skills development unit by unit. However, the targets for each unit are different. As the instruction suggests, this activity should be completed in relation to the targets of the particular unit and also to how they have done in previous units. This activity may provide opportunity for peer support, for weighting the syllabus as the teacher picks and chooses certain tasks, resulting in effective course tailoring.

Notes to the students

You are an active participant in the simulated case study. Whilst this course has been conceived as a teacher-led programme, it has also been designed to allow students to work though the materials and tasks at their own individual pace autonomously.

Key features that support you as students include:

- **Appendix 1**: A comprehensive guide to the words and expressions **bolded** in the reading and listening texts as an alphabetically arranged dictionary. The particular meanings of the words/expressions are derived from the context in which they occur in the coursebook.
- **Appendix 2**: Listening transcripts for each of the units. The recordings can be accessed as an e-resource.
- **Appendix 3:** Relevant academic journal studies underpinning the knowledge and skills presented in each of the units. Postgraduate and undergraduate applied linguistic students may find these of particular interest, where theory informs practice.

Activity 1: Readings and 'The story So far... You may be asked to read the two background texts before you come to class and be ready to discuss the key topics raised in the unit. The dictionary of words and expressions will assist your understanding and appreciation of the two readings. As well, 'The story so far...' provides an engaging narrative around the people and events in the case study CommunicAsian project. Apart from providing a human interest element in the case study, the story broadens the context and gives depth to your understanding of the protagonists, thus making your roleplays and email exchanges realistic and well targeted. We hope that in the activities where you produce spoken and written texts your teacher and peers might say things like:

> *But Dawn would never say something like that!*
>
> *Do you think Tony would think about that as a challenge?*
>
> *That message is a bit too aggressive if it's coming from Melinda?*
>
> *Is Samantha saying that just to appease Vivek?*
>
> *Trevor would want much more depth than that in the report!*

These are all real-life concerns when you are working and communicating with colleagues and clients at work.

Activity 2: Input: Understanding and modelling spoken and written texts. Whilst this book does not provide generic templates for students to blindly replicate, it does provide knowledge and skills in being able to see, for example, what makes for a good presentation or a good proposal report. It does this by providing guides to how good samples of business spoken and written model texts may be ***organised***, and what particular ***linguistic features*** they contain. In class the teacher will assist in deconstructing these model texts for organisation and language and then scaffold your attempts to produce these in the Activity 3 tasks. These models can be unpacked by yourselves if you are working autonomously.

Activity 3: Output: Spoken and written skills development tasks. Building on the knowledge and skills of unpacking the model texts in Activity 2, students are then invited individually, in pairs and/or in groups to produce these texts themselves as part of the case study. As a classroom activity, teachers will scaffold this process as you create your own texts and, importantly, will provide both feedback and an evaluation of what you have done. If, however, you do the activities on your own, you may want to refer back to the models provided in the previous activity to guide you.

Activity 4: Self-evaluation. You will be invited to complete the self-evaluation and reflection task when you complete each of the units. You will be asked to reflect not only on how you have done in previous units, but also against the specific learning targets of each unit. In so doing you become aware of where your strengths and weaknesses are and consider these going forward.

6. The Business Scenario: GlobeNet and CommunicAsian

GlobeNet is a broadband and mobile phone network service provider working directly with customers in United Kingdom and, to a small extent, in Europe. It has provided CommunicAsian with a Request for Proposal (RfP) paper on the marketing work they would like them to complete. In summary, GlobeNet plans to introduce a SIM contract which gives unlimited talk and text minutes and allows a subscriber to nominate two Asian countries to be included at no extra cost. The plan is tentatively called 'Roam like you're Home'. GlobeNet believes that the target market for this service is Asian people based in the UK with family connections back in Asia. The RfP is looking for confirmation of the demographic, the market size and what the potential market might be. It is also looking for advice on how advertising can use social media, and how to measure the campaign performance.

The key participants from GlobeNet are:

- Chief Executive Officer (CEO) – Trevor Lavender – UK
- Marketing Director – Celia Tang (HK Chinese) – based in Hong Kong

The Players

<u>**GlobeNet**</u>

Trevor Lavender
UK based CEO, English, over 20 years in Telco Industry

Celia Tang
Hong Kong based Marketing Director, Responsible for Asian Region, over 10 years IT and Telco sales experience

CommunicAsian is a young Singapore-based marketing business with offices around Asia; management is primarily based in Singapore and Hong Kong, with specialist services in Manila and Bangalore. CommunicAsian develops advertising and messaging for companies together with the plans to deliver these messages to the target audiences. Last year they developed a campaign for a sports broadcast subscription company in Tokyo which was introducing a Sumo wrestling channel in Europe as well as a campaign to roll out a new drink: a spirit distilled in the USA and launched in the Asian market.

CommunicAsian has been in business for over 5 years and employs about 80 people around Asia, but now Dawn Chen (CEO) is wanting to build the company to 200 in the next 2 years; winning more UK and European business in order to diversify the client portfolio and expand the range of business areas served is a high strategic priority.

The problem-solving authentic scenarios are around project-bidding, product development and roll out. Different departments and personnel in CommunicAsian are involved at different stages of the project, and they all confront challenges. The departments are:

(i) **Talent Management (sometimes called HR)** – responsible for hiring staff, salary management, discipline and other 'people related' issues
(ii) **Creative Direction** – responsible for advertising and customer acquisition
(iii) **IT Development and Support** – responsible for developing and supporting IT solutions
(iv) **Finance** – responsible for budgets, billing and expense approvals

CommunicAsian, like many companies, sets up a project team to work with each customer. In this scenario the team comprises the key stakeholders shown in the box on pages 17–18. These are based in different Asian regional offices.

It is important for students to identify with these mostly young global professionals, as they will simulate their work transactions and interactions, spoken and written, in each of the units. For this reason, the course includes human interest situations (e.g. The story so far…) affecting the characters and their work situations, as well as pure work issues.

The Players

CommunicAsian

Dawn Chen
Singapore based CEO, 5 years with CommunicAsian, last 2 years as CEO, 3 as Chief Operating Officer

Tony Tanaka
Hong Kong based Creative Director, American born Japanese, 2 years with the company, previously with global advertising agencies

Samantha Greenwood
Singapore based Talent Manager, Australian, 8 years in HR and Talent Management

Melinda Rodriguez
Manila based Finance Manager, 10 years in finance, set up the Manila office for CommunicAsian 2 years ago.

Vivek Sengupta
Bangalore based IT Development and Support Director, over 15 years IT experience, very detail minded

Prasad Patel Bangalore based Project Manager, working in Singapore, 3 years with the company detail minded	Peter Lee Singapore based Marketing analyst, Australian born Chinese, 2 years experience in UK

Typical **work** problems include:

- Intercultural misunderstandings around leadership and participation
- Need to contain costs of the project
- Importance of monthly reporting and metrics
- Different ways of working and expectations both internally and externally
- Working together in virtual teams across locations
- Following corporate policies and guidelines

Typical **human interest** problems include:

- Building diversity within the organisation
- Bullying/sexual harassment at work
- Personality conflict
- Managing and resolving conflict

7. Detailed content by Unit

Unit	Activity 1 – Input readings and discussion ➢ Learning targets (see table in next section) ➢ Readings and discussion ➢ The story so far… (I.5 hours)	Activity 2 – Input Understanding and modelling spoken and written texts and tasks (2 hours)	Activity 3 – Output Spoken and written skills development tasks (3 hours)	Activity 4 – Reflection and further reading (0.5 hours)
1	**INTRODUCTION TO THE COMPANIES AND PERSONNEL OF GLOBENET AND COMMUNICASIAN**			
	Readings: *Reading 1. Business globalisation in Asia: The impact on business exchange* *Reading 2. The use of Business English as a Lingua Franca (BELF)* ***The story so far …*** *The Players and the Game*	**Reading and writing texts and tasks:** (i) *Reading and understanding the GlobeNet entry in Globepedia* (ii) *Reading and understanding collateral documentation for CommunicAsian* (website text) **Listening and speaking text and task:** *(iii) Audio listening: The CommunicAsian welcome speech*	**Output skills tasks:** (i) *LinkedIn writing exercise for Samantha and Tony* (followed by personal LinkedIn writing) *(ii) Roleplay – The CommunicAsian networking event*	**How did you do in this unit?** (i) *Reflection* (ii) *Further reading* ➢ Kankaanranta, A. & Louhaila Salminen, L. (2010) 'English? Oh it's just work' – A study of BELF user's perceptions. *English for Specific Purposes*, 29(3), 204–209. ➢ Lockwood, J. (2013) International communication in a technology services call centre in India. *World Englishes*, 32(4), 586–600.

2	OPPORTUNITY KNOCKS FOR COMMUNICASIAN			
	Readings: *Reading 1. The function and fit of twenty-first century business communication texts: What is 'intertextuality'?* *Reading 2. Business emails and webchats* ***The story so far …*** *Opportunity Knocks for CommunicAsian*	**Reading and writing text and task:** (i) *Deconstructing a Request for Proposal (RfP)* **Listening and speaking text and task:** (ii) *Audio: Internal meeting between Dawn, Samantha and Melinda about the GlobeNet RfP*	**Output skills tasks:** *(i) Written texts for business* *(ii) Spoken texts for business* *(iii) Email exchanges (internal)* *(iv) Meeting roleplay at CommunicAsian* (v) *Email exchanges (external)*	**How did you do in this unit?** (i) *Reflection* (ii) *Further reading* ➢ Bremner, S. (2008) Intertextuality and business communication text books: Why students need more textual support. *English for Specific Purposes*, 27(3), 306–321. ➢ Kameda, N. (2009) *Contrastive rhetoric in business writing across cultures.* Paper presented at the 8th ABC Asia Pacific Conference at Nanyang Business School, Nanyang Technological University, March 2008.

3	BUILDING A BUSINESS RESPONSE			
	Readings: *Reading 1. Communication challenges of virtual business meetings* *Reading 2. The importance of making your writing readable* ***The story so far …*** *Building the Project Team*	**Reading and writing texts and tasks:** (i) *Tips and techniques for virtual meetings* (iii) *Reading and deconstructing the Himeno proposal as a model for the RFP* **Listening and speaking texts and tasks:** (ii) *Listening to virtual meetings Audios 1 & 2* ➢ *Meeting 1. CommunicAsian meets virtually with internal team members* ➢ *Meeting 2. CommunicAsian holds a follow-up meeting virtually with internal team members*	**Output skills tasks:** (i) *Roleplay: Virtual meeting between GlobeNet and CommunicAsian* (ii) *Preparing to write the RfP response (The Proposal)* (iii) *Email exchange* (iv) *Writing the proposal for GlobeNet* (v) *The winning project proposal*	**How did you do in this unit?** (i) *Reflection* (ii) *Further reading* ➢ Beamer, L. (1994) Teaching English business writing to Chinese-speaking business students. *The Bulletin of the Association of Business Communication*, 57(1), 12–18. ➢ Lockwood, J. (2015) Virtual team management: what is causing communication breakdown? *Language and Intercultural Communication*, 15(1), 125–140.

4	WINNING THE BID			
	Readings: *Reading 1. Workplace bullying and harassment* *Reading 2. Accommodation strategies in global business exchange* ***The story so far ...*** *Problems in the Team*	**Reading and writing texts and tasks:** *(i) Sexual harassment policy at CommunicAsian* *(ii) What makes a good presentation?* **Listening and speaking text and task:** *(iii) Video: PowerPoint – CommunicAsian presentation*	**Output skills tasks:** (i) *Preparing, presenting and feeding back on your PowerPoint* (and delivering the presentation for GlobeNet) *(ii) Congratulations email from GlobeNet and responses* *(iii) Accommodation scenarios*	**How did you do in this unit?** (i) *Reflection* (ii) *Further reading* ➢ Lockwood, J. & Song, F. (2016) Strategies for accommodation in a virtual business project based in China. *Journal of Business Communication*, 57(1), 113–144. ➢ Salem, Ashraf Atta M.S. (2009) A Sage on the Stage, to Express and Impress: TED talks for improving oral presentation skills, vocabulary retention and its impact on reducing speaking anxiety in ESP settings. *English Language Teaching*, 12(6), 146–160.

5	BUILDING THE TEAM			
	Readings: *Reading 1. Diversity at the workplace – a global issue?* *Reading 2. Intercultural and linguistic differences* ***The story so far…*** *Getting Ready to Deliver*	**Reading and writing texts and tasks:** *(i) Understanding the job advertisement* *(ii) Deconstructing the applicant resumes and cover letters* **Listening and speaking text and task:** *(iii) Audio listening: Internal meeting at CommunicAsian to prepare for the interviews*	**Output skills tasks:** *(i) Email summary of interview question decisions* *(ii) Applying for a job with CommunicAsian* (i.e. writing resumes and cover letters) *(iii) Preparing for an interview* *(iv) Forum on diversity awareness*	**How did you do in this unit?** (i) *Reflection* (ii) *Further reading* ➢ Choy, W. (2007) Globalisation and workforce diversity: HRM implications for multinational corporations in Singapore. *Singapore Management Review*, 29(2), 1–19. ➢ Wong, Irene. F.H. & Lai Phooi-Ching (2000) Chinese cultural values and performance at job interviews: A Singapore perspective. *Business Communication Quarterly*, 63(1), 9–22.

6	PLANNING THE PROJECT: PEOPLE, PROCESS AND TECHNOLOGY			
	Readings: *Reading 1. Interview skills* *Reading 2. Problem-solving projects and team work* ***The story so far …*** *Planning the Project*	**Listening and speaking text and task:** (i) *Audio listening: Interviewing and discussing the three candidates* **Reading and writing text and task:** (ii) *Read the email below from Prasad with the attached project plan from the Himeno Media project*	**Output skills tasks:** (i) *Interviewing for a graduate internship roleplay* (ii) *The project schedule* (keeping a project plan)	**How did you do in this unit?** (i) *Reflection* (ii) *Further reading* ➢ Lockwood, J. & Forey, G. (2016) Discursive control and power in virtual meetings. *Discourse and Communication*, 10(4). ➢ Mayer, J. (2019) Managing culturally diverse teams. *Applied Information Management Program. University of Oregon. USA.* ➢ Pullen, P. & Prokopi, E. (2016) Leading virtual teams: dos and don'ts. Presented at PMI® *Global Congress 2016–EMEA* Barcelona, Spain. Newtown Square, PA: Project Management Institute.

7	WORKING ON THE PROJECT: THE BIG IDEAS			
	Readings: *Reading 1. Collaborative teams and creativity at work* *Reading 2. The language of problem-solving in the workplace* ***The story so far …*** *Project Management Has Some Issues*	**Listening and speaking text and task:** (i) *Audio listening: Internal meeting at CommunicAsian to discuss project changes* **Reading and writing text and task:** (ii) *Project status monthly report*	**Output skills tasks:** *(i) Email exchange* *(ii) Campaign meeting roleplay* *(iii) Writing a monthly report* *(iv) Covering email*	**How did you do in this unit?** (i) *Reflection* (ii) *Further reading* ➢ Bremner, S. (2010) Collaborative writing: Bridging the gap between the textbook and the workplace. *English for Specific Purposes*, 29(2), 121–132. ➢ Peirson-Smith, A., Bhatia, V.J., Bremner, S. & Jones, R. (2010) Creative English and public relations in Hong Kong. *World Englishes*, 29(4), 523–535.

8	PROBLEMS, PROBLEMS, PROBLEMS			
	Readings: *Reading 1. Dealing with conflict with your clients and customers* *Reading 2. Texting in a business context* ***The story so far ...*** *Managing Cost and Scope*	**Reading and writing texts and tasks:** (i) *Deconstructing webchat* (ii) *Email exchanges of complaint* **Listening and speaking text and task:** (iii) *Audio listening: Internal meeting at CommunicAsian: Project problems*	**Output skills tasks:** *(i) Texting and emailing* *(ii) Writing to complain* ***(iii)*** *Roleplay – confronting problems and expressing your concern.*	**How did you do in this unit?** (i) *Reflection* (ii) *Further reading* ➢ Lacity, M. & Willcocks, L. (2017) Conflict resolution in business services outsourcing relationships. *The Journal of Strategic Information Systems,* 26(2), 80–100. ➢ Lockwood, J. (2016) An analysis of web chat exchange in an outsourced service account in the Philippines. *English for Specific Purposes,* 47(July), 26–39.

9	SOLUTION AND RESOLUTION			
	Readings: *Reading 1. Resolving conflict* *Reading 2. The language of active listening* ***The story so far...*** *Back on Track*	**Listening and speaking texts and tasks** (i) *Audio of active listening on Prasad's performance on the project* **Reading and writing texts and tasks:** (ii) *Deconstructing and responding to written business complaints*	**Output skills tasks:** *(i) Active listening roleplays* *(ii) Email exchange: Writing an adjustment email*	**How did you do in this unit?** (i) *Reflection* (ii) *Further reading* ➢ Koester, A. (2006) *Investigating Workplace Discourse*. Chapter 6: Negotiating consensus and conflict in workplace talk. Taylor & Francis. ➢ Ruiz-Garrido, M.F. (2011) Complaining in the business world: Complaint and adjustment emails. Chapter 5. In Perez-Llantada, C. & Watson, M. (2011) *Specialised Languages in the Global Village – A Multi-Perspective Approach*. Cambridge Scholars Publishing, UK.

10	DECLARE SUCCESS: PROJECT PRODUCT LAUNCH AND LEADERSHIP			
	Readings: *Reading 1. The product launch* (and winding down and transitioning the project) *Reading 2. Intercultural issues in corporate leadership* **The story so far …** *Prasad Steps Up* *Looking Back and Looking Forward*	**Listening and speaking texts and tasks:** (i) *Audio listening: Meeting to prepare for client presentation* **Reading and writing texts and tasks:** (ii) *Writing the storyboard outline* (iii) *Email exchange*	**Output skills tasks:** *(i) The launch presentation* *(ii) Email exchanges*	**How did you do in this unit?** (i) *Reflection* (ii) *Further reading* ➢ Groysberg, B., Lee, J., Price, J., & Cheng, J. Y.-J. (2018) The leader's guide to corporate culture *Harvard Business Review*. January–February. ➢ Lockwood, J. (2019) What do we mean by workplace English? A syllabus framework for course design and assessment. Chapter 2. In Hyland, K. & Wong, L. (eds) *Specialised English: New Directions in ESP and EAP Research and Practice*. Routledge.

8. Learning targets by unit

LEARNING TARGETS BY UNIT				
UNIT 1	**UNIT 2**	**UNIT 3**	**UNIT 4**	**UNIT 5**
• Understand how globalisation has impacted business communication with specific reference to Asian business contexts • Understand why Business English as a Lingua Franca (BELF) is common in business communication in Asia and its impact on business communication • Understand the background details of GlobeNet from an on-line information text on Globepedia	• Understand how different spoken and written texts (e.g. email, webchat) function and fit together within and across the twenty-first century workplace • Develop email writing skills for specific workplace purposes, content and audiences • Understand the purpose and structure of a Request for Proposal (RfP) • Understand the principles of responding to an RfP	• Understand the communication demands of virtual team meetings • Practise the skills of leading and participating in internal and external virtual meetings • Understand how an RfP response is organised and written in English • Plan and write a proposal response to an RfP	• Understand workplace policy documents and how they impact business practices • Understand what makes a good business presentation • Prepare and deliver a successful business presentation • Understand and use a range of accommodation strategies	• Understand how diversity impacts business workplaces • Understand how to read and interpret job advertisements • Explore how to adapt and tailor resumes and cover letters for specific jobs • Practise preparing interviews for specific types of jobs

LEARNING TARGETS BY UNIT				
UNIT 1	**UNIT 2**	**UNIT 3**	**UNIT 4**	**UNIT 5**
• Read and understand collateral documents of CommunicAsian as an example of a website persuasive text • Model, understand, deconstruct and write LinkedIn texts • Listen to, and understand in detail, the welcome address of the CEO of CommunicAsian • Provide an opportunity for participants to introduce themselves in a professional setting and get into and out of casual conversation in a workplace context	• Generate questions and an agenda for the RfP virtual internal meeting • Discuss some preliminary ideas for the written proposal for GlobeNet RfP	• Understand and practise how to make your writing readable		and the types of questions asked.

LEARNING TARGETS BY UNIT				
UNIT 6	UNIT 7	UNIT 8	UNIT 9	UNIT 10
• Understand what makes for good interview skills from the perspectives of both the interviewee and interviewer • Understand how interviews may vary face-to-face and virtually • Understand how to plan a project ensuring progress is reported and deliverables completed on time • Collaboratively develop a project plan for GlobeNet	• Understand the language of, and practise, collaborative problem-solving in English • Work in teams in English to come up with a range of project/campaign ideas • Package your ideas creatively for GlobeNet through a virtual presentation • Understand the structure of the monthly report and practise writing one • Practise language modality choices for a range of CommunicAsian scenarios	• Understand and practise how to deal with external client and customer conflict • Explore the nuance of business chat exchange • Understand and practise texting/chatting in a business context • Understand the written genre and language of business complaints	• Understand the process of resolving problems in internal business contexts • Explore and practise the principles and skills of 'active listening' • Understand and develop skills in the language of responding to external and internal business complaint texts	• Understand the components of a successful product launch • Explore the thinking behind the narrative of a successful project • Produce a presentation from a business storyboard • Understand the importance of leadership in global business contexts • Explore intercultural and linguistic challenges when leading and mentoring teams and individuals

UNIT 1

Introduction to the companies and personnel of GlobeNet and CommunicAsian

The **learning targets** for this unit are to:

- Understand how globalisation has impacted business communication with specific reference to Asian business contexts
- Understand why Business English as a Lingua Franca (BELF) is common in business communication in Asia and its impact on business communication
- Understand the background details of GlobeNet from an on-line information text on Globepedia
- Read and understand collateral documents of CommunicAsian as an example of a website persuasive text
- Model, understand, deconstruct and write LinkedIn texts
- Listen to, and understand in detail, the welcome address of the CEO of CommunicAsian
- Provide an opportunity for participants to introduce themselves in a professional setting and get into and out of casual conversation in a workplace context

Activity 1. Input readings and discussion

- **Before you complete Reading 1, in pairs/groups discuss the questions below:**

(i) What do you understand by the term 'globalisation'?

....

....

....

(ii) What implications does this trend have for different countries in Asia doing business?

....

....

....

- **Look at the vocabulary and idiomatic expression items in bold. If you don't understand them, refer to the dictionary in Appendix 1 and/or try and guess the meaning from the context.**

Now read the text below:

Reading 1 **BUSINESS GLOBALISATION IN ASIA: THE IMPACT ON BUSINESS EXCHANGE**

The last 20 years have seen many Asian countries build whole new industries working with developed countries – notably the United States of America (USA) and the United Kingdom (UK) and Europe – in a movement known as 'globalisation'. Globalisation refers to the movement of work across the world where **economies of scale** are to be found, and **supply chains** ensure products are made cheaply and moved. Globalisation also refers to customer service and back office work that can be carried out for multinationals for less cost in developing countries. Examples of this are where such companies are re-locating work from **on-shore to off-shore** places such as the Philippines and India to achieve a **competitive advantage** for the business. For example, India produces more Information Technology (IT) Engineering graduates than the United States, so most American

continued . . .

cont. technology companies have established centres for IT software development and support off-shore in India.

As well, customer service is now **outsourced** to developing countries – the first **contact centre** was established in India in 1998 with 18 people; there are now more than a million Indian **customer service representatives** working in India and supporting overseas companies, and that support is provided almost 100% in English. The Philippines has a similar story; from a few thousand support workers in 2000, it now has more than a million seats in the outsourced contact centre industry. Add to this the opening up and internationalisation of the People's Republic of China where **foreign investment** continues to grow. In 1979 there were only 100 foreign-owned companies in China, but this rose to nearly 300,000 by the end of the century. China's trade with the United States continues to grow; exports grew by almost 60% from 2008 to 2018, although recent events are slowing this down.

However, this is not just a story of individual countries. The **network effects** of globalisation mean that global project teams may come from a range of countries: Marketing from USA, customer service from the Philippines, IT from India, and manufacturing from Vietnam and Pakistan; and the common language (or **lingua franca**) for the group is English. Therefore, developing better English is no longer about 'sounding American' but about being **globally comprehensible** and being able to communicate effectively with both first (L1) and second (L2) language speakers of English in a business context. By 2025 there will be more English speakers in Asia than in all the 'English-speaking countries' combined. This is the new world order for English communication and it has huge implications for what we now mean by good communication for Asian businesses and workplaces.

This course is based on a case study where two global businesses work and communicate with each other. GlobeNet is a large **mobile virtual network operator** (MVNO) based in the United Kingdom, and CommunicAsian, based in Singapore, provides **outsourced public relations** (PR) services for companies such as GlobeNet (UK) in Asia. GlobeNet recognises the expertise outside of the UK in software development, and also the developing expertise in Asian-based businesses to provide a range of services including creative design. CommunicAsian is just such a company.

CommunicAsian is a young Singapore-based marketing and public relations business with offices around Asia; management is primarily based in Singapore and Hong Kong, with specialist support services in Manila and Bangalore. CommunicAsian develops **research-based advertising and messaging** for companies together with the plans to deliver these messages to the target audiences. Last year they developed a campaign for a sports broadcast subscription company in Tokyo which was introducing a Sumo wrestling channel in Europe as well as a campaign to **roll out** a new **distilled spirit** in the USA and now for the Asian market. CommunicAsian has been in business for 7 years and employs about 80 people around Asia, but now Dawn Chen (CEO) is wanting to build the company to 200 employees in the next 2 years and winning more UK and European business in order to diversify the client portfolio and expand the range of business areas served is a **high strategic priority**. This Singaporean company employs a team throughout Asia and the common language at work is English. This course is about how these two companies interact as they develop an exciting business relationship and work together on an **innovative product** to be rolled out globally.

GlobeNet is a broadband and mobile phone network service provider working directly with customers in the United Kingdom and, to a lesser extent, in Europe. It has issued a Request for Proposal (RfP) looking for a partner company to undertake a market planning project to build a subscriber base in Asia. In this RfP, GlobeNet plans to introduce a SIM contract which gives unlimited talk and text minutes and allows a subscriber to nominate two Asian countries to be included at no extra cost. The plan is tentatively called 'Roam like you're Home'. GlobeNet believes that the target market for this service is Asian people planning to be based in UK, such as students or nurses, who have family connections at home in Asia. The RfP is looking for confirmation of the demographic, the market size and what the market might be. It is also looking for recommendations on how to present the service through advertising and social media, and how to measure the campaign performance.

Now read the text below:

Reading 2 THE USE OF BUSINESS ENGLISH AS A LINGUA FRANCA (BELF)

It is now estimated that there are more L2 English speakers of business globally than L1 speakers. This **phenomenon** has been steadily growing over the last 20 years and has huge **implications** for business communication in Asia. Whilst there are going to be transactions between L1 speakers and L2 speakers, most of the transactions are between L2 speakers (e.g. Mandarin speakers talking to Korean speakers) where they use English as the 'lingua franca'; this has become known as Business English as a Lingua Franca (BELF). The use of BELF in Asia challenges the **traditional notions** of needing to have L1-like proficiency in English in order to communicate successfully. The use of **'accommodation strategies'** are equally, if not more, important in the business exchange in Asia where at least one of the participants is an L2 speaker.

Many communicators in English show common-sense ways of working professionally with those whose English is not so good in the workplace; these are called 'accommodation strategies'. A good example of accommodation is where the better speaker will slow down his/her rate of speech to allow comprehensibility for the other party. A bad example of accommodation is where the better speaker may shout so as to be understood. Shouting carries its own meaning of frustration and impatience so this will **jeopardise**, rather than assist the communication. In this course you will learn how to use a range of effective language accommodation strategies in a business context. Although there are lots of suggestions for stronger communicators accommodating weaker speakers and writers in a business context, attention should also be paid to weaker speakers asking for clarification and repetition from stronger speakers; accommodation works both ways.

Finally, just as we accommodate for language differences, we also need to accommodate for cultural differences. In this course we talk about

continued . . .

cont. cultural **adaptability** strategies in business, where people from different backgrounds think about how to adapt their behaviours towards, and expectations of others at work, and not assume there is a **universal norm**. For example, different cultures have different norms of privacy. Think about how you would respond to questions at the workplace such as 'Are you married?'; 'What is your salary'; or to colleagues who volunteer excuses for absence such as 'I am **menstruating**'? In Western countries such information is felt to be private, whereas in some parts of Asia, there is more openness on such topics.

- **Now in pairs/groups discuss the questions below:**

(i) What do you think are some of the other features of 'accommodation' making for successful communication in BELF?

....

....

....

(ii) BELF is commonly used in Asian business contexts. How does this challenge current views on what 'good' communication is? What are the implications for business communication in Asia?

....

....

....

(iii) Do you agree there is a cultural as well as a language dimension to 'accommodation' called cultural adaptability? If yes, can you give some examples?

....

....

....

The story so far ...

At the beginning of each unit, 'The story so far ...' texts tell you what is going on in the two companies. This background information provides extra professional and personal information to bring the case study alive.

- **Look at the vocabulary and idiomatic expression items in bold. If you don't understand them, refer to the dictionary in Appendix 1 and/or try and guess the meaning from the context.**

Now read the story below:

THE PLAYERS AND THE GAME

Dawn Chen was in a **good mood**. She had just finished making her annual report presentation to the board of directors. Dawn was the CEO – Chief Executive Officer – of CommunicAsian, a marketing and communications consultancy based in Singapore and with offices across Asia. The board had congratulated her on delivering a good year's performance: **revenues** and **growth** had both **beaten** the **forecasts**. And, more importantly, they had accepted her **strategic plan** for the next year: more growth, expand the services offered, and build a **portfolio** in Europe. As she was leaving the meeting, the Board Chairperson had stopped her and said:

"Dawn, I'd like to congratulate you personally. I supported your appointment when you **took over** as **CEO**, and you've done even better than I'd hoped. But you've given yourself some hard targets for next year."

Dawn smiled her thanks. "That's what motivates me," she said. "I love the challenge and being a boss."

Back in her office Dawn **wondered** how to celebrate. Maybe a dinner at Fisherman's Wharf with a friend. She wondered who to call first.

In Hong Kong, Celia Tang was finishing a Zoom call with her London boss, Trevor Lavender. Celia was Marketing Director and, effectively, head of the Asian region for GlobeNet, a **telecoms** and **broadband** provider based in the UK. Celia was also making a presentation but, unlike Dawn's, it was not going easily.

"I'm still a bit worried that your **Request for Proposal** is too broad," said Trevor. "I would prefer more **precise** instructions to **suppliers**."

Celia sighed. They had covered this about three times, but Trevor kept on coming back to it **like a dog gnawing a bone**. "We agreed on this. We want the responders to our RfP to give us their best creative ideas, so I want to give them as much freedom as possible to deliver the best solution. And it doesn't commit us to taking any of the solutions if we aren't satisfied."

"No, but we could waste a lot of time."

"Trevor, you've given me the task of building the Asia subscriber base and this is my solution. If I'm going to run this project, I need to have some freedom."

"Yes, that's fair," said Trevor, "but do you think you've chosen the right companies to respond? CommunicAsian seems a bit small."

"Yes," said Celia, "but they're good. I've done **reference checks** and they seem to be good with **creative branding** and with social media. Anyway, they are only one of four – the **outlier** if you like."

"Like you said, it's your project," said Trevor. "I'll sign off on the RfP and the **short list**, and we'll talk next week."

Celia disconnected and **pumped her fist** in the air. She wondered how to celebrate. Maybe a coffee on the way home.

Activity 2. Understanding and modelling spoken and written texts

Task (i). Reading and understanding the GlobeNet entry in Globepedia

- **Read through the information about GlobeNet on 'Globepedia', and in pairs answer the question below:**

Before you start to read the text, what kind of text do you think this is? What kinds of information do you think this text will provide?

....

....

....

- **Look at the vocabulary and idiomatic expression items in bold. If you don't understand them, refer to the dictionary in Appendix 1 and/or try and guess the meaning from the context.**

From Globepedia, the free encyclopedia

GlobeNet	
Industry	Telecommunication
Founded	2015
Headquarters	United Kingdom
Key people	Richard Park (Chairman) Trevor Lavender (CEO) Celia Tang (Asia Marketing Director)
Products	Mobile telecommunications services Broadband services
Market	Focus on UK customers originating from East and South Asia
Website	GlobeNet.com

GlobeNet is a mobile virtual network operator (MVNO) operating primarily in United Kingdom. The bulk of GlobeNet **revenue** is generated from its SIM products. GlobeNet built its market by targeting customers within **expatriate** and **ethnic markets** who want to make international calls to their home countries.

GlobeNet sells international pay-as-you-go SIM cards to customers wanting to make international telephone calls, and it forms partnerships with the operators in each country it serves. GlobeNet has also developed **subscription** or contract SIM card products. It positions itself as a low-cost provider to acquire market share.

The GlobeNet brand was launched in 2010, and it now has more than 15 million pay-as-you-go and subscription customers worldwide. Over 70% of these customers are pay-as-you-go, but GlobeNet has announced that it plans to invest to build its contract business customer numbers to 50% of its total in the next 3 years and plans to penetrate the Asian markets.

In 2018, ten GlobeNet employees were **arrested** for knowingly providing unregistered SIM cards to people on the Security Services watch list. The case is pending.

Operations

The company currently has partnerships with providers of telecom services in 42 countries all of Greater China, ASEAN, and the Indian sub-continent. GlobeNet has provided services in Hong Kong since 2015, and in Singapore a year later.

Deconstructing the text

- **In pairs/groups answer the questions below:**

(i) What are the two sales systems GlobeNet uses to charge its customers for SIM cards?

....

....

....

(ii) How does GlobeNet want to improve its proportion of how customers pay for their SIM cards, and what is its time frame?

....

....

....

(iii) Can you think of ways in which they could achieve customer subscriptions?

....

....

....

Task (ii). Reading and understanding collateral documentation for CommunicAsian

Website text for CommunicAsian

Before you start to read the text, what kind of text do you think this is? What kinds of information do you think this text will provide?

....

....

....

■ **Look at the vocabulary and idiomatic expression items in bold. If you don't understand them, refer to the dictionary in Appendix 1 and/or try and guess the meaning from the context.**

Now read the website text below.

CommunicAsian Website (four web pages)

Home Page

We produce communications that work for your business and for your audience in Asia

Asia is home to almost 50% of the world's population and is home to some of the fastest growing countries. With our deep knowledge and focus on Asian cultures, CommunicAsian develops campaigns which **drive business success** across the region.

What We Do	Our Clients	Our Team

What We Do

The greatest ideas will achieve nothing without people being made aware of them. That is why we believe that the delivery of the communication is as important as getting the communication right. Our Creatives work closely with our IT and Social Media experts to ensure that the right people – your prospects – get the message you want to **get across**.

Our Clients

Our clients range from regional powerhouses to local companies and campaign groups. For a selection of case studies go here.

Our Team

CommunicAsian sets up a project team to work with each customer depending on needs, and with team members typically based in different Asian regional offices to ensure that local knowledge is applied. Key players are:

- Our CEO **Dawn Chen** – based in Singapore and takes an oversight role in all major projects

- IT Development and Operations – led by **Vivek Sengupta** in Bangalore
- Talent Management – **Samantha Greenwood**
- Creative Director – **Tony Tanaka**
- Finance Manager – **Melinda Rodriguez** – based in Manila.

We believe that our people's diverse backgrounds and locations let us build the right team for any project.

Deconstructing the text

- **In pairs/groups discuss the purpose of this text, the audience and how is the text organised. Put your ideas in the box below:**

Purpose	
Audience	
Organisation	

Are there any distinctive linguistic features (e.g. types of grammar and vocabulary items)? How do these strengthen this text as an information text? Jot your ideas below.

....
....
....

Task (iii). Audio listening: The CommunicAsian welcome speech (Transcript – Appendix 2).

Deconstructing the welcome speech to all new interns at CommunicAsian

Before you listen, what do you think a welcome speech will include for new employees?

....
....
....

- **Listen to the welcome speech of Dawn Chen who is CEO of CommunicAsian and answer the questions below.**

- **Look at the vocabulary and idiomatic expression items in bold. If you don't understand them, refer to the dictionary in Appendix 1 and/or try and guess the meaning from the context.**

(i) How would you describe the overall tone of Dawn's welcome speech? Give your reasons.

……………………………………………………………………………………
……………………………………………………………………………………
……………………………………………………………………………………

(ii) Why was Dawn proud of their 'Scotts' campaign?

……………………………………………………………………………………
……………………………………………………………………………………
……………………………………………………………………………………

Activity 3. Spoken and written skills development tasks

Task (i). LinkedIn writing exercise

- **Look at Samantha and Tony's LinkedIn profiles below:**

Samantha Greenwood (Human Resource Manager) CommunicAsian

Headline

Talent management in media industry and public relations/global experience/intermediate Mandarin speaker/workplace mediator

Profile Summary

With a postgraduate degree in psychology and 8 years' experience in workplace talent acquisition and development in Australia and Asia, I bring a global and culturally sensitive perspective to the recruitment and management of the workforce. Throughout my career, I have worked to recruit and retain the best talent for a range of companies including banks, insurance and public relations companies. By combining my analytical approach with a passion for problem-solving, I have identified and confronted complex issues directly, whilst ensuring accountability.

My commitment to diversity in the workplace has meant talent has been recruited and supported across a range of ethnic and demographic profiles to build effective teams. This has entailed supporting a range of workplace initiatives to get the best out of our people. This has involved supporting a range of training and coaching programmes and providing mentoring opportunities to prospects for promotion. It has also involved internal workplace mediation sessions where conflict has occurred.As a collaborative voice in the executive team, I have provided an objective perspective, offered constructive challenges and managed the expectations of key stakeholders effectively.

Areas of Expertise

Talent Acquisition | Workplace Mediation | Mentoring and Coaching Skills | Programme Management | Impact Analysis | Stakeholder Engagement | Strategic Planning

Tony Tanaka (Creative Director)

Headline

Creative and account management experience across internal departments and agencies in the USA and Asia, now based in Hong Kong. Marketing awards for large bank and from Industry Associations. Global experience and multilingual ability including English, Cantonese, and basic Japanese.

Profile Summary

Educated in the USA and postgraduate degree from Hoover Business School in global marketing. Proven ability to lead complex campaigns and winner of international creative marketing award. With 15 years' experience in creative marketing design, I bring an ability to work collaboratively on complex briefs.Specific campaigns have included CommunicAsian 'Sumo for all' which penetrated Europe and won the runner-up campaign award in Europe. Works collaboratively and provides unique insights to analytics and measurement data.My passion in life is to get your message across in the right way to the right people and so help your business succeed.

Areas of Expertise

Marketing Campaigns | Creative Messaging

■ **Discuss how these texts are organized and what kind of language is used. Are these two LinkedIn entries the same or different?**

....
....
....
....
....
....

Do you have a LinkedIn account?

■ **Write a 250-word entry for yourself in the box below:**

Task (ii). Roleplay – The CommunicAsian networking event

What is 'small talk' and why is this important?

In this roleplay you are at the CommunicAsian welcome drinks party and you'll need to circulate and introduce yourself to as many people as possible.

Making 'small talk' and casual conversation with colleagues can be stressful, but it is a necessary part of building business relationships with the people who you work with. Topics such as income, wealth and marital status can be sensitive for some people to reveal. Different cultures, personalities and interests can impact how successfully you communicate professionally in a business context, and therefore listening carefully and 'profiling' the people you interact at work and with external clients and customers is important. One of the things you are constantly trying to do is to identify common ground you might have with the person you are talking to.

Who are you?

Allocate the following CommunicAsian roles:

- CEO – Dawn Chen (Singaporean)
- Talent Manager – Samantha Greenwood
- Creative Director – Tony Tanaka

These current managers need to try and meet all the new interns and welcome them to the company.

- **Ask the remaining students to complete their 'new employee' identity in preparation for the CommunicAsian welcome party in the box.**

All new employees need to complete the following at the party:

- Introduce yourself to at least three other employees and all the CommunicAsian current members of senior staff
- Find someone who works in the same field as you

Now spend 15–20 mins talking to colleagues at the CommunicAsian welcome drinks event.

New CommunicAsian Employee Form

My name is:

Nationality:

Hired into CommunicAsian dept:

Other interesting facts to share at the welcome party:

- **Feedback and discuss.**

Activity 4. Reflection and reading

Reflection

How did you do in this unit?

- **Look back at the original learning targets of this unit and evaluate your own strengths and weaknesses. Tick either + (positive) or – (negative) in the table below. Specify which tasks in each skills areas and activities you are evaluating. Then reflect on these and make notes in the final column.**

Tasks	**+**	**–**	**Reflection notes**
The reading tasks:			
The writing tasks:			
The speaking tasks:			
The listening tasks:			

Further reading

Kankaanranta, A. & Louhaila Salminen, L. (2010) 'English? Oh it's just work' – A study of BELF user's perceptions. *English for Specific Purposes*, 29(3), 204–209.

Lockwood, J. (2013) International communication in a technology services call centre in India. *World Englishes*, 32(4), 586–600.

UNIT 2

Opportunity knocks for CommunicAsian

The **learning targets** for this unit are to:

- Understand how different spoken and written texts (e.g. email, webchat) function and fit together within and across the twenty-first century workplace
- Develop email writing skills for specific workplace purposes, content and audiences
- Understand the purpose and structure of a Request for Proposal (RfP)
- Understand the principles of responding to an RfP
- Generate questions and an agenda for the RfP virtual internal meeting
- Discuss some preliminary ideas for the written proposal for GlobeNet RfP

Activity 1. Input readings and discussion

Task (i).

- **In pairs/groups discuss the questions below:**

(i) How do you think business spoken and written texts have changed over the last 20 years? Why do you think this has happened and give some examples.

....

....

....

(ii) What do you understand by the term 'intertextuality'? Can you guess and give a brief example of this?

....

....

....

■ **Look at the vocabulary and idiomatic expression items in bold. If you don't understand them, refer to the dictionary in Appendix 1 and/or try and guess the meaning from the context.**

Now read the text below:

Reading 1

THE FUNCTION AND FIT OF TWENTY-FIRST CENTURY BUSINESS COMMUNICATION TEXTS: WHAT IS 'INTERTEXTUALITY'?

Business communication does not occur **in isolation**. Think, for example, of when you make an on-line purchase. You may first look at the sites, make your selections, ask questions, confirm your orders and delivery times, and even complain once the product has arrived. In this routine type of business exchange there is an **ebb and flow** of spoken and/or written textual exchange, with each exchange influenced both by what has come before and what you are doing right now, and what you **predict** will come after. This has been **coined** by business communication researchers as **'intertextuality'**; this is where one text (spoken and written) builds on the ones before and suggests the next. It is obvious that the context of, and people involved in these exchanges heavily influence the texts. It is therefore nonsense to talk about 'how to write a business email, letter or report' if it exists out of context with no purpose or audience.

continued . . .

cont. Businesses use all sorts of text types to communicate in context. One of the most common text types is the report. However, there are many different kinds of reports depending on the *purpose*, the *audience* and the *content*. Reports may be **informational** (e.g. progress/status report, annual report, implementation report, compliant report, incident/accident report, etc), others are **analytical** (e.g. risk/opportunity report, an audit report, feasibility study report, etc) and others are **persuasive** (a marketing report, funding proposal, etc). Some may have features of all three report functions. Furthermore, some reports are only for **internal distribution** whereas others may only be for external parties. In this unit, CommunicAsian receives a request for proposal (RfP) and this will generate a persuasive proposal report. The RfP will be primarily trying to persuade GlobeNet that they are the best choice to run their project. However, this report will also have information sections e.g. CommunicAsian's experience and skills. As the document name suggests, an RfP is a formal business-to-business invitation competing for work; often these are sent out by companies to several businesses that may be able to supply the services. The document itself is full of **specifications, timelines** and other relevant information. In order therefore to prepare a good proposal response, this document needs to be read carefully and adhered to. As well, it is often the case that a meeting is called where the **bidders** can clarify their understanding of what is required and ask questions. A knowledge of these events and key people impact the preparation and writing of the proposal report. This is intertextuality in action.

- **Look at the vocabulary and idiomatic expression items in bold. If you don't understand them, refer to the dictionary in Appendix 1 and/or try and guess the meaning from the context.**

Now read the text below:

Reading 2 BUSINESS EMAILS AND WEBCHATS

Perhaps the most common written text used in business is email. Emails do not exist in isolation but as part of **a chain or thread** of texts that are referencing other emails and other written and spoken texts that have already taken place. This referencing of other texts may be done **implicitly** and **explicitly** in the exchanges; for example, Tony may respond implicitly to an angry email from Dawn requiring more numbers in his monthly report by simply writing a tag line 'the amended report' and saying in the email: ***FYI**, the amended report attached. Regards, Tony.* The implicit message is 'I'm sorry that the report did not contain the numbers to support what was reported. I hope you respond well to this one that is attached'. If he were referencing explicitly, his tag line would be *Re: your email of xx date*, or simply a reply email keeping the same original subject line.

A guiding principle for email writing is to consider the *purpose* for writing (is it a response to an initial email or part of an on-going thread?), the *audience* (is it your colleague or an external party?) and the *content* (does it contain the right amount of key information based on the purpose and audience being addressed?). The **formality or informality** of the email/webchat exchange will depend on the answers to these questions too. It is important to note that many companies have their own **style guides** that regulate the **'dos and don'ts'** of written communication to external parties, and these often cover how to address a client with the appropriate tone and style. It is also important to note that the way we organise our business texts in English are not universal, and intercultural differences may impact the flow of the text. For example, Japanese writers and speakers tend to 'background' their business requests/information much more than is the case in English, where 'getting to the point' and being direct is seen as good business practice.

The biggest challenge in writing good emails and webchats is to **balance all these considerations** in a response, and it is critical to read and understand the nuances of emails and webchats you have received. Embedded in the message may be **criticism**, **sarcasm** or

continued . . .

cont. even **praise**. These messages need to be well understood and taken into account before responding.

As a customer, have you ever used webchat to make your enquiry/ complaint?

How is email and webchat different? Normally we would say that email is **asynchronous**, meaning it is not written in real time, whereas webchat is **synchronous**, meaning it is exchanged in real time. Does this make a difference to how it is structured and communicated? It seems it does.

Webchat is **ubiquitous** in social interaction nowadays and this **media** is **creeping into** business exchanges globally. In fact, in customer service this new media is becoming the **preferred option**, especially in the **contact centre** industry environment globally. In this context, studies have shown however that there are business regulations **mandating** how webchat should be approached at work. Despite the fact that businesses want to protect 'relationship building' in webchat, some are concerned that using **social media strategies** such as the emoticons, emojis, **punctuation deviations**, and abbreviations for meaning making may communicate to an external customer an **unprofessional image**. Such regulations generally are not applied to the internal use of business webchat, where colleagues will use chats formally and informally to communicate with each other.

Webchat for business exchange is becoming increasingly common. What do you think are some of the advantages and disadvantages of webchat in a business context?

....

....

....

- **Discuss.**

The story so far ...

- **Look at the vocabulary and idiomatic expression items in bold. If you don't understand them, refer to the dictionary in Appendix 1 and/or**

try and guess the meaning from the context. Look at the questions at the end of the text and keep these in mind as you read the story.

Now read the story below:

OPPORTUNITY KNOCKS FOR COMMUNICASIAN

Dawn Chen arrived at her Singapore office at about 8.30 a.m. As the CEO of CommunicAsian, she liked to arrive early as an example to her employees. She **booted up** her computer and reviewed her emails and her schedule for the day. Nothing too stressful: a couple of project reviews and a performance **appraisal** with Samantha Greenwood, the HRO Manager, who was coming up to a year's service in the company. Suddenly a mail alert popped up on her computer and she saw 'urgent mail' in the title. She clicked it open. It was forwarded by the Administration Group and said

> "You'll want to see this RfP from GlobeNet. It looks big."

Dawn read quickly through the RfP and then re-read more slowly. Then she forwarded it to Tony Tanaka, the Creative Director who worked out of Hong Kong. Tony was responsible for major accounts and for managing business opportunities.

> "Tony – look at this – it could be a big one and we'll have to do a lot of work in a short time. Can you call me at 10.00 to discuss how we respond and who we put on it?"... Dawn.

Dawn was too excited to sit still, so she stood at the whiteboard listing her ideas to discuss with Tony. The problem with Tony – like all marketing people he likes to promise everything to the customer, and then Finance and Operations get upset that they have to deliver with an **overtight budget** or an impossible schedule. She would have to **keep strict control** over this one.

At 10.00 her WeChat tone burbled. Tony was as excited as her.

"If we win this bid and the project **takes off** we could **double our size**. And it gets us some serious UK **exposure**."

"Agreed," said Dawn, "but we need to win the proposal stage before we can think of the implementation. We need to put a team together today to build our response."

"I'm happy to lead it," said Tony, but Dawn **cut him off**. "No, I'd like you to coordinate but I'll take a hands-on leadership on this one. But I think you should come to Singapore for a few days so we can work closely."

Dawn knew Tony would not be happy that he was not the head, but he would get over it.

"The RfP talks about related experience, so we'll need to have Vivek on the bid team. He did all the app design and metrics measurement for the Sports channel launch into UK last year."

Vivek and Tony **did not get on**, and it was good that one was in Bangalore and the other in Hong Kong. Vivek was a logic guy: his IT work was based on **metrics and processes**, and he could not relate to Tony's **impetuous**, emotional decision making. Tony was quiet: he was obviously trying and failing to think of reasons why Vivek should not be included. Dawn decided to **quit** while she was winning.

"Okay, Tony, why don't we both spend some time thinking of next steps and who to include, and we'll talk again at 4 p.m. I am cancelling everything else today and it would be good if you can too."

- **Discuss your answers to the questions below:**

(i) How does Dawn feel about the project?

....

....

....

....

(ii) How does Tony feel about the project?

....

....

....

....

(iii) Is there any tension between Dawn and Tony? Explain your answer.

....
....
....
....

(iv) What do you know about other members of the team at CommunicAsian?

....
....
....
....

Activity 2. Understanding and modelling spoken and written texts

Task (i). Deconstructing a Request for Proposal (RfP)

An RfP is commonly sent out to potential providers for specific product development and/or services. It is usually a competitive process and it takes time to produce a good proposal.

- **In pairs/groups discuss the following questions:**

(i) What is the function of an RfP?

....
....
....
....

(ii) What kind of information do you think it should contain?

....
....
....
....

(iii) How do you think it could be structured?

....
....
....
....

(iv) What kind of language could you use?

....

....

....

....

- **Read the following RfP GlobeNet sent to CommunicAsian inviting them to bid for software development work.**

GlobeNet Communications Request for Proposal

Project: "Roam like you're Home"

1. Project Overview

GlobeNet has a 10-year history of successful mobile phone SIM card sales in the United Kingdom, focused on short term SIM cards for visitors to the country. GlobeNet has partnership agreements with network providers in Middle Eastern countries so that visitors from there can call home at reduced rates.

Some 70% of its business is 21-day duration SIM cards offering unlimited call minutes and texts and 8 GB data downloads. The other 30% offers similar services but allowing top-up on a pay-as-you-go basis.

GlobeNet has recently signed agreements with network providers throughout East and South East Asia, and wants to offer SIM cards to these citizens visiting United Kingdom. The project is code named 'Roam like you're Home', and will allow the SIM purchaser to nominate two Asian countries to be included in the free call minutes.

The project has three key deliverables:

- **Develop the message** to market the product throughout Asia, but initially in three test markets to validate the concept
- Develop the strategy to **deliver the message** (including social media, influencers, placements, and partnerships)
- **Propose measures** to track the success of the project and programme

1.1 Timeline and Point of Contact

Please confirm within 72 hours if you plan to respond to the RfP.

All respondents are invited to a meeting next week at which any questions and explanations on the RfP will be addressed. Respondents may submit questions in advance of the meeting. All questions and answers will be shared with all respondents.

Your proposal response is requested within 4 weeks and should be sent to Celia Tang, Marketing Director. Celia will also be the point of contact for any questions. Please note our offer of a virtual meeting for all potential bidders on September 27th at 9 a.m. GMT.

1.2 Selection Criteria

GlobeNet is looking for a partner in Asia for the first time, so the creativeness of the message and the ability to track its performance and adapt as necessary will be most important.

Relevant previous experience will also be considered.

Celia Tang will make recommendations to the final decision maker, Trevor Lavender, the London-based CEO.

2. Project Goals and Audience

Based on our experience and statistics of travel, we believe that there are three main segments to target:

- Students planning to study in UK
- Holidaymakers planning longer than 10 days in UK
- Nurses recruited to UK from Asia

These segments may require different messages and value propositions.

The goal of the project is to build awareness of the offering and to sell the SIM cards within the home country (in local currency) rather than depend on the customer choosing GlobeNet when he or she arrives in UK.

3. Budget and Analytics

GlobeNet does not intend to set a budget for the project at this stage. However, in your response we want you to segregate cost estimates between **fixed**: the costs we will be committed to regardless of the project's success performance, and **controllable**: the costs we will incur based on successful revenues from sales.

Most importantly, we are looking for your proposals on how the project outcomes are to be measured, including possibly a mixture of brand awareness surveys, SIM card sales figures, and trends over time. These will need to be related to country, region, and/or target demographic.

4. Next Steps

Please sign up to our virtual meeting on 27th September 9 a.m. GMT by emailing Celia Tang on ctang@globenet.com

What do you notice about this text in terms of (i) how it is structured and (ii) the language used?

....
....
....
....
....
....

- **Have a feedback discussion about the structure and language used in the RfP.**

What is explicit and implicit in this text?

....
....
....
....

Remember to refer back to your answers to these questions when you are writing your response proposal.

Task (ii). Audio: Internal meeting between Dawn, Samantha and Melinda about the GlobeNet RfP (Transcript – Appendix 2)

Pre-meeting before the whole team meeting.

The scene is Dawn's office where Samantha has joined Dawn and Melinda is about to phone in. Samantha enters.

Pre-listening tasks

What do you think the meeting is going to be about?

....
....
....
....

- **Look at some of the words and expressions in the box below. These are all used in the meeting. In pairs/groups write your own meanings. Discuss.**

Words and expressions	Meaning
I'll fill you in	
I don't have to go through it again	
Your appraisal will need to slip a bit	
I'll save that up	
We're going to go for it	
Smart analytics	
Track its success	
Support people	

A first cut Chalk and cheese Say so	

- **As you listen to the meeting the first time, write down in the table below what you think the purpose of the meeting was, what content was covered and how all the participants felt during and after the call.**

Purpose of the meeting	Content covered	Feelings of the participants during and after the meeting

Now share your ideas on content, purpose and feelings in this meeting.

Activity 3. Spoken and written skills development tasks

Task (i). Written texts for business

There are many written texts, particularly emails and reports, required in the workplace.

- **Working in pairs/groups complete the table below thinking of all the different *written* types of business texts and then comment on:**

- their priority function(s) (e.g. informational, analytical, persuasive, relationship building, complaining, etc) within the workplace depending on their purpose
- whether it is directed to an internal and/or external audience(s)

The first one has been done for you.

WRITTEN texts	Purpose, function and audience
Sales Report to external client	*Purpose is to inform and provide some analysis of sales performances of the business. This kind of external report is also designed to be persuasive.*

Now think about the departments within CommunicAsian. What kinds of reports would they do collaboratively across departments? What sorts of emails might they write?

....

....

....

....

Task (ii). Spoken texts for business

- **Working in pairs/groups complete the table below thinking of all the different spoken text types and then comment on:**

- their priority function(s) (e.g. informational, analytical, persuasive) within the workplace depending on their purpose
- whether it is directed to an internal and/or external audience(s)

SPOKEN texts	Purpose, function and audience
An internal monthly Presentation	*Purpose may be to inform and provide some analysis of monthly performances of the business. This kind of internal presentation may also contain a set of recommendations in which case it may also be persuasive.*

Now think about the departments within CommunicAsian. What kinds of meetings would they do internally and externally? What sorts of presentations might they do?

....
....
....
....

Task (iii). Email exchanges (internal)

Look at the series of emails that are about to be sent and received.

Before you start writing responses, think about the purpose of each email and what the appropriate length and style might be.

Email invitation to join meeting

- **You are Dawn, the CEO and keen to get this new work. Circulate the RfP and invite colleagues to read it, think about it and attend a meeting to prepare for the virtual meeting next week with the client.**

To: Vivek, Sam, Tony, Melinda
From: Dawn
Subject: Re. RfP meeting in Singapore

Hi everyone,

This opportunity (see attached RfP) looks very exciting for us and as key people in your departments I'd like to get your input for the virtual meeting we'll have next week with GlobeNet.

I would like as many of you present physically as possible in Singapore to discuss this next week Wednesday 15th at 10 a.m. I'll book Meeting Room C on the 3rd floor.

Can you get back to me by tomorrow first thing with your availability and your preliminary ideas?

All the best,
Dawn

- **Based on the previous email, you are Vivek. You write a response back cc-ing everyone saying you are away for 2 weeks starting the day after tomorrow and won't be able to attend a meeting next week, but you think you have a suitable deputy, Prasad, to ensure the IT department has a voice.**

To: Dawn
From: Vivek
Cc:
Subject:

- **Based on Vivek's email, you are Dawn. You write a response to everyone commenting on Vivek's solution whereby his department can provide input, and attach an agenda for the meeting.**

To:
From: Dawn
Cc:
Subject:

How was each email affected by what had come before? How was each email affected by what you wanted to achieve by sending it? Write your ideas below:

....
....
....
....

What made you choose the length and style for each email? Write your ideas below:

....
....
....
....

Task (iv). Meeting roleplay at CommunicAsian

Split into groups of six. You all work for CommunicAsian and you have received and read the RfP.

You are meeting to prepare for the virtual question and answer meeting with GlobeNet. You have a number of comments and questions to ask at that meeting.

■ Take the following roles or departments:

1. CEO (Chair) – Dawn (writes the agenda, give skeleton)
2. IT Development and Operations – Vivek and Prasad
3. Talent Management – Samantha – minute taker
4. Creative Director – Tony
5. Finance head – Melinda

Vivek, Prasad, Tony and Melinda are attending the meeting virtually.

Step 1: Each role/department will meet separately to discuss ideas/ concerns in preparation for the meeting (10–15 mins). Dawn will chair the meeting and Samantha will take the action point minutes from the meeting.

- **Write down your questions/concerns/comments for your department/ role based on your reading of the RfP in the box below:**

Step 2. You now attend the CommunicAsian internal meeting roleplay meeting with your ideas and concerns.

Feedback from each department. What are the main questions, concerns and comments from each department?

Task (v). Email exchanges (external)

Dawn has just received the following email from GlobeNet:

> To: Dawn Chen
> From: Celia Tang
> Cc: Trevor Lavender
> Subject: Re. Your proposal
>
> Dear Dawn,
>
> Thank you for your expression of interest in submitting a proposal for our Telecom work; we were very pleased to receive it.
>
> Given that we have had a number of strong expressions of interests we would like to invite you to a meeting where you may want to seek further information and advice. This will take place individually for each of our invited bidders Wednesday 2 p.m. on September 28th.
>
> Can you confirm this invitation by reply and access our conference site by ringing the toll free number:
> 659-265-552-6296
> Password code: 74750732

We look forward to meeting your team soon and any questions can be sent before the meeting to ensure we cover all your concerns.

Best wishes,
Celia Tang (Marketing Director)

- **Based on GlobeNet's email and your internal meeting last week and your own ideas, what questions do you want to ask?**

- **Given these concerns/questions raised in the meeting, now write an email as Dawn to GlobeNet, copying your team in and outlining CommunicAsian's questions to be addressed at the invited bidder's meeting.**
- **Before you start writing think also about the *purpose* and *audience* for this email.**

To: Celia Tang
From: Dawn Chen
Cc: Vivek, Tony, Samantha, Melinda
Subject: Our questions about the RfP
Dear Celia,

- **Feedback and discuss.**

Activity 4. Reflection and further reading

Reflection

How did you do in this unit?

- **Look back at the original learning targets of this unit and evaluate your own strengths and weaknesses. Tick either + (positive) or – (negative) in the table below. Specify which tasks in each skills areas and activities you are evaluating. Then reflect on these and make notes in the final column.**

Tasks	+	–	Reflection notes
The reading tasks:			
The writing tasks:			

Tasks	**+**	**–**	**Reflection notes**
The speaking tasks:			
The listening tasks:			

Further reading

Bremner, S. (2008) Intertextuality and business communication text books: Why students need more textual support. *English for Specific Purposes*,27(3), 306–321.

Kameda, N. (2009) *Contrastive rhetoric in business writing across cultures.* Paper presented at the 8th ABC Asia Pacific Conference at Nanyang Business School, Nanyang Technological University, March 2008.

UNIT

3

Building a business response

The **learning targets** for this unit are to:

- Understand the communication demands of virtual team meetings
- Practise the skills of leading and participating in internal and external virtual meetings
- Understand how an RfP response is organised and written in English
- Plan and write a proposal response to an RfP
- Understand and practise how to make your writing readable

Activity 1. Input: Readings and discussion

Task (i). Pre-reading discussion

- **In pairs or groups, discuss the differences between face-to-face and virtual meetings. Make your notes in the table:**

Face-to-face business meetings	Virtual business meetings

■ **Discuss the following questions:**

(i) What do you think is/are the most important difference(s) between 'virtual meetings' and 'face-to-face' business meetings? Why?

....

....

....

(ii) How common do you think virtual business meetings are now in Asian countries (and globally)?

....

....

....

(iii) What do you think the major challenges might be?

....

....

....

■ **Look at the vocabulary and idiomatic expression items in bold in the readings below. If you don't understand them, refer to the dictionary in Appendix 1 and/or try and guess the meaning from the context.**

Now read the text below:

Reading 1 COMMUNICATION CHALLENGES OF BUSINESS VIRTUAL MEETINGS

Due to advances in technology in globalised Asian workplaces and the communication challenges posed by **geographically dispersed teams**, it is likely that we will be working increasingly with colleagues living and working all over the world. The global Covid 19 pandemic has accelerated this trend, where **'work from home'** (WFH) guidance was given in most countries. The trend is therefore both local and international. Businesses with **remote global teams** may be **synchronously communicating** with team members in Hong Kong, India, USA, Singapore, South Korea, UK, Japan and Vietnam, just to name a few. What are the challenges of communicating effectively for such remote business teams and colleagues?

The **implications** of such virtual communication practices are enormous for how we communicate, especially where **English is the lingua franca** used for business. Not only are we faced with having to understand a range of different accents and cultures, but we are doing all this using technical platforms **and mobile devices** that may not have **video capability**. This means that **synchronous listening** in a second language, without the **affordance of** face-to-face interaction, becomes very demanding because facial and body gestures no longer **augment the meaning** of what we are saying. Another big challenge is that our team members will be on different time zones, so virtual communication practices may involve attending project meetings remotely, at the **dead of night**, for some of the project team members.

Unsurprisingly recent studies exploring virtual business communication, even where there is video capability such as on Zoom, have shown that communication breakdown is very common. In one of these studies it was found that managers complain that their virtual teams sometimes are not fully participating in meetings, they are not putting forward their ideas, not asking questions and not having the kind of **normal social chit-chat** and unplanned conversation that often happens in face-to-face meetings. At the same time, team members

continued . . .

cont. complain about not being heard because managers take all the meeting time to talk, without **eliciting the views** of the team, so participation and collaboration become problematic in the team. Allowing time for participation and actively encouraging this is a key management responsibility. However, team members must also take responsibility to actively engage. There is also the problem that there may be differences in language competency levels across teams and participants, and knowing how to accommodate these differences and make cultural adaptations is also a key business communication skill.

A final challenge for successful virtual meetings is to ensure they are well-organised. Often a meeting is booked on a meeting platform for 45–60 minutes, and making the most of that booked time is critical. One of the ways that managers have found to **maximise time** and effectiveness in these meetings is to send out documentation for review before the meeting, have **clear agendas** and allocate time for each of the team members to talk. Of course, these ideas all need to be considered in relation to the purpose(s) of the business virtual meeting. Is the purpose to make weekly/monthly reports; is the purpose to provide a **one-off** forum to collaboratively resolve a problem, or is it to brainstorm a new idea? The purpose, content and participants dictate roles and contributions expected in the virtual meeting and these need to be **explicit** and agreed by everyone attending the meeting.

This unit will describe and help you practise virtual meeting skills in the context of the case study where CommunicAsian is regularly communicating with project members in India, the Philippines, Singapore and Hong Kong, as well as with the client GlobeNet which is based in the UK.

Post-reading questions

(i) According to the text, what are the challenges of communicating in English in virtual meetings? Can you think of any others?

....

....

....

(ii) What are the virtual team strategies that are suggested in the text? Can you think of any other ones?

....
....
....

■ **Look at the vocabulary and idiomatic expression items in bold in the readings below. If you don't understand them, refer to the dictionary in Appendix 1 and/or try and guess the meaning from the context.**

Now read the text below:

Reading 2 THE IMPORTANCE OF MAKING YOUR WRITING READABLE

The use of **'plain English'** has now become common in many English-speaking business and legal contexts ensuring the customer is able, for example, to read a complicated legal document or a business guarantee and understand them before they sign and purchase.

As with all business communication, when writing your proposal response to an RfP be careful not to the use **ambiguous, complex** and **jargonistic** language. It is your responsibility to make your writing readable for your audience. Look at the free downloadable guide on plain English http://www.plainenglish.co.uk/free-guides.html.

Use plain English that is easy to read! Here are some common problems in writing business documents. Examples (X poor) replaced by (√ good) are given below.

1. **Long sentences.** Write short sentences and use punctuation to enable easy understanding. For example:
   Each of our team members have experience and skills in understanding and meeting your company's needs and we focus on results of our efforts. (X)
   Our highly experienced team will provide results. (√)

continued . . .

cont.

2. **Poor use of the passive voice.** In business communication, where relationship building and interaction is key, this is enabled by the use of personal pronouns and active voice. For example:

   Technical decisions are made based on your requested specifications. (X)

   Our technical team creates quality results based on your needs. (√)

3. **Overuse of personal pronouns.** This is problematic where the main purpose of the communication is on the area of concern (e.g. the quality or the product), not the relationship. For example:

   We are the right team to take your company to success and ensure the quality product and set of processes you are looking for. (X)

   Your high quality product and set of processes ensuring success, are the focus of our expert team. (√)

4. **Omit superfluous or redundant words.** Too many words are often used that do not add to the meaning and are therefore distracting to the communication of your message. For example:

   Our well-renowned company comprising a very experienced and highly skilled team of experts is always ready to actively listen to your every need and respond efficiently and appropriately in a timely way with their advice and recommendations. (X)

   Our team of experts is always ready to provide needs-based, timely advice. (√)

5. **Write in the positive; the problem of double negatives.** Using double negatives in the same sentence, common in legal English, often threatens a clear understanding. For example:

   We are not liable to refund you if you are not in Hong Kong (X)

   We are not liable to refund you if you are out of Hong Kong (√)

6. **Develop parallelism in your writing.** Use the same grammatical clause structure to exemplify or list advantages/disadvantages. For example:

   The CEO gave guidance on how to deal with shortage of supplies and said that any new purchases need to be cleared with the FO because the IT department would need new equipment. (X)

   The CEO gave guidance on dealing with shortages of supplies and the need to clear new purchases with reference to IT with FO. (√)

Ensuring your writing is readable is a writer's responsibility not a reader's responsibility in English. Some studies have suggested that this is a cultural issue where, for example, the Chinese reader also has a responsibility to **decipher** the meanings of Chinese written texts. This finding has implications for teaching good business writing skills when working in global business contexts, particularly where the audiences are first language speakers of English.

As you write your first draft of the GlobeNet proposal report think about ensuring it is readable.

The story so far ...

- **Look at the vocabulary and idiomatic expression items in bold. If you don't understand them, refer to the dictionary in Appendix 1 and/or try and guess the meaning from the context.**

Now read the story below:

BUILDING A PROJECT TEAM

At four o'clock Singapore time there were five people logged into the Zoom virtual meeting. Dawn and Tony were joined by Vivek and Prasad from Bangalore, Melinda, the finance manager from the Philippines, and Samantha, the head of Talent Management, who was sitting opposite Dawn in Singapore. Dawn checked that everyone had read the RfP and said:

"Okay. I can confirm that we are definitely going to respond. We have four weeks to put together a **killer proposal**, so this meeting is about who should be on our response team and how we should run it. I shall lead this one."

"I've been thinking about the name," said Tony. "I think 'Roam like you're home' is too **dated**, it **doesn't speak to** smartphone users. How about something like Connection Selection?"

"Tony, we're not **coming up with** the campaign now. This is about planning." Dawn grinned at Samantha and **mouthed the words** "how do we **rein him in**?"

Samantha smiled too, and moved in front of the screen. "I have a few questions," she began. "What skills are we going to need on the team, and do we have them **in-house** at the moment? Do we want all the team members to be **full-time** on the proposal until it's done?"

"I can't be full-time," said Vivek. "I can't just drop everything. I can do my bits and we can conference at the end of each day."

Dawn **cut in** "I was thinking we'd bring the team to Singapore and give them one of the conference rooms. Face-to-face is more productive, it builds the team spirit more." Dawn looked to Samantha for support, and she nodded, but before she could speak, Vivek **came back**.

"We **spent a fortune** on technology and networks and then we don't want to use it?"

Tony added his comment. "I'm going to need to be in Hong Kong because that's where the client manager, Celia is based, right? I can send my best account manager to Singapore if that's useful."

"I can do that too," said Vivek.

"Who do we have who knows the mobile phone business, especially in UK?" said Samantha. "I can't think of anyone. If we need a **consultant** they will probably be in the UK."

There was a silence that lasted almost a minute before Melinda, the finance manager, **broke it**. "I was hoping to **get clarity** on what the budget should be for the proposal preparation, but it seems we are not even close."

Dawn knew she had to do something or else what started as an exciting opportunity would become a list of problems.

"Right," she said, "there were a lot of good points raised. I would like everybody to consider those and send me their thoughts by tomorrow morning 10.00 a.m. Vivek and Tony, consider what you would need to do, and how it could work virtually, oh, and list any problems you **foresee**. I will put all your ideas together and **set the direction**. We should aim to have the team in place by next Monday."

There were smiles and goodbyes as everyone exited the meeting, and Dawn breathed a sigh of relief. This team was not going to be easy.

Why does Dawn think this team is not going to be easy?

....
....
....

Activity 2. Input: Understanding and modelling spoken and written texts

Task (i). Tips and techniques for virtual meetings

To make sure virtual meetings are effective, there needs to be **plenty of preparation** to ensure the meeting has:

(i) **An agenda**

- **An agenda** that is circulated with relevant documents before the meeting with time to read. This should be written in **plain English** to ensure comprehensibility
- Clear understanding of **who** is on the call and the **purpose** of his/her presence

(ii) **During** the meeting-tips and techniques:

Opening and closing the meeting the manager needs to:

- Welcome and introduce participants at the beginning of the meeting
- Summarise the main points of the meeting and next steps at the end of the meeting

■ **What are some of the other important things to consider when running or attending a virtual meeting?**

Put your ideas down in the box below:

Below is a virtual team checklist for the successful management of a virtual meeting.

<table>
<tr><th colspan="2">5-min Virtual Meeting Checklist</th></tr>
<tr><td rowspan="10">Advance Preparation</td><td>Preparation and Agenda</td></tr>
<tr><td>• Sent minutes/actions from last meeting to everyone</td></tr>
<tr><td>• Sent agenda and access to everyone with confirmations</td></tr>
<tr><td>• Time of meeting suits all locations</td></tr>
<tr><td>• Meeting responsibilities agreed with relevant people</td></tr>
<tr><td>• Meeting materials/supporting documents sent</td></tr>
<tr><td>Technology</td></tr>
<tr><td>• Instructions and access requirements sent to everyone</td></tr>
<tr><td>• Contingency plan agreed if network problems</td></tr>
<tr><td>• Zoom/Team Meet connections checked</td></tr>
<tr><td rowspan="6">Meeting in Progress</td><td>In Progress</td></tr>
<tr><td>• Check all expected attendees connected</td></tr>
<tr><td>• Confirm responsibilities for minutes/actions/agenda items</td></tr>
<tr><td>• Announce who is on the call (and why)</td></tr>
<tr><td>• Remind people to give their name before they speak</td></tr>
<tr><td>• Control time allocation for items</td></tr>
<tr><td rowspan="4">Meeting Conclusion</td><td>Wrap Up</td></tr>
<tr><td>• Ask for any other business (AOB)</td></tr>
<tr><td>• Confirm when minutes and actions will be sent</td></tr>
<tr><td>• Close</td></tr>
</table>

Task (ii). Listening to virtual meetings (Transcripts-Appendix 2)

There are two virtual meetings in this task for you to listen to and evaluate, compare and contrast.

Audio Meeting 1. CommunicAsian meets virtually with internal team members

Pre-listening question

- **How would you rate the success of this meeting on a scale of 1 (poor) to 10 (excellent)? Use the virtual meeting checklist above to help you assess the success of this meeting and comment on it.**

....
....
....
....

- **Look at the words and expressions in the box below and discuss the meanings. If you don't understand, try and guess the meanings as you listen. The words and expressions are explained in Appendix 1.**

Words and expressions	Meanings
Roll call Invited bidders People from their side Just like to point out Take it out ... travel budget Getting off track Open up the discussion Message/the measures Dashboards Cloud based/local servers Evolves Market segments	

Post-listening question

Are there any aspects of this virtual meeting that you would improve? Comment.

....
....
....
....
....

Audio Meeting 2. CommunicAsian holds a follow-up meeting virtually with internal team members

- **Now listen to *Meeting 2* and note down how communication was improved in this meeting in the box below:**

Post-listening questions

(i) How did this meeting compare to Meeting 1? How would you rate it? Refer to your notes.

....
....
....
....

(ii) What are some of the questions you think the team members would like to raise in the bidders' meeting with GlobeNet?

....
....
....
....

■ **Now write Dawn's email to GlobeNet with the questions CommunicAsian would like to address:**

To: Celia Tang
From: Dawn
Cc: Tony, Melinda, Vivek
Subject:

Now go to Activity 3 Task (i) for the meeting roleplay.

Task (iii). Reading and deconstructing the Himeno proposal as a model for the RfP

■ **Read Dawn's email below and check you understand the meaning of the words in bold.**

From: Dawn
To: Samantha; Melinda; Tony; Vivek; Prasad; Rory
Subject: Proposal Preparation for GlobeNet
Sent: Thursday, April 2, 11:13 a.m.

Hi all

Congratulations on getting the team set up so quickly and starting the project.

So let's agree Tony, Prasad and Vivek to go to the meeting. Tony you could delegate it to Prasad but that's **your call**.

I agree with Tony's suggestion that we refer back to our Himeno project documents (Sumo channel) and they should be available on our **archive**. However, remember that for GlobeNet we want to **pitch** for the implementation as well as the strategy – we didn't do that for Himeno.

A couple of points: can you let me know who is responsible for the final proposal document because I'd like to discuss my thoughts on that before you get too far in. I'll need a day at the end to review and edit so please build that into the schedule. Second, can you set up two or three progress meetings (depending on your schedule) so you can brief me on what your thinking is on approach and pricing for the actual project?

It'll be a busy three weeks so let's make it worthwhile!

Best

Dawn Chen (Direct line: +65 379 6133)
Chief Executive officer

The Himeno Media Group proposal

- **Look at the vocabulary items in bold and discuss with your partner if you are not sure of the meanings. Try and guess the meanings from the context and/or refer to Appendix 1.**

Now read this successful proposal written by CommunicAsian.

Proposal to:

Himeno Media Group

For

Sumo Into Europe: Market Analysis and Planning for Launching a Dedicated Sumo Wrestling Channel in Europe

1. INTRODUCTION

CommunicAsian thanks you for the opportunity to respond to your Request for Proposal dated May 14th.

We were established four years ago in Singapore as a new company within the XXX **conglomerate**, and we now have offices in four South East and South Asian countries with plans to open in North Asia within the next year.

We believe we are **unique** in the advertising and marketing sector for two reasons:

- Our full-service coverage: we have specialists in market analysis and **segmentation**; branding and messaging; effective use of social media to deliver messages, and developing and tracking analytics to manage the campaign.
- Our geographic and multicultural coverage: as well as having operations across Asia, we ensure that our teams are culturally diverse so that we incorporate cultural intelligence in all our solutions.

We set out to deliver a great Customer Experience (CX), and our belief is that CX makes Success.

Our work in the media industry includes **relaunching** the career of singer Bryan Tyco with a social media campaign measured through Twitter (over 100,000 followers) and YouTube (90,000 views), and his album is now **top-selling** in the Philippines and Indonesia.

Our experience in Europe includes working with the Far Eastern News Digest to build a **subscription base** in UK and Germany. This involved building audiences for their weekly podcast and using that to **generate** subscriptions, resulting in over seven thousand subscribers in three months.

2. PROPOSAL SUMMARY

This project is essentially looking at two phases:

- **Market research and analysis** to identify whether there is a viable market in Europe for a dedicated Sumo channel, measured by potential annualised revenue of US$ 1 million achievable within six months; and
- **Pilot strategies** for brand building and audience awareness for the initial six months and ongoing.

These are discussed more fully in Section 3 – Our Approach.

We expect the project to be completed within 10–12 weeks, depending on the results and timing of social media and focus group responses, and we propose weekly review meetings with Himeno Management so that any **potential hold-ups** can be addressed and **resolved** quickly.

Himeno requested a **fixed price** for this project to include all media costs and data analysis fees. The price is therefore set at USD32,000 at a maximum. If our estimated social media costs are lower than planned, we shall **rebate** the difference to Himeno. This is explained in Section 5 – Pricing, Terms and Conditions.

3. OUR APPROACH

Given Himeno's requirement for the Sumo channel to be **viable** within six months, the market survey and analysis must be highly focused. From our experience with products and services like this, we believe that the minimum size of any market segment should be 50,000–100,000 people, or 25,000 households. These segments must then be **qualified** through surveys and focus groups to understand their degree of interest and, importantly, what they would be prepared to pay for it.

Based upon those findings, we design **campaigns** (which may be different for different market segments) to **convert** that interest into an actual subscription.

The overall schedule is:

Task	Description	No of days	Comment
1.	**Demographic study** of European populations and market segment identification	5	Japanese residents will be one segment; others will depend on size
2.	Address the interest of **identified** segments	10	Surveys, focus groups, analysis of search engine activity

Task	Description	No of days	Comment
3.	Develop **pilot** 'Sumo Awareness' campaign to build interest and knowledge of new channel availability	10	Measure awareness before and after; follow up focus groups
4.	Run pilot on Social Media	28	Four-week **teaser** campaign
5.	Report to Himeno for decision on whether to proceed to a launch	5	Report to be a presentation as well as a document so the team can answer questions

We plan to complete the project by July so that Himeno can launch in late summer, which is the **peak** buying season for streaming services in Europe.

4. OUR TEAM

Our team will be led by our Creative Director, Tony Tanaka. Tony is from a Japanese family and raised in the United States. He has been with CommunicAsian for three years, and his work includes leading the Far Eastern News Digest project referred to above. The case study is available on our website. Tony won a gold award at the Advertising Association last year in the *Slogan of the Year* category for the anti-knife crime campaign **'Just cut it out.'**

Tony will be supported by the demographics and analytics team based in India.

Our CEO, Dawn Chen, will attend the weekly meetings with Himeno together with Tony.

5. PRICING, TERMS AND CONDITIONS

Himeno requested a fixed price for this project. Pricing for this project is of two types:

Type of cost	Description	Amount
Internal		22,000
External		10,000
Total		**32,000**

The external costs may be lower if, for example, market analysis shows only a limited potential, and if that occurs the difference would be rebated to Himeno.

US$32,000 is thus the maximum price for the project.

We can start the project within two weeks of your acceptance of this proposal.

This proposal and pricing are **valid** for two weeks from your receipt.

We look forward to working with you on this exciting project and to a successful outcome.

Dawn Chen
Chief Executive Officer

Deconstructing the proposal

Each of the five sections of the Himeno proposal response has a particular purpose. Each section also has its own kinds of vocabulary and grammar.

- **As you read through each section again note down the purpose and the kind of language that is used to achieve this purpose. Section 1 has been completed for you.**

Section	Purpose	Grammar and vocabulary choices and format
1. Introduction	This section thanks the client for the invitation and introduces the bidder. It provides an opportunity for the bidder to show how well they are positioned to deliver, relying on descriptions of work that has been completed elsewhere. This is an informative, descriptive and persuasive text.	**Past and present tense** is used to describe when and where CommunicAsian was set up, what it does and what has been achieved with other clients. **Adjectives** e.g. *unique, great, top-selling*. Choice of **key business words/ expressions** e.g. *conglomerate, full-service coverage, tracking analytics, operations, customer experience (CX), media campaign, subscription base*. Use of **third-person plural subject and possessive pronouns** *'we'* and *'our'* to communicate business solidarity Use of **clear headings, short paragraphs** and **bullet points** ensuring easy reading.
2. Proposal summary		
3. Our approach		
4. Our team		
5. Pricing, terms and conditions		

Use this model to help structure and choose appropriate language when writing your own proposal response for GlobeNet in the next activity.

Activity 3. Output: Spoken and written skills development

Task (i). Roleplay: Virtual meeting between GlobeNet and CommunicAsian

Situation

GlobeNet has offered a Q & A session with potential providers.

The GlobalNet bidders' meeting has been organised for today at 2 p.m. and the CEO will chair this virtual meeting.

■ **Divide the class into groups of four:**

- Two students work for GlobeNet: CEO (Trevor) and Marketing and Sales Manager (Celia)
- Two (or more) students are CommunicAsian employees: (Tony), Vivek and Prasad

■ **Read the GlobeNet and CommunicAsian role cards below and make comments and questions:**

*GlobeNet is keen to find a provider that is **creative** , **cost efficient** and has the technical expertise to deliver the project on time.*

Trevor (CEO) and Celia (Sales and Marketing)

- *You will first confirm the questions that Dawn has already sent in (see email in Activity 2), and elicit any further questions from CommunicAsian*
- *You want to check on the credibility of the team in terms of their software capability and experience*
- *You heard that CommunicAsian have located a number of software jobs to India from Singapore, so you want to know whether the development work will be done in Bangalore.*

Read the CommunicAsian company profile. You are Singapore based with increasing amounts of work off-shored to India.

Use the outcomes and questions of the internal meeting and Dawn's consolidated email to GlobeNet in Activity 2 for the meeting.

To make the roleplay 'virtual' make the roleplay groups sit in a circle where they are facing outwards. This way they have to rely on listening and speaking clearly.

- **Elect an observer for each group who will assess the success of the virtual meeting using the checklist provided in Activity 2 Task (i). Allow the roleplay to run for 30 minutes.**

Makes notes of the answers to the questions in the box below:

These will be useful as your write the proposal.

- Feedback and discuss.

Task (ii). Preparing to write the RfP response (The Proposal)

- In groups, use the ideas from the meeting above and the model Himeno proposal to structure and write the proposal.
- Once you have the structure, make notes on what you think should be included in each of the sections. Use the space provided below.

Structure: The headings	Content: The key information

Task (iii). Email exchange

Dawn has sent the following email to the team after the virtual meeting.

To: Samantha; Melinda; Tony; Vivek; Prasad; Rory
From: Dawn Chen, CEO.
Subject: Team membership suggestions.

Hi everyone,

Good to have you all on the call to plan our response to the RfP. One of the key things is to have in place our dream team so we can list them all out in the document and highlight their credentials. Yes budgets are also important so Melinda and I will work on that very soon.

My main concern right now is to seek Vivek's and Tony's advice about who you think would contribute well to this project and put those names forward. Please provide me with good justification for your suggestions and I will assume they will be available for the life of the project ... and may also like to relocate to Singapore to join the team.

Let's say something to me by Wednesday? That gives you a couple of days. And please copy Sam in.

Talk soon, Dawn

- **Respond to Dawn's email by taking the role of either Vivek or Tony.**

To: Dawn Chen
From:
Cc:
Subject:

Task (iv). Writing the proposal for GlobeNet

- **Working in groups, assemble all the information that is relevant to this proposal bid including the information you learned from the virtual meeting using your output from Task (ii) above.**

In groups draft your proposal. It should be no longer than 2–3 pages.

Read and discuss each other's proposals. They look at the winning one below.

Task (v). The winning project proposal

This is the one used for the rest of the project.

Proposal to:

GlobeNet Communications

for

Roam like you're Home: Market analysis, Branding and Planning for Selling UK based SIM Cards in three Asian Markets

1. INTRODUCTION

CommunicAsian thanks you for the opportunity to respond to your Request for Proposal dated April 4th.

We set up more than five years ago in Singapore as a company within the XXX conglomerate, and we now have offices in five Asian countries. We are now over 100 people, with plans to expand considerably over the next two years.

We believe we are unique in the advertising and marketing sector for two reasons:

- **Our full-service coverage:** we have specialists in market analysis and segmentation; branding and messaging; effective use of social media to deliver messages, and developing and tracking analytics to manage the campaign.
- **Our geographic and multicultural coverage:** as well as having operations across Asia, we ensure that our teams are culturally diverse so that we incorporate cultural intelligence in all our solutions. In the past year we have developed specific expertise and experience working with Asian companies expanding markets into Europe.

Examples of this experience in Europe include:

- Working with the **Far Eastern News Digest** to build a subscription base in the UK and Germany. This involved building audiences for their weekly podcast and using that to generate subscriptions, resulting in over seven thousand subscribers in three months.
- Working with **Himeno Media Group** to successfully launch a subscription streaming service in the UK for Sumo Wrestling. The target of US$1 million in annual subscriptions was exceeded within six months of project initiation. We provided the full range of services from market analysis and branding to campaign management.

Case studies for these and other projects, as well as client testimonials, are available on our website www.CommunicAsian.com.

2. PROPOSAL SUMMARY

This project is essentially looking at four areas of work:

- **Market research and analysis** to identify target market segments, initially in three countries for the launch. Initial reviews of travelers to the UK suggest four likely market segments based solely on numbers: students from the People's Republic of China (some 150,000 per year according to census data), health workers and care workers from the Philippines (30–40,000), students from Hong Kong (30–40,000 including secondary and tertiary students), and school students from Thailand (20,000 estimated). These and other potential segments will be analysed through surveys, focus groups, and social media responses to identify the true potential for GlobeNet products. As an estimate, we would expect 50% of any validated segment to be a likely customer for GlobeNet.
- **Brand building and audience awareness** is a critical success factor for consumer products. Our creative team will test different branding ideas (including your project name 'Roam like you're Home') with target groups to maximise awareness and positivity towards GlobeNet products.
- **Planning and piloting the campaign** to look at all the aspects of delivering the message: language used, social media and/or print in relevant publications, and evolution of the messaging over the 10-week campaign.
- **Measurement and analytics** are key to tracking effectiveness and identifying where things need to be changed. Our team will identify the right measures and develop the tracking reports and dashboards so that GlobeNet managers can quickly see progress.

These are discussed more fully in Section 3, Our Approach.

We expect the project to be completed within 10–12 weeks, depending on the results and timing of social media and focus group responses, and we propose weekly review meetings in Hong Kong between Tony Tanaka, our Head of Creative, and Celia Tang so that any potential hold-ups can be addressed and resolved quickly. Other managers from Singapore and Bangalore can join as needed.

Based on our experience, we estimate a price for the project of USD40,000 to US$50,000, depending on the market segments selected and the campaign. We will be able to refine this estimate at the end of the market research phase. The basis for our costing is shown in Section 5 below.

3. OUR APPROACH

Given GlobeNet's requirement to expand the top-up, pay-as-you-go SIM cards, we shall focus on groups spending a minimum of three months in UK as part of our segment analysis. From our experience with products and services like these, we believe that the minimum size of any market segment should be 30,000 people, and with an expected 50% take-up rate. These segments must be qualified through surveys and focus groups to understand their degree of interest and, importantly, what they are prepared to pay for it.

Based upon those findings, we design campaigns (which may be different for different market segments) to convert that interest into an actual purchase.

The campaigns are tracked so that messages or service offerings can be changed to improve results if necessary.

The overall schedule is:

Task	Description	No of days	Comment
1.	**Market research and analysis** Demographic study of East Asian temporary residents of UK and market segment identification	5	This should lead to decisions on where to run campaigns
2.	Assess the strength of the interest of identified segments	10	Surveys, focus groups, analysis of search engine activity

Task	Description	No of days	Comment
3.	**Brand building and awareness** Test that the brand and message generate positive feelings in the audience Test the product and features knowledge	10	Test responses to different messages and tag lines Measure awareness before and after; follow up focus groups
4.	**Planning and piloting, measurement** Run pilot on Social Media	30	Six week campaign with tracking and modifying
5.	Report to GlobeNet with recommendations for ongoing management	5	Report to be a presentation as well as a document so the team can answer questions

We plan to complete the project by July so that GlobeNet will access the large student market which tends to travel to the UK in August and September.

4. OUR TEAM

Our team will be led by our Creative Director, Tony Tanaka. He has been with CommunicAsian almost five years, and his work includes leading both the Far Eastern News Digest project and the Himeno Media project referred to above. The case studies are available on our website. Tony won a gold award at the Advertising Association in the Slogan of the Year category for the anti-knife crime campaign 'Just cut it out.'

Day to day project management will be handled by Prasad Patel, who will also head up the analytics and reporting team. Prasad joined us originally to work on the Himeno Media project with a background in data analysis and statistics, and has contributed to several projects since.

Our CEO, Dawn Chen, will lead a project steering committee to oversee the work, and members will include the heads of Talent Management and Finance.

5. PRICING, TERMS AND CONDITIONS

Our best estimate of costings is shown below, and will be refined at the end of the market research phase when target segments and countries are agreed with GlobeNet.

Type of cost	Description	Amount
Internal	Market research and segment identification Focus groups, surveys, analysis Develop branding and messaging Develop and agree success measures and tracking Plan and implement campaign Formal report to GlobeNet with further recommendations	25,000
External (assuming 3 countries and English only)	Fees to Facebook, Google etc. for analytics reporting Fees to Survey app Licenses for use of photographs and other images	15,000
Language/app changes	Possible translation services Additional fees to use WeChat, Weibo etc	5,000
Total		45,000

How does this compare to your own group's proposal? Discuss.

....
....
....

Activity 4. Reflection and further reading

Reflection

How did you go in this unit?

- **Look back at the original learning targets of this unit and evaluate your own strengths and weaknesses. Tick either + (positive) or – (negative) in the table below. Specify which tasks in each skills areas and activities you are evaluating. Then reflect on these and make notes in the final column.**

Tasks	+	–	Reflection notes
The reading tasks:			
The writing tasks:			

Tasks	**+**	**–**	**Reflection notes**
The speaking tasks:			
The listening tasks:			

Further reading

Beamer, L. (1994) Teaching English business writing to Chinese-speaking business students. *The Bulletin of the Association of Business Communication*, 57(1), 12–18.

Lockwood, J. (2015) Virtual team management: what is causing communication breakdown? *Language and Intercultural Communication*, 15(1), 125–140.

UNIT 4

Winning the bid

The **learning targets** for this unit are to:

- Understand workplace policy documents and how they impact business practices
- Understand what makes a good business presentation
- Prepare and deliver a successful business presentation
- Understand and use a range of accommodation strategies

Activity 1. Input: readings and discussion

■ **Look at the vocabulary and idiomatic expression items in bold. If you don't understand them, refer to the dictionary in Appendix 1 and/or try and guess the meaning from the context.**

Now read the text below:

Reading 1 WORKPLACE BULLYING AND HARASSMENT

Global workplaces are very aware about the need to **safeguard** their employees from bullying and harassment. These safeguards are usually written into contracts and policy documents, and are overseen by human resource departments.

Workplace bullying and harassment can be defined as **harmful** and **targeted behaviour** that takes place at work. It might be **malicious**, **offensive**, and/or **intimidating**, and may be **systematically applied** over a period of time. Examples of workplace bullying may include **victimising** by:

- targeted **practical jokes**
- malicious **gossip**
- being **misled** about work duties, e.g. incorrect deadlines or deliberately unclear directions
- **unreasonable denial** of requests for time off; early departure etc.
- **threats**, **humiliation**, and other **verbal abuse**

Such unreasonable behaviours can result in stress and workplace **absenteeism**. However, it should be noted that **criticism or monitoring** in the workplace is not necessarily bullying. For example, **objective** and **constructive** criticism that typically takes place as part of team monthly reports and annual **appraisals** does not constitute bullying and harassment.

■ **Now discuss and answer the questions below**

(i) Do you think these sorts of problems are common in Asian workplaces?

....

....

....

(ii) Do you know of any victims of such behaviours?

....

....

....

(iii) What do you think could be some of the language and cultural issues in such behaviours at work?

....

....

....

To prevent misunderstandings at the workplace, language accommodation and cultural adaptability strategies are key to safeguarding the workforce and providing a healthy workplace environment.

- **Look at the vocabulary and idiomatic expression items in bold. If you don't understand them, refer to the dictionary in Appendix 1 and/or try and guess the meaning from the context.**

Now read the text below:

Reading 2 ACCOMMODATION STRATEGIES IN GLOBAL BUSINESS EXCHANGE

Given that English is now spoken by more second language than first language speakers, it is often the case that in business communication situations, your English may be much better than the person you are speaking or writing to. What can you do about this to ensure smooth communication?

In order to ensure your business message is understood, it is important that you use **plain standard forms of English** combined with appropriate **accommodation strategies** where you may be constantly adapting your language, and using your cultural knowledge as well, to make sure your exchange is understood by the other party. Accommodation strategies are explained and exemplified below.

What are examples of accommodation strategies?

If your English is better than the business colleague you are talking to, you may find that s/he avoids responding because s/he may be trying to translate what you are saying word by word. So as a more proficient speaker you may find that the following 'accommodation strategies' **facilitate** successful business exchange.

cont.

- Don't shout or raise your voice; this is not a volume problem! This is an **instinctive thing** to do but raising your voice will carry its own meaning of **impatience**, **disapproval** and even **annoyance**.
- Slow down your pace of speech and stress the important words as these carry the main meaning.
- Be prepared to repeat what you have said as many times as is necessary.
- Check your colleague has understood by asking her/him to repeat the message back to you. This is important if you have weak speakers of English in your team and you have, for example, given an important instruction and want to be sure it has been well understood.
- Use visuals and other media to ensure your message is understood. Mobile devices have some great translation software now.
- Standardise your English. This means using simple English avoiding **complex idiomatic language** and **unfamiliar** technical and workplace jargon.

Being proficient in English makes for smooth communication at work in a BELF context, but this also needs to accompanied by the skilled use of accommodation strategies where colleagues from different language and culture backgrounds are communicating. Being able to accommodate linguistically and **adapt** culturally to a range of business situations ensures that businesses can be successful in this new global business environment. **Cultural adaptability** refers to your ability to understand the communicative and behavioural styles of different ethnicities, ages, personalities, professional groups and other orientations. For example, it is often said that Americans tend to be more aggressive and confrontational about what they want compared to their Asian counterparts. Without falling into the trap of stereotyping, this kind of knowledge may provide the business communicator with opportunities of trying different communication approaches in English to ensure messages have the best prospect of being understood and acted upon.

In Activity 3 Task (iii) in this unit you are asked to discuss appropriate cultural adaptability approaches in a series of authentic situations.

A recent study has expanded the notion and value of linguistic accommodation and cultural adaptability to include the **structuring** *cont.* and **scaffolding** around the business communication event.

For example, in one of the studies, a large on-line American travel business subcontracted a Chinese company in Beijing to do major development work to update their on-line booking function. The Chinese company employed engineers who were technically very good but whose communication in English was very low, apart from the team lead. The **rules of engagement** for each daily meeting were mandated in an informal **project charter** where the format of the meeting was to be the same every day and **spelt out** strict turn-taking, the use of standardised English and very limited social chit chat. Social chit chat is unpredictable and often comprises **idiomatic expressions** and **slang** that the Chinese members might find difficult. This study mirrored the findings of what makes good virtual meetings as discussed in the previous unit where **forethought** and good organisation result in successful virtual team meetings.

- **Now discuss and answer the questions below**

(i) Do you think it is only the stronger language speaker that needs to accommodate? Why?/Why not?

....

....

....

(ii) What are some accommodation strategies you could use if you don't understand what has been said to you?

....

....

....

The story so far ...

- **Look at the vocabulary and idiomatic expression items in bold. If you don't understand them, refer to the dictionary in Appendix 1 and/or try and guess the meaning from the context.**

Now read the story below:

PROBLEMS IN THE TEAM

The bid process was going well. Vivek and Tony worked mainly in their home cities, but were planning to go to Singapore for a day or two to work on the final presentation. Each had sent someone to be part of the Singapore team; Tony's Account Manager, Rory, was a small man with a big voice and a strong American accent. Many people found him **irritating**, but he was good at his job, so they **put up with him**. Prasad, from Vivek's department, proved an expert at identifying and specifying analytics, and was always prepared to help other members with technical issues. In short, Dawn thought, not having the **impetuous** Tony and **negative** Vivek on site had proved a really good thing. The team had been creative, worked to a schedule, and was now close to completing the response. She was quietly confident.

Tony and Vivek would arrive around noon the next day, and Dawn was planning to surprise them by proposing that Rory and Prasad deserved to be part of the team presenting the proposal to GlobeNet management. She wondered if Tony and Vivek would see that as a **compliment** to their management skills or a threat.

Her thoughts were interrupted by a knock at the door, and Samantha, the HR Manager, came in.

"Hi Sam," she smiled. "Sit down. I was just thinking that the team has worked really well. We should organize some sort of recognition."

"Sorry," said Samantha, "I'm about to **rain on your parade**. I've had a serious complaint about Rory from a female team member. She says that Rory has been making **suggestive** remarks to her since the project started, and she has ignored it as she did not want to disrupt the team. She says that yesterday he put his arms around her."

"Do you believe her? Have you spoken to Rory?"

"I do believe her," said Samantha, "and I haven't spoken to Rory. Our policy on **sexual harassment** says that a possible offender should be **suspended from work** so they cannot contact their **accuser**. I think we have to suspend Rory, and that is going to **send a shock through** your team."

"Do we have an option?" said Dawn. "Could we send him back to Hong Kong while we investigate? That would avoid upsetting the project and buy us some time."

Samantha shook her head. "If we ignore it and it **comes out** that we didn't follow our own policy we would be in real trouble. If you want to keep Rory and send him to Hong Kong, you would need to **be upfront about it** and explain the circumstances. I don't think it's likely that he or his accuser would agree to that."

Dawn stood up and **paced** across the office. She thought better when she could move around.

"Sam, would it be possible for me to talk to Rory unofficially before you have to **tackle** him formally? I'd like to see if there's any way ..."

"**No way**," said Samantha, "we have a **complainant** to consider as well."

Dawn walked around some more and then decided. "Very well, Sam. Start the process and follow the policy."

■ Now discuss and answer the questions below

(i) How does Dawn's mood switch in this episode of the story so far....? Why?

....

....

....

(ii) What does Sam persuade her boss to do?

....

....

....

In the next section, you'll read CommunicAsian's company policy.

Activity 2. Input: Understanding and modelling spoken and written texts

Task (i). Sexual Harassment policy at CommunicAsian

- As you read the policy in the CommunicAsian employee manual, look at the words and expressions in bold and discuss the meanings; can you guess any of them from the context? Refer to Appendix 1.

We do not tolerate sexual harassment in our workplace in any form. Our culture is based on *mutual respect* and collaboration. Sexual harassment is ***a serious violation*** of those principles.

Scope

This policy applies to every person in our company *regardless* of gender, sexual orientation, or level.

Policy elements

(i) What is sexual harassment?

Sexual harassment has many forms of *variable seriousness*. A person sexually harasses someone when they:

- *Invade* another person's *personal space* (e.g. inappropriate touching.)
- Comment on someone's looks, dress, sexuality or gender in a *derogatory* or *objectifying* manner or a manner that makes them uncomfortable.
- Make *obscene* comments, jokes or gestures that *humiliate* or offend someone.
- Pursue or *flirt* with another person *persistently* without the other person's willing participation.

Sexual harassment may be *unintentional* or *inadvertent*, but that does not excuse it.

(ii) How to report sexual harassment?

If you are being sexually harassed please report it to the Manager, Human Resources (HR Manager).

Disciplinary action

Employees who are accused of sexual harassment will be suspended from work so that they do not contact the complainant or interfere in the investigation process.

Employees who are found guilty of sexual harassment for the first time may:

- Be *reprimanded* and fined.
- Get a "below expectations" performance review and suspension of promotion and/or pay rise.
- Be *terminated* if the HR Manager deems it appropriate.

HR responsibilities

When HR receives a complaint that an employee harasses another employee, they will:

- Ask for as many details and information as possible from the person or people making the complaint.
- *Launch an investigation.* If the matter is complex, the HR person can defer to a more senior manager.

Contact the harasser and set up a meeting to explain the complaint and explicitly tell the person that he or she will be *suspended* from work until the investigation is completed.

Given the CommunicAsian policy above, and given the sexual harassment complaint made about Rory, how should the company respond?

....

....

....

Task (ii). What makes a good presentation?

- **In pairs, think about a good presentation you have been to recently. What was it and why was it so good? Jot your ideas down in the box below and discuss.**

■ **Feedback as a whole class and read the text below.**

Key questions to think about when designing and delivering your PowerPoint presentation

As with any other business communication tool (e.g. email), PowerPoint is a TOOL not a template that works the same way in every situation.

Three key questions to think about before you start developing your slides are:

- What is/are the *main purpose(s)* of my presentation? (Is it to inform, persuade, stimulate discussion, report results or a combination of these? Which is the most important?)
- What is the audience of my presentation? (Is my audience internal colleagues? External client?)
- What is the content of my presentation? (How much content should be included and how should it be presented?)

Steps in preparing your PowerPoint:

Step 1: Consider the *purpose, audience and content* of your PowerPoint. Then think of your PowerPoint as a narrative – a story you want to tell.

Step 2: Decide on, and prepare, *handouts* before you start developing your PowerPoint. This simple step will help you keep the presentation format simple as the audience will already have the detail numbers and tables.

Step 3: Select *visuals* that will communicate the key points you are making in your presentation.

Step 4: *Less is more. Limit the amount of text* and the *number of slides* you put on your PowerPoint. Adult audiences lose interest if your PowerPoint is too long. If each slide is densely packed with text, your audience may not be able to read it and you may be tempted to read it verbatim which reflects your lack of preparation and/or expertise.

Step 5: Having developed and revised your PowerPoint, *rehearse it* and be prepared to keep *revising* it. *Rehearsing does not mean memorising the content.*

One of the most difficult things to do well is *transitioning* between one slide to another especially where you are introducing a new topic.

Tips in delivering your PowerPoint.

Tip 1: *Ensure your technology works.* This is particularly important if you are doing a virtual PowerPoint presentation. Don't give your PowerPoint centre stage, it is your slave not your master.

Tip 2: *Strong start.* Make your introductions, then *preview the main purpose/content the presentation* will cover and have a *'hook'* to engage your audience (this may be a question, a joke, an anecdote, even something personal about yourself).

Tip 3: Ensure your *slide headings are clear and there is a logical flow* e.g. who we are/the brief/the approach etc. These headings will differ for different purposes and audiences.

Tip 4: Strong finish. Depending on the purpose of your presentation, you may want to summarise the key points, or highlight the key takeaway form your PowerPoint.

Tip 5. *Thank* your audience and *open up* for questions and comment.

Task (iii). Listening audio: PowerPoint – CommunicAsian presentation to Himeno Media Group (Transcript – Appendix 2)

Before you watch the PowerPoint for the first time note down what you think the purpose, audience and content of the PowerPoint is:

....
....
....
....

PowerPoint made to the Himeno Media Group by CommunicAsian

- **Look at the words and expressions used in the PowerPoint. Discuss in pairs and if you don't understand try and guess from the context in which it is used.**

Words and expressions	**Meaning**
On top of	
Leverage	
An annualised amount	
Standalone service	
Brand building	
Pilot	
Identify market segments	
Correlate	
Compensate	
Teaser campaign	
Census data	
Obscure facts	

■ **As you listen to the PowerPoint for the first time, note down the how each slide is functioning:**

Slide	Title and function(s)
1.	
2.	
4.	
5.	
6.	
7.	

Slide 1: Sumo into Europe

Sumo into Europe

Slide 2: The Brief

The Brief

- Himeno Media Group have recently acquired the worldwide rights to broadcast all Sumo Wrestling tournaments in Japan.

- Himeno contracted CommunicAsian to identify the potential in Europe and to develop a brand campaign. The requirements are:
  - Subscription revenue to be minimum USD1 million within 6 months
  - Sumo channel to be standalone, not part of a bundle

Slide 3: What we did

What we did

- Identified target market segments for the initial 6 month pilot
  - Japanese people living in Europe
  - Local students studying Asian subjects
  - Self selecting with an interest in Sumo

- For each of these we conducted a survey followed by focus groups to give us information on
  - How many would be interested in subscribing to a Sumo channel
  - What extras might make them subscribe
  - How much they would be willing to pay

- Conducted a 'Sumo awareness' study with a small campaign to measure before and after impact

Slide 4: Findings

Findings

- UK is home to about 100,000 Japanese residents. Italy is second largest with 50,000. We estimate that UK has about 40,000 Japanese households.

- UK has over 100,000 tertiary students studying Japanese and Asian subjects.

- 50% of Japanese focus groups and 40% of student groups would be interested in a Sumo channel. Price point was around $10 per month. At that price, Himeno would need about 10,000 subscribers to meet its minimum revenue target.

- As a comparison, the badminton channel charges $15 per month and has 22,000 subscribers in its last filing.

Slide 5: Our campaign

Our campaign: Who knows Sumo?

Different fact each week for 4 weeks on Facebook and Twitter

Slide 6: Results

Results

- There is a viable market for the Sumo channel in UK, and we recommend focusing on that market rather than trying to cover all of Europe.
- The pilot campaign using social media to generate interest in Sumo had more than 200,000 visits and likes in four weeks.

Slide 7: Thank you

■ **As you listen for the second time, note down the language Tony uses to transition from one slide to another. The first one has been done for you.**

Slides	**Transitioning and introducing the next topic**
1–2	*So, let's remind ourselves of what you asked us to do.*
2–3	
3–4	
4–5	
5–6	
6–7	

- **Use the Presentation Feedback Form in Activity 3 Task (i) to assess the effectiveness of this PowerPoint presentation.**
- **Discuss in groups and feedback.**

Activity 3. Output: Spoken and written skills development

Task (i). Preparing, presenting and feeding back on your PowerPoint

Using the model proposal for CommunicAsian's bid for GlobeNet in Unit 3, Activity 2, and using the model presentation for the Himeno project, prepare slides for a 15-minute GlobeNet presentation bid.

Now use the feedback form to peer assess other groups as they make their presentation

PRESENTATION FEEDBACK FORM			
Focus points	**Needs work**	**Good**	**Comments**
1. Content			
• Information was accurate, interesting, relevant			
• Balance of text and visuals			
• Used examples, anecdotes, and facts/ cited source to support main ideas			

PRESENTATION FEEDBACK FORM			
Focus points	**Needs work**	**Good**	**Comments**
2. Organisation			
• Presentation was organised in logical, clear manner with good transitioning			
• Presentation included a clear introduction			
• Presentation had conclusion			
3. Audience			
• Presentation was appropriate for the audience			
• Presentation held audience's attention.			
4. Presentation skills			
• Presentation reflected preparation and rehearsal			
• Presentation was well paced			

PRESENTATION FEEDBACK FORM			
Focus points	**Needs work**	**Good**	**Comments**
• Presenter used technology/ visual aids effectively			
5. English communicative competence			
• Selection of language for interpersonal effect			
• Selection of language for transitions, openings and closing for discourse effect			
• Grammar accuracy, range, selection of vocabulary and accommodating where appropriate			
• Voice quality and phonological features are appropriate			
Strengths			

PRESENTATION FEEDBACK FORM			
Focus points	**Needs work**	**Good**	**Comments**
Challenges			
Reflection space			

Task (ii). Congratulations email from GlobeNet and responses

Dawn has just received the following email from Trevor at GlobeNet.

To: Dawn
From: Trevor
Cc: Celia Tang

Congratulations

Dear Dawn,

I am very pleased to announce that you are our preferred partner for the 'Roam like you're Home' project. It was a competitive process but we thought your team provided a good balance between a creative and analytical approach in your proposal.

Celia will manage this project out of Hong Kong and will set up an initial meeting next week to confirm timelines and deadlines.

Again, our congratulations and we look forward to a productive partnership.

Kind regards,

Trevor Lavender
CEO GlobeNet

Just as Dawn was reading this, her phone pinged and there was chat message from Celia Tang in HK:

> *Congratulations! (Hands clapping) Celebrations all round! Champagne on me when we next meet. (Popping champagne bottle)*

You send back responses to both.

- **Write an email to Trevor. What is your purpose, audience and content?**

To: Trevor From: Dawn Cc:? Subject:

- **Now respond to Celia's text.**

Justify your different text responses to Trevor and Celia.

....
....
....

- **Now write a 'good news' email to the team.**

To: CommunicAsian team
From: Dawn
Subject:

Task (iii). Accommodation scenarios

- **Read the different scenarios and decide the appropriate ways of communicating in these difficult situations.**

Discuss what the key culture and language issues may be in these encounters.

(i) You are a European business person sourcing camping tents in Shenzhen from a Chinese supplier. You have no Chinese language ability and your Chinese supplier does not speak your European language although he speaks a very little English. What strategies might you use to complete the purchase of 100 tents? Give your reasons.

....
....
....
....

(ii) You are a Japanese educational agent based in Tokyo and you recruit students on a commission basis to attend educational courses for colleges in New York City. One of the NYC colleges is visiting and pressing you to commit to sending 50 students to study this summer; he wants an immediate commitment. You have not worked with this college before. What strategies might you use to avoid being pressurised into such an immediate agreement? Give your reasons.

....
....
....
....

(iii) You are an American travel company and you have outsourced the design of the new travel platform to a China-based group of IT engineers based in Shanghai. The project must be delivered within a 6-month period. The levels of English of the China team are variable with only one member who is able to understand English well. What strategies might you use to ensure this project is delivered on time to a high-quality specifications, and where English is the lingua franca. Give your reasons.

....
....
....
....

Activity 4. Reflection and further reading

Reflection

How did you do in this unit?

- **Look back at the original learning targets of this unit and evaluate your own strengths and weaknesses. Tick either + (positive) or – (negative) in the table below. Specify which tasks in each skills areas and activities you are evaluating. Then reflect on these and make notes in the final column.**

Tasks	+	–	Reflection notes
The reading tasks:			
The writing tasks:			
The speaking tasks:			
The listening tasks:			

Further reading

Lockwood, J. & Song, F. (2016) Strategies for accommodation in a virtual business project based in China. *Journal of Business Communication*, 57(1), 113–144.

Salem, Ashraf Atta M.S. (2009) A Sage on the Stage, to Express and Impress: TED talks for improving oral presentation skills, vocabulary retention and its impact on reducing speaking anxiety in ESP settings. *English Language Teaching*, 12(6), 146–160.

UNIT
5

Building the team

The **learning targets** for this unit are to:

- Understand how diversity impacts business workplaces
- Understand how to read and interpret job advertisements
- Explore how to adapt and tailor resumes and cover letters for specific jobs
- Practise preparing interviews for specific types of jobs and the types of questions asked

Activity 1. Input and discussion

■ **In groups, discuss the following questions:**

(i) What do you understand by the term 'diversity'?

....
....
....
....
....

(ii) How can diversity impact the workplace?

………………………………………………………………………………
………………………………………………………………………………
………………………………………………………………………………
………………………………………………………………………………
………………………………………………………………………………

- **Look at the vocabulary and idiomatic expression items in bold. If you don't understand them, refer to the dictionary in Appendix 1 and/or try and guess the meaning from the context.**

Now read the text below:

Reading 1 DIVERSITY AT THE WORKPLACE – A GLOBAL ISSUE?

'Diversity' has become a 'must have' when taking on staff and forming teams in globalized workplaces, and it makes a lot of sense.

Workplaces and businesses, particularly in English-speaking and developed countries in Europe, America and Australia, put great effort into ensuring that their management and their teams **comprise** the kind of diversity that is **reflected in** society. This means that achieving a balance of gender, race, age, **sexual orientation**, socio-economic background and religion plays an important role when recruiting diverse team members into the workforce. In many countries it is unlawful to **discriminate against** applicants on any of these grounds; however, there are also good business reasons to be promoting diversity in the workplace.

Diversity can be defined as **'inherent'** diversity and 'acquired' diversity. The former relates to racial, gender and age where diversity is something you are born with and is naturally part of what is 'you'!

continued . . .

cont. The latter relates to things like education, socio-economic advancement, values and culture, skills and religious beliefs; these are things that are more **fluid** and can develop or evolve over time. In fact, sexual orientation could now also be described, for some, as 'acquired' diversity.

Most businesses would agree that diverse teams enable companies to be more innovative, creative and high performing. The different **perspectives** in a problem-solving work environment are bound to contribute to innovative and **balanced solutions**, thus leading to improved performance in our fast-changing global businesses.

However, the topic of diversity goes beyond just business results and performance. This policy of diversity falls within the business's own **corporate social responsibility** agenda where qualified candidates, **irrespective of** who they are, **signals** a step towards true equality in the workplace.

But what about diversity views in business and workplaces in the different countries and business contexts in Asia? To what extent is this 'diversity' trend evident in businesses in countries like Japan, Korea, Hong Kong and the Philippines? What are the contextual and even cultural issues that make the notion of 'diversity' relevant, or not relevant, to workplaces in these countries?

■ **Discuss the following questions:**

(i) How is 'diversity' reflected in business workplaces in your country?

....

....

....

....

....

(ii) Think about the challenges of inherent and acquired 'diversity' in workplace and business contexts in your country. Jot your ideas down in the table below.

Inherent diversity challenges	Acquired diversity challenges

Diversity amongst virtual teams working globally is a given. Australian banks, for example, have team members working around the world in India, China, the Philippines etc, so this necessarily means that managers of these banks have to manage language and cultural diversity all the time. Understanding these differences are critical to effective management and good communication.

- **Look at the vocabulary and idiomatic expression items in bold. If you don't understand them, refer to the dictionary in Appendix 1 and/or try and guess the meaning from the context.**

Now read the text below:

Reading 2 INTERCULTURAL AND LINGUISTIC DIFFERENCES

Much has been written about the intercultural and linguistic differences in the workplace. Countries such as the USA, UK and Australia, where immigration has been **sizeable**, have taken an

continued . . .

cont. **'assimilationist'** approach to welcoming **immigrants** into their English-speaking workplaces. This essentially means that immigrant workers are encouraged to **conform** to the host workplace culture and language. Some researchers have explored, for example, the particular role of **humour** in the New Zealand workplace and others have looked at the role of **casual conversation** in the Australian workplace; these studies have, in the past, informed the language and culture training of immigrants going into Australasian workplaces. Another context in which the **host** culture and language dominates is in the **offshored contact centre** work where Filipino and Indian customer service representatives deal with American, British and Australian customers' enquiries and complaints. Knowledge of the intercultural and language **norms** of these customers is key to their successful service. So, for example, understanding American accents, spending patterns and customer service expectations are key; these are trained and coached for to ensure the customer is satisfied. This assimilationist or **'integrative'** approach to the language and culture training is understandable where immigration is high, and where American and British companies off shore their back offices and contact centres to developing countries.

However, much of the rest of the global business world appears to be more pragmatic and **'instrumental'** in its use of English. In a business context where second language speakers are talking to each other, English as a lingua franca is often selected simply because it can be used by both parties to get business done. Thus the use of the term Business English as a Lingua Franca (BELF) is now **commonplace**. We have talked about the importance of 'accommodation strategies' in the previous unit where, as the stronger speaker, you may be required to slow down, repeat and standardise your English in order to be understood by your business colleague. Or, on the other hand, as the weaker speaker, you might need to ask for your colleague to slow down, repeat or explain a difficult word or expression being used as you do business transactions in English. Interestingly, having a high proficiency in English is no longer a guarantee for success in such a global business communication context. Language

continued . . .

cont. accommodation strategies using the lingua franca are a relatively new consideration when wanting to achieve successful communication. BELF is therefore a **two-way and two-pronged** process where language proficiency and accommodation strategies are highly valued.

The same can be said for achieving successful intercultural communication. In global business and workplace settings in Asia, professional and organisational cultures are often **prevalent**, and ethnicity differences may need to be understood and accommodated by everyone at work. National stereotyping however, is not helpful where, for example, members of a Japanese team may be labelled as **'reserved'** or American members are labelled as **'brash'**. This can lead to assumptions that such behaviours are set and can't be changed. However, these general characteristics can be impacted by understanding and promoting organisational cultures and values where, for example, punctuality, meeting deadlines and being **transparent** are important. If such differences are at odds with the prevailing or desired business culture, these will need to be worked though by everyone to ensure colleagues are **on the same page**. Adapting and negotiating these kinds of cultural differences are important skills for business success.

■ Discuss the questions below

(i) How would you define the difference between integrative and instrumental approaches to English language learning and success?

....

....

....

....

(ii) Imagine you have just got a job in a new team of soft-ware engineers in a large multinational company with headquarters in the USA. You will be working and reporting to managers in the USA, Bangalore and Tokyo.

What do you think are the language and culture challenges ahead? Jot down your ideas before you discuss in pairs/groups.

....
....
....
....

The story so far ...

- **Look at the vocabulary and idiomatic expression items in bold. If you don't understand them, refer to the dictionary in Appendix 1 and/or try and guess the meaning from the context.**

Now read the story below:

Getting Ready to Deliver

Some days later Samantha was alone in her office at the end of the day's work. It was the first time she'd had a moment to sit and reflect on the week. Overall, she was happy: the issue with Rory was **resolved fairly painlessly**, and the announcement that CommunicAsian won the GlobeNet contract had **lifted the spirits** of the whole organisation. Samantha made a note that she should look at all the company policies. "We just assume that they are okay until we actually have to use them," she thought, "I wonder what the policy is for appraisals."

Rory had been truly apologetic, saying that he had misinterpreted the complainant's response, while she was upset that her complaint led him into so much trouble. Rory chose to resign and the complainant chose to **withdraw the complaint**, so the problem passed. "We **dodged a bullet** with that," thought Samantha. "I must make changes to our harassment policy to give more flexibility in how we respond. Maybe **mediation** is as an alternative to a formal process."

Discipline was always Samantha's least favourite part of the job, but now she was starting her most favourite: building the team and recruiting, or as her position description put it **'Talent Acquisition'**. She had already made a good start with her recommendation that Prasad be the team leader and report to a project board including Tony and Vivek. It would test his ability to **manage upward**, but that's good. He would need support, and Samantha made a note to call the finance manager, Melinda, **to stress** her important role in the project.

Meanwhile, she reviewed the resumes – CVs they called them in Singapore – that had been **shortlisted** by Vivek and Prasad. They were looking for someone who could bridge the creative side and the analytical side, with solid experience in both. All five shortlisted candidates seemed to fit that: two had answered a posting on JobStreet and three had been **sourced** by Vivek from LinkedIn. All were happy to be based in Singapore. She decided to speak to all of them, and left a note for the Administration Assistant she shared with Dawn to schedule calls the next day.

She sighed. Her 'to-do' list seemed to be getting longer, so she decided to try and deal with Melinda before going home. Melinda had 'available' as her status so she tried a call. After the **usual pleasantries** Samantha **got down to business**.

"Mel," she said, "I want to talk about the GlobeNet project. We are putting Prasad in as PM/TL (Project Manager/Team Lead), and he'll do a fine job, but he hasn't had much experience with project budgets and **cost control**. We look to you to do a lot of that."

"I could put one of my staff on it full time," said Melinda.

"I think it needs to be you," said Samantha. The next bit was **tricky**. "You know, Mel, that there is **some concern** about your **assertiveness**. It was **highlighted** in your last appraisal that you **don't push back** enough or **stand up for** yourself. We want you in this project to own the budget and any changes, and your performance will be measured on the outcomes."

"Are you saying that I am **on trial**?" asked Melinda.

"Not exactly, but ... this is a chance to **raise your profile** in the organization and really make a great contribution. And we need your seniority and status on the project to give your decisions the right amount of authority."

Samantha **wound up** the call with a promise to resume tomorrow, after Melinda had time to think. Talking of Melinda's appraisal reminded Sam that her appraisal from Dawn, scheduled for the day the RfP arrived, had been forgotten in the activity. She added another item to her to-do list.

Activity 2. Input: Understanding and modelling spoken and written texts

Task (i). Understanding the job advertisement

- **Look at the vocabulary and idiomatic expression items in bold in the CommunicAsian advertisement below. If you don't understand them, refer to the dictionary in Appendix 1 and/or try and guess the meaning from the context.**

Marketing Analyst – Singapore or Hong Kong contract or permanent

CommunicAsian

Posted 10th April

Job description:

This is a role at Team Lead/Supervisor level with the focus on **integrating** the **creative branding** and messaging work of our creative team with ongoing measurement of performance through data analysis and systems. Our focus for this will be primarily social media.

As CommunicAsian operates a **matrix management structure**, the successful applicant will report jointly to the Head Creative manager and the Data and Systems manager.

Job responsibilities:

- Participate in marketing group planning to ensure that ideas can be **implemented** by technical teams
- Provide ideas for new solutions or identify opportunities to **optimise** existing solutions/tactics
- Develop **reusable** Marketing information **templates, segments** etc.
- Create and share **best practices**, respond to queries, **troubleshoot** issues, and create and maintain often complex solutions

Experience, skills and capabilities:

- Working knowledge of HTML, Python or similar, and Excel
- Ability to lead customer/project meeting(s)
- Willing to work hands-on at all levels of system problem-solving, design and implementation
- Serve as the subject matter expert on marketing **automation developer** best practices.

Qualifications:

- Bachelor's degree in a relevant subject
- 2+ years of marketing analytics experience
- 2+ years' experience with projects involving marketing communications/ branding
- Experience with virtual and **geographically dispersed teams**
- Salesforce.com or similar experience is a plus

Job specialisations (related to LinkedIn categories):

Information Analytics, IT – Software, Sales/Marketing, E-commerce, Marketing/Business Dev, Digital Marketing

Company overview – CommunicAsian:

We are a young Singapore-based marketing business with offices around Asia; management is primarily based in Singapore and Hong

Kong, with specialist services in Manila and Bangalore. CommunicAsian develops advertising and messaging for companies together with the plans to deliver these messages to the target audiences.

Last year we developed a campaign for a sports broadcast subscription company in Tokyo which was introducing a Sumo wrestling channel in Europe and a campaign to roll out a new spirit distilled in the USA and now for the Asian market. We are building a team for a new project opportunity which will need both creative and analytical skills as we develop ideas, track their effectiveness, and make effective changes over the next year.

CommunicAsian has been in business for over 5 years and employs about 60 people around Asia. We are targeting growth to 200 in the next 2 years, with more UK and European business.

Applications:

Please send your application to HR@CommunicAsian.com

If you were applying for this job, what would you highlight in your CV and cover letter. Discuss.

....

....

....

- **Look at the words and expressions in the box below and discuss the meanings. If you don't understand, try and guess the meanings. The words and expressions are explained in Appendix 1.**

Words and expressions	**Meanings**
Integrating	
Creative branding	
Matrix management structure	

Words and expressions	Meanings
Implemented	
Optimise	
Reusable	
Templates	
Segments	
Best practices	
Troubleshoot	
Marketing automation developer	
Dispersed teams	

From the position description of 'Marketing Analyst', and your knowledge about CommunicAsian, what do you think the ideal knowledge and skills set would be of prospective candidates? Read through the position description, jot down your ideas and discuss.

....
....
....
....

Task (ii). Deconstructing the applicant resumes and cover letters

Applying for a position in a multinational firm may be a very different process from applying for a job in a government department. It is also the case that some kinds of professions e.g. IT and sales, marketing and public relations will attract different candidates needing to showcase different types of skills and experience. This means you have to tailor your application, i.e. both the CV and cover letter, carefully for the specific job.

In total, CommunicAsian received over 20 applications for the advertised position above. The following three have been shortlisted for interview.

The resumes

Compare and contrast the shortlisted three resumes below and complete the table. Think about how they differ and why the applicants have chosen to do their resumes in a particular way.

Resume 1: Rayyan Shukor

RAYYAN SHUKOR

Marketing Analyst email: rayyanmajidshukor@hotmail.co.nz

I have built my career over 15 years in the Malaysian banking industry, starting as a teller and then taking on roles as a reporting analyst and then as a marketing analyst. With a degree in information technology, I have been able to apply business and project management skills in this role. I also achieved a qualification in project management.

Since I moved to Malaysia's premier international bank seven years ago, I have worked with teams in the United Kingdom, Australia and Asia.

PROFESSIONAL EXPERIENCE

MAYFINANCE – Kuala Lumpur and Singapore Jan 2013 – Present

Marketing Analyst – Responsible for ensuring that our internet based interactions with our customers and prospects deliver targeted results in sales and **upsales**.

Managed as a matrix manager teams in both the IT group and the marketing group (measuring and messaging) with two direct reports developing content and **customer experience navigation**.

FORWARD OUTSOURCING SERVICES (FOS) – Kuala Lumpur Dec 2011 – Dec 2012

Consultant – This was a chance to apply my experience in a broader marketplace. FOS specializes in operational efficiency and effectiveness in retail financial services. Our clients included Sumitomo Bank and Ping An Insurance.

My responsibilities included conducting needs analysis, developing solutions, client training, as well as being part of the sales team.

BERHAD BANK – Malacca March 2006 – Jan 2007

Operations Associate – From starting as a teller, I became highly competent across the whole range of branch banking administration and compliance. I was appointed **Subject Matter Expert** and referral point for junior staff within my branch.

I was responsible for an 8-month project to study the local market opportunities for a new on-line banking app and to advise management on how they might approach this. The report was accepted and commended.

Previous work while at school and university included setting up websites both for friends and customers.

EDUCATION AND PROFESSIONAL QUALIFICATIONS

Bachelor in Computer Science from University of Malaya.

PMP Certification from Project Management Institute.

HOBBIES AND INTERESTS

Creative writing, travel, software programming, continuous learning.

Resume 2: Asmitha Murthy

Asmitha Murthy
Mobile +91 946464682
asmitha_murthy@yahoo.com

An accomplished professional of 9 years; reflecting strong leadership qualifications coupled with "**hands-on**" project experience. Team-based management style, excellent interpersonal and communication skills. Strong in systems design and implementation.

Major Achievements

- Responsible for implementing a lead tracking system for a consumer products company. This resulted to an increase of 15% in sales volumes in the first year.

- Design and implementation of a new dashboard-based recruitment system for a multi-national which allowed their hiring managers to track candidates through the process. This reduced drop-out rate from 17% to 8%.
- Selected as 'Employee of the Month' six months ago with the success of lead tracking.

Certifications Attained

- Certified Agile Professional – Sharma Training Institute.
- Lean Six Sigma Green belt – Taga Global Services, Inc.

EMPLOYMENT HISTORY

1. **Taga Global Services (Bengaluru) 2015 – present**

   Current Position: Development Team Lead (2 years)

⇨ Responsible for building and deploying lead tracking system to measure website and media effectiveness, processes and delivery.

⇨ Works directly with the stakeholders from various lines of business/programs to ensure each group's reporting needs are addressed.

⇨ Coaches and develops a team of up to 8 people.

Position: Associate Team Lead and SME (2 years)

3 years of experience as an Associate Team Lead

⇨ Responsible for converting screens and reports to mobile formats.

⇨ Involved in team meetings such as planning, scheduling, weekly reviews and performance reviews.

2. **Gentech Outsourcing Services (Bengaluru) (4 years)**

   Positions: Graduate trainee to Testing Team Lead

⇨ Responsible for converting screens and reports to mobile formats.

⇨ Led the testing team for quality reviews of reporting systems for a year.

EDUCATIONAL QUALIFICATIONS

- **Bachelor of Engineering** Chandra College Mumbai

Resume 3: Peter Lee

Peter Lee
Communications and Marketing

Address | Oxford and Cambridge Mansions, [illegible] London

Contact | peterlee@me.com
+44777282000

Citizenship | United Kingdom
Hong Kong (Permanent Resident)

SUMMARY

Growing up across four cities on three continents, I have always found communications fascinating. Having been accepted onto the Marketing Association Account Management Fellowship this past summer has provided a tangible direction to this passion and I hope to continue learning in the future

EDUCATION

September 2012 to July 2015 | London, United Kingdom
BA with Honours in Politics with focus on China, Taiwan and Southeast Asia
Minor in Political Islam
SOAS, University of London
Second Class Honours

September 2007 to July 2011 | Hong Kong
International Baccalaureate Diploma
General Certificate of Secondary Education
Sha Tin College, English Schools Foundation
(Chinese A, English A, Mathematics A, Science AA)

WORK INTERESTS

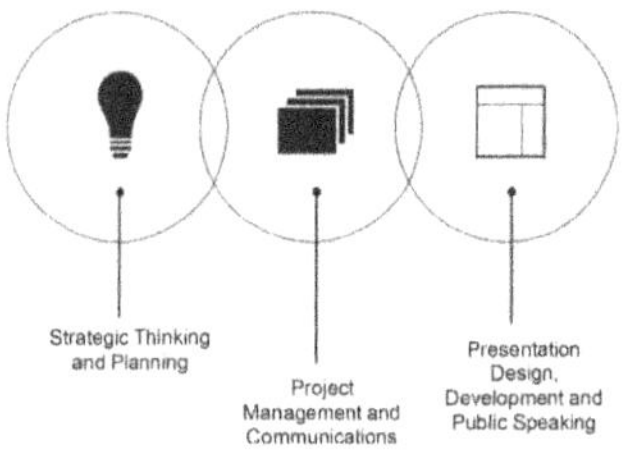

REFERENCES

Harriet Harris: Global Account Director, TipTop Agency
Harriet.Harris@yahoo.com
Andrew Zorro: Head of Global, Council Planning
AndrewZorro@gmail.com

LEADERSHIP

2015 **Politics Department Student Representative**
- University of London
- Elected by peers to be the fulcrum between staff, students and university management on student welfare issues and satisfaction while also responsible for providing input into the future direction of the department. Also founded a peer-to-peer mentoring scheme open to all students studying politics modules and am a tutor for China, Taiwan and Southeast Asia studies.

2011 **Head of House**
- Kai Wee College, English Schools Union
- Captained house team of over 200 students aged 11 to 18 to first place in the annual house cup, rewarding excellence in the fields of creativity, action and community service.

EXPERIENCE

1

Account Management Summer Fellow | London
July – August 2015
Marketing and communications giant, TipTop Agency
- Worked with the corporate teams on global fast food restaurants as well as gaining experience with Social@Market social media management
- Assisted the complete project management for roll out
- Researched and developed a presentation on employee engagement and workplace trends and contributing this information to a major rebranding project
- Worked across the global wind farm teams
- Conducted primary research and organised various local teams to compile a global competitive review on the industry

Throughout this time also prepared a full strategic and creative response to a live brief for WWF in conjunction with other fellows and presented this to the TipTop Agency.

2

Reed Ellis, Online Marketing Project Manager | London
June – September 2014
FTSE 500 company specializing in publishing and information solutions.
- Led digital team to develop and report a marketing strategy to enhance online presence of Global Risk Team through website development, content management and SEO
- Built realistic timeline for execution through extensive stakeholder consultation and budget analysis
- Reported directly to senior-level (Head of Global Risk Team)

3

Future Perfect, Market Analyst | Hong Kong & Manila, Philippines
June – September 2013
Multinational communication start-up dealing in cross-cultural assessment and consulting.
- Spearheaded project for the Philippine government to revamp marketing strategy and material for the International Contact Centre Conference & Expo, the largest of its kind in the world
- Facilitated research partnership with The Workplace Foundation (Lancaster University) and devised articles for publication
- Assisted the redesign and drafting of Future Perfect's flagship product and managed the social media marketing for the launch

4

Sun Yat-sen University, Instructor | Guangzhou, China
September 2011 – February 2012
Top 10 university in China and national leader in research.
- Worked on curriculum and assessment development of a first year phonics course specifically for Chinese learners of English
- Planned and taught all seminars to first year English major students, including class lectures and one-to-one consultations
- Oversaw a dramatic rise in student participation of extracurricular English classes and English Language events

LANGUAGES

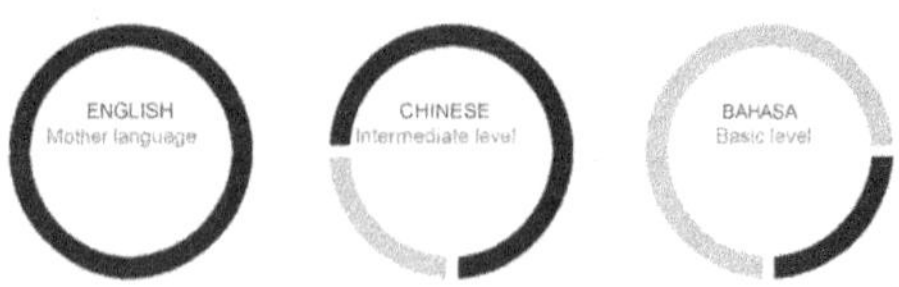

PETER LEE

- **Now jot down your ideas when comparing and contrasting these 3 resumes. Think about things such as format, the use of visuals and choice of language.**

Resume 1 – Rayyan Shukor	Resume 2 – Asmitha Murthy	Resume 3 – Peter Lee

- **Discuss.**

The cover letters

As you read and compare the different cover letters below think about the following questions:

(i) How are the cover letters organised; how does each section of the cover letter function; are they the same or different?
(ii) What kind of language choices (vocabulary and grammar) are made; are they the same or different?
(iii) Do they all make explicit/implicit links to the advertisement?

■ **After reading the cover letters and thinking about the above questions, complete the table below.**

Cover letter 1: Rayyan Shukor

From: rayyanmajidshukor@hotmail.co.nz
Sent: Thursday, April 2, 11:13 AM
To: HR@CommunicAsian.com
Subject: Application for Marketing Analyst Position with CommunicAsian

Dear HR Manager

I reviewed your opening on JobStreet, and I believe that I am an excellent fit for the position.

I have, for the last seven years, been involved with the inspiration of creative marketing together with the analytic rigour that is necessary to measure its effectiveness. My teams at MayFinance are responsible for both areas, and much of my role is to ensure that the bridge between them is effective. I manage these teams on a matrix basis where I serve as project manager cutting across their line management, and, because we are geographically separate, my management style has to operate successfully in a virtual manner.

My IT and application skills are consistent with your requirements. I have been an expert user of Excel since my undergraduate time, and also used HTML in my website business.

Perhaps my best feature for fitting the position is that I am an adaptable and a fast learner. In my first job I became the expert for staff who needed advice on what to do in complicated situations. Three years ago, while working full time, I studied and successfully passed the Project Management Institute (PMI) Certificate exams – the first in our company in Malaysia to do so.

I should also add that I am a keen user of social media. I am active in special interest groups on both Facebook and LinkedIn, and I have more than 800 followers on Twitter.

I can be available for an interview either in person or virtually at any time. My telephone number is at the top of my attached CV.

Kind regards
Rayyan Shukor

Cover letter 2: Asmitha Murthy

From: asmitha_murthy@yahoo.com
Sent: Thursday, April 2, 11:13 AM
To: HR@CommunicAsian.com
Subject: Application for Marketing Analyst Position

Dear Sir/Madam,

I am writing to apply for the Marketing Analyst role which you posted on JobStreet. I have also spoken to your Development Manager in Bengaluru.

I am currently leading a development team lead with Taga Global Services in Bengaluru, and my projects have all focused on using and tracking analytics. I recently completed a project for tracking e-commerce inbound and outbound marketing, enabling the marketers to react quickly on what was working, and increasing sales by over 15%.

I have over nine years of experience working on projects, both development and implementation, as well as testing and reporting and dashboard design.

I have done a little work in Singapore as Taga has an office there, and they are often part of my "virtual team", so I am familiar with the culture. I am single, so I can locate anywhere.

I attach my resume.

Yours truly
Asmitha Murthy

Cover letter 3: Peter Lee

To: HR@CommunicAsian.com
Subject: Application for Marketing Analyst

Dear HR

I am excited to apply for the Marketing Analyst role which you posted on JobStreet. The blend of creative conceptualisation and then making it happen is exactly what I am looking for. While my work since university has focused on the creative side, this position would enable me to pick up the interest in project management and systems which I developed and practised while getting my degree. Furthermore, having studied and/or worked in Hong Kong, Singapore and the United Kingdom I love the Asian and European focus of CommunicAsian (also love the name!), and I truly believe I could play a big part in helping you triple your size in the next two years.

I am currently working in London, as you will see from the attached CV, and I would be happy to relocate to either Hong Kong or Singapore. I'd also be happy to fly down for an interview or, of course, connect by Zoom.

Look forward to hearing from you ... Peter

- **Now jot down your ideas for comparing and contrasting these three cover letters.**

Cover letter 1	Cover letter 2	Cover letter 3

■ Discuss.

Final discussion

Which of the candidates do you think it most suitable for the position and why?

....
....
....
....
....

Task (iii). Audio listening: Internal meeting at CommunicAsian to prepare for the interviews (Transcript – Appendix 2)

Given that Samantha, Tony, Vivek and Prasad will be interviewing the three candidates, what do you think will be areas they will want to probe for each? Write your ideas below:

....
....
....
....
....

■ Before you listen to their pre-interview discussion for the first time, think about the words/expressions listed in the left-hand column.

If you don't understand them, refer to the dictionary in Appendix 1 and/or try and guess the meaning from the context.

Write your meanings in the table provided.

Words and expressions	Meanings
Standard questions	
Specific/tailored questions	
Consistent	
On my behalf	
It makes sense	
Administrative issues	
References	
Notice period	
Eliminated	
First impression	
Probe	

Spearheaded	
Pin him down to details	
Interrogated	
Substance underneath the sizzle	
Solid	
Thin	
Dealing with	
Supplementary question	
Doesn't have to last that long	

■ Now listen to the internal pre-interview meeting at CommunicAsian.

Look at the comments below made by different members of the CommunicAsian interviewing panel, and discuss what the underlying concern they express of the applicant.

(i) *Vivek: If he (Peter) spends as much time doing proper work as he did in formatting his resume, he would be outstanding.*

....

....

(ii) *Vivek: There's lots of words like 'led' and 'spearheaded'. What was he (Peter) actually doing, what was the team structure, and let's pin him down to details.*

(iii) *Tony: That's what worries me a little. 15 years, and he's (Ryyan) applying for a team leader position.*

(iv) *Tony: We need to know more about her (Asmitha) customer knowledge. Did she do customer needs or just build to a specification from another department?*

(v) *Samantha: Okay, so with Peter we want to find out what is the substance underneath the sizzle*

Who do you now think is the front runner? Why?

Activity 3. Output: Spoken and written skills development tasks

Task (i). Email summary of interview question decisions

- **You are Samantha. After the internal job interview preparation discussion in the previous section, write to Prasad and Tony with your summary of decisions made about questions and approach for the interviews.**

Would you cc Dawn and Vivek in? Why/Why not?

To: Tony, Prasad
Cc:
From: Samantha
Subject:

You will have to wait until Unit 6 to see what happens!

Task (ii). Applying for a job with CommunicAsian

An exciting new job advertisement has been posted by CommunicAsian below. They are looking for new graduate trainee. You have decided to apply.

- **Look at the words and expressions in bold and try and guess the meaning.**

InfoGraphics Graduate Trainee CommunicAsian

About the company

We are a young Singapore-based marketing business with offices around Asia; management is **primarily** based in Singapore and Hong Kong, with **specialist services** in Manila and Bangalore. CommunicAsian develops advertising and **messaging** for companies together with the plans to deliver these messages to the target audiences.

About the role

The Graphics and Clients Presentations department plays a key role within this organisation, producing internal and external reports and presentations.

You will be presenting often complex information using clear, simple, and meaningful images and **infographics** for our client presentations, website, and internal communications.

Candidate profile

The successful candidate will understand the information **generated** by data and **qualitative research** including surveys and discussions, and present this in a simple but effective way.

Requirements

- A strong **numerical mindset** and comfortable working with data and design
- Some knowledge of design software such as Photoshop & Acrobat would be **a plus**
- Confident and **proactive** with a **'can-do' attitude**
- Able to collaborate and communicate efficiently and effectively within a team

- Competence with languages such as SQL, HMTL would be **advantageous**

Personal competencies

- Results focus
- Creative, self-motivated and a self-starter
- Proactive and **results orientated**
- Teamwork and communication
- Strong speaking, writing and presentation skills in English and **preferably** in another language
- Experience and desire to be part of a team

Benefits

We offer a **highly competitive** graduate benefits package.

Application process

Please submit your application online and include CV and other relevant material (such as design examples).

Having read the application, what kind of knowledge/skills do you think CommunicAsian is looking for?

....
....
....
....
....
....

■ **Individually write/adapt your resume for this position.**

There is no one right way to do this! Your resume is a reflection of yourself, your qualifications and experience, and your understanding of the job you are applying for. Look back at the models in Activity 2 to get some ideas. Highlight the relevant parts of the advertisement and jot some ideas down in the box below.

Your CV should be one or two pages only.

■ **Now write your covering letter.**

There is no set length for your cover letter. Look back at the models in Activity 2 to get some ideas. Highlight the relevant parts of the advertisement and jot some ideas down in the box below.

Task (iii). Preparing for an interview

Congratulations, you have been shortlisted!

You now need to do some interview preparation.

- **Write down the questions that you think might be asked in this interview in the box below. Discuss why these questions might be asked.**

In Unit 6 you will do the interview.

Task (iv). Forum on diversity awareness

Samantha has invited all the new graduate trainees to a 'Forum on Diversity' run by a workplace communication consultancy group. Before attending this forum she has asked everyone to complete the following survey and bring it along.

■ **Now spend 30 minutes answering these survey questions.**

Thanks for attending our Forum on Diversity where we are able to raise awareness about the importance of diversity and how to manage it in the workplace.

Please complete this survey and bring it along!

1. How would you react to your colleague saying they were 'trans'? Comment on the challenges and benefits this may bring to the workplace.
2. What do you know about different cultural approaches to business problems such as meeting deadlines; managing conflict with your colleagues; offering money (or other incentives) to get favourable decisions; pushing back on management decisions; working with younger female bosses? Comment.
3. Would you hesitate to hire someone over 65 years of age? Comment.
4. How would you respond to the rationale for hiring more women into the organisation, being that they provide 'emotional intelligence' in the workplace?

5. When you hear comments like 'Winnie is really bossy' and Iris 'doesn't say boo to a goose' and Kelvin is a 'show pony', what are the messages being communicated? Do you think they are positive/negative?
6. The dress code at your workplace is 'smart casual'. What do you think this code means in a diverse workplace?

- **Discuss your answers in pairs/small groups.**

Activity 4. Reflection and further reading

Reflection

How did you do in this unit?

- **Look back at the original learning targets of this unit and evaluate your own strengths and weaknesses. Tick either + (positive) or – (negative) in the table below. Specify which tasks in each skills areas and activities you are evaluating. Then reflect on these and make notes in the final column.**

Tasks	+	–	Reflection notes
The reading tasks:			

Tasks	+	–	Reflection notes
The writing tasks:			
The speaking tasks:			
The listening tasks:			

Further reading

Choy, W. (2007) Globalisation and workforce diversity: HRM implications for multinational corporations in Singapore. *Singapore Management Review*, 29(2), 1–19.

Wong, Irene. F.H. & Lai Phooi-Ching (2000) Chinese cultural values and performance at job interviews: A Singapore perspective. *Business Communication Quarterly*, 63(1), 9–22.

UNIT

6

Planning the project

People, process and technology

The **learning targets** for this unit are to:

- Understand what makes for good interview skills from the perspectives of both the interviewee and interviewer
- Understand how interviews may vary face-to-face and virtually
- Understand how to plan a project ensuring progress is reported and deliverables completed on time
- Collaboratively develop a project plan for GlobeNet

Activity 1. Input: Readings and discussion

- **Look at the vocabulary and idiomatic expression items in bold. If you don't understand them, refer to the dictionary in Appendix 1 and/or try and guess the meaning from the context.**

Now read the text below:

Reading 1 INTERVIEW SKILLS

There is so much written about how to prepare for job interviews and 'Youtube' videos provide examples – good and bad ones. However, there are no **universal truths** about what may or may not work beyond your basic **common sense** of doing your homework, dressing appropriately, projecting a **positive disposition**, and thinking carefully about what the questions are really asking and **crafting** your best responses.

No one size fits all. An interview, like a presentation, is a spoken forum which has a purpose, a context and a specific audience; so how you prepare for it requires thinking about the context carefully and **tailoring your approach**. This means preparing well.

If, for example, you were applying for a public relations/advertising job, your designed CV and interview techniques would be different for a private young 'go ahead' type company as opposed to a more **staid** government department running a health campaign. The former may want someone who thinks very creatively and **'out of the box'**, whilst government campaigns may need to ensure a safe and accurate message, and this message therefore may need to be more **mainstream**. Not only will **nuances** like this be reflected in your CV and cover letter, but also in how you might dress for, and present, in an interview. You wouldn't **turn up** for a government interview in a T shirt and jeans ... or would you?

Think about the questions being asked in the interview, and trust yourself to answer them as 'you', not **second guessing** what you think they want to hear. **Coming across** as professional and confident can only be a good thing, even if you are feeling nervous. Don't be afraid to ask for repetition or clarification of the question, and also be prepared to ask questions showing you have thought about the position deeply. This will require you doing your homework on the

continued . . .

cont. company and the position you are applying for. Finally, you wouldn't ask for information about salary and your likelihood of securing the position ... or would you?

So, in summary, the key issues relate in doing a successful job interview relate to:

(i) Doing your homework about the company you hope to work for and the position itself; this demonstrates your interest and **commitment** to working at this workplace. It may also provide you with questions to ask during or at the end of the interview.
(ii) Dress appropriately for the interview; and smile – the first impressions are very important and remember to be yourself.
(iii) **Anticipate** some of the questions that may be asked, and prepare and rehearse what you are going to say. However, do not **memorise** your answers as this may come across as being **'robotic'**.
(iv) Think about some questions you may want to ask; some of these may arise from the interview itself. Whilst your questions about the selection process and start dates may be appropriate, questions related to salary and benefits may be seen as **premature**.

■ **Look at the vocabulary and idiomatic expression items in bold. If you don't understand them, refer to the dictionary in Appendix 1 and/or try and guess the meaning from the context.**

What do you think is meant by the 'life cycle' of a project?

....
....
....
....

Now read the text below:

Reading 2 PROBLEM-SOLVING PROJECTS AND TEAM WORK IN VIRTUAL BUSINESS SETTINGS

The problem-solving project

Any business project is going to go through a number of stages, and these can be roughly divided into five, some of them **overlapping**:

continued . . .

cont.

(i) Getting ready to start
(ii) Project planning
(iii) Executing the project
(iv) Monitoring and controlling the project
(v) Closing the project phase

Teamwork in the twenty-first century workplace involves colleagues working **collaboratively** and problem-solving together. Obviously, however, there are all sorts of different teams and different projects. **On one end of the spectrum** we have project teams doing highly complex projects that require high levels of **interdependence** and problem solving; other projects may be doing more routine work and require less interdependence. However, they all require good and regular communication between team members and the project managers.

Problem solving with your team refers to the ability to **systematically** work through a problem, using **critical thinking** skills to arrive at a solution. This is not necessarily a **lockstep process**, but more an **iterative** one. In the workplace, teams have to solve problems every day and this collaborative and creative ability is what companies have come to value a great deal. Problem-solving as a team improves the chances of **coming up** with the best solution or result. When people work together they can share and compare ideas and choose the best one to solve the problem. Currently, there is much written in the business manuals about **Agile Teams**. These are essentially teams that work creatively, quickly and flexibly end-to-end on processes and problems, solving each one collaboratively, thus improving products and services as a result.

What are the key stages in effective problem-solving? As already mentioned, it is just as much **an iterative process** as a **linear** one. The first thing to do is to carefully identify the problems and challenges. This seems as if it should be straightforward, but **jumping to** quick **assumptions** about the nature of the problem may lead the project in the wrong direction. Once the problem has been carefully identified and defined, the exact nature of the problem can be described, analysed and diagnosed. From here the project team can get to work to test the diagnosis by working out the possible solution. There may be various points of views and **hypotheses** as to the best solution,

continued . . .

cont.

and this is key work of the project team; it takes time and care. Once a solution has been found, then the team needs to test and evaluate it.

For the translation of all this into a successful workplace project, the business needs to select the right team and get their input as the project is planned. Then you need to:

(i) Align on the nature and scope of your project; you need a **shared vision**.
(ii) Write the project plan or charter i.e. the project targets, steps and responsibilities for achieving these targets. This schedule of tasks and responsibilities, with timelines, gives clarity to the project.
(iii) Schedule the project tasks designating the operational, management and reporting roles and responsibilities.
(iv) Estimate costs for each phase of the project, and ensure **contingency** arrangements.
(v) Measure your progress and quality on a regular basis.

There are a number of project planning software packages and templates and your company will train you to use one and a standard approach is exemplified in this unit.

The team work

What are going to be some of the challenges in putting an effective team together for the GlobeNet project? In groups/pairs, think of at least 3.

....

....

....

High performing project teams are a **huge asset** to any company in the twenty-first century. This means that new employees need to have great communication and collaborative skills. Furthermore they need to be working together towards what are often **tight deadlines**.

In a globalised context, however, where teams are **dispersed**, they have to work with their project teams virtually. This adds another

continued . . .

cont.

layer of complexity to these business work practices as colleagues are not physically located together and need to be communicating on a regular basis. In a recent study (Pullan & Prokopi, 2016) employees were asked about the challenges they found most difficult when working virtually. Over three quarters of the respondents reported **'engaging remote participants'** to be most difficult, citing the main challenges to be:

- Missing out on **dynamics and nuances** of conversation (58%)
- Working across time zones (56%)
- Working across different cultures (56%)
- Building trust (55%)

The same study then explored what made virtual project teams working more productively together. The most common response identified the opportunity of face-to-face meetings at the start of the project; and then to meet as regularly as possible, even if it only on an annual basis.

Other responses included:

- regular, clear communications, without lengthy gaps in between
- clear roles and responsibilities
- the use of meeting agendas
- being clear about how the team will work together in meetings to achieve overall
- **shared vision**, outcomes, and sense of purpose
- an **open team culture**, with each person listened to and able to ask for help from the others
- time to get to know each other and **build rapport** and **trust**
- understanding each team member's **perspectives** and how they prefer to work
- technology should be easy to use and up to the challenge
- the use of video over audio alone
- widespread use of screen sharing technology
- the use of a **common repository** that everyone can access easily

Interestingly, while some people preferred to use the telephone, others preferred to use instant messenger. Perhaps these people were from different generations? Other than on this point, the feedback was very **consistent**.

The story so far ...

- **Look at the vocabulary and idiomatic expression items in bold. If you don't understand them, refer to the dictionary in Appendix 1 and/or try and guess the meaning from the context.**

Now read the story below:

PLANNING THE PROJECT

Prasad was preparing for his first Project Board meeting. He had led teams before, and been a project manager on a small project, but this was the highest profile one with heads of department and even the CEO on the board. He would have called it a Steering Committee, but Dawn preferred the name 'Project Board' as she said it showed the importance of the project. Whatever it was called, its role was to review the progress, agree any changes, especially financial, and resolve any policy issues or disagreements between CommunicAsian and GlobeNet. Members were Dawn, Vivek, Tony and Samantha, and they would receive weekly updates from Prasad and Melinda.

Prasad had prepared a detailed **Project Charter** for the first meeting. This set out plans, budget, **milestones**, risk management and other project controls. The agenda was essentially for the Board to agree the charter.

The meeting started well, with Dawn **praising** the hard work of the team in producing so comprehensive a document, and then Vivek agreed and added that there should be a sign-off by the client, and also it should have an **escalation person** on both parties in case there were problems at the project level.

"I will be the escalation person," said Tony. I'm already in their office three or four times a week."

"I think it should be someone more distant," said Dawn, "so we are not pushed to have an answer straightaway. I propose Samantha to be our person."

That was quickly settled, but Tony was not finished.

"I don't see enough time for **brainstorming** or focus groups. You've got a lot of systems and apps and metrics, but it's the creative ideas that are going to deliver. How can we plan social media until we've decided the market segment demographic?"

Vivek came back, "This plan is about the process and checkpoints. So, it says you need your social media strategy by x date so the plan can be developed, and then delivered by y date."

Tony was not convinced. "You say it's all about process, but the project's all about ideas and outcomes. I can't decide to have a great idea on Thursday, because that's what the plan says. Some of my best ideas come when I'm in the bath. Will we have a bath in the project room on Thursday?"

Dawn decided to say nothing and see how Prasad **made out**, but before he could speak Vivek came back again.

"I think this is a good schedule and we should approve it. Otherwise we can go back to GlobeNet and say to them: 'we'll deliver a solution sometime but it will depend on when inspiration strikes'."

Prasad said, "I take the points from both of you, and there's no point in being **sarcastic**. I have a deadline to deliver the project given by Dawn and based on the contract with GlobeNet, so I am working within those constraints. The final date will not change. Let me update the Charter with your comments and suggestions, and with more emphasis on the creative needs, and I'll go through it with you individually before the next Board meeting. Thank you."

Samantha smiled at Dawn, her choice had done well. Now they just had to get that extra person on the team.

Activity 2. Input: Understanding and modelling spoken and written texts

Task (i). Audio listening: Interviewing and discussing the three candidates (Transcript – Appendix 2)

There are four sections to this listening task divided into interview questions (1 & 3) and discussions between the interview panel (2 & 4).

- **In the previous unit you met the CommunicAsian candidates Rayyan, Asmitha and Peter. Think about the following questions before you listen to snippets of the interviews:**

(i) Which of these job candidates do you think will get the job offer and why?

....

....

....

....

....

(ii) Do you think the same questions will be asked of all the job applicants, or will the interviewers vary them? Comment.

....

....

....

....

....

Section 1. CommunicAsian interviews: there are 4 sections in this interview

- **Now listen to the interview snippets in Section 1 and note down what each candidate was asked. Also give your rating out of 10 (1 being poor and 10 being excellent) on how they answered the questions. Use the table at the end of Section 1.**

Candidate	**Questions**	**Response evaluations 1–10 and commentary**
Rayyan		
Asmitha		
Peter		

■ **How did they do? Discuss.**

Section 2. CommunicAsian Interview Team discussion: Tony, Samantha, Prasad

■ **Now listen to the Interview panel discussion so far.**

Do you agree? Comment.

....
....
....
....
....
....

Section 3. CommunicAsian interviews – more questions

Candidate	Questions	Response evaluations 1–10 and commentary

Candidate	Questions	Response evaluations 1–10 and commentary

Who do you think gets the job? Comment.

....
....
....

Section 4. Interview Panel discussion and decision: Tony, Samantha, Prasad

- **Now listen to the final interview discussion.**

Do you agree with their evaluations of each of the candidates? Comment.

....
....
....

Task (ii). Read the email below from Prasad with the attached project plan from the Himeno Media project

To: Samantha, Tony, Vivek
Cc: Dawn
From: Prasad

Dear everyone,

Thanks for your efforts with interviewing yesterday and I think we have the best candidate. Let's get the offer letter out asap and as soon as he has accepted, I assume you'll contact the other candidates Samantha?

Now we need to get on with the project planning schedule. I've attached the archived schedule that was done for Himeno Media last year, so let's use this as a template for our GlobeNet project.

Let's meet next Wednesday to discuss.
Talk soon,
Prasad.

■ **Now look at the attached project plan Himeno Media template below.**

(i) What is the purpose, content and audience of the project plan?

....
....
....
....
....

(ii) What do you notice about the format of this project plan and the kind of language that is used?

....
....
....
....
....

■ **Look at the common business terminology in the box below and discuss the meanings.**

Business terminology	Meaning
Deliverables	
Annualised revenue	
Demographic	
Census data	
Collate findings	

Business terminology	Meaning
Demonstrated marker	
Awareness campaign	
Creative campaign	

HIMENO MEDIA PROJECT PLAN TEMPLATE

Project Name: **Sumo into Europe** Project Manager: **Tony Tanaka**

Project Deliverables: **Market study and proof of concept for a Sumo streaming channel in Europe**

Project Success Measures: **$1m annualised revenue achievable within 6 months; demonstrated marketing and community building approach through social media**

Start date:__**10 May**_ End date:__**18 July**__ % Complete:____________

Task No.	Task Description	Task Owner	Start Date	End Date	Status
1	Demographic study of European populations and market segment identification	Tony	10 May	15 May	
1.1	Get Japanese residents' data (population and census data) in Europe	Prasad	10 May	11 May	
1.2	Identify other market segments with Sumo potential	Prasad/ Rory	12 May	13 May	

Task No.	Task Description	Task Owner	Start Date	End Date	Status
1.3	Select country(ies) and segment groups for further analysis	Tony	14 May	14 May	
2	Address the interests of identified segments				
2.1	Design survey questions and delivery	Rory	15 May	18 May	
2.2	Plan and conduct focus groups	Rory	19 May	31 May	
2.3	Collect and analyse data from search engines, media	Prasad	19 May	5 June	
2.4	Collate findings and agree pilot marketing plan	Tony	6 June	6 June	
3.	Develop pilot 'Sumo Awareness' campaign to build interest and knowledge of new channel availability				
3.1	Set up measurement systems and reports	Prasad	7 June	12 June	
3.2	Plan creative campaign for social media	Tony	7 June	10 June	

Task No.	Task Description	Task Owner	Start Date	End Date	Status
4	Run pilot on social media	Rory	10 June	6 July	
5	Report to Himeno				
5.1	Draft findings and recommendations	Rory	8 July	12 July	
5.2	Present to Tony and produce second draft	Rory/ Prasad	12 July	13 July	
5.3	Present to Dawn, Vivek, Management and finalise for delivery to Himeno	Tony	15 July	18 July	

Activity 3. Output: Spoken and written skills development tasks

Task (i). Interviewing for a graduate internship roleplay

- **Look back at your notes you prepared in Unit 5 Activity 3 Task (iii).**

Divide into groups of 3; allot members A –the interviewers, B – the applicants, and C –the observers.

Allow 10 minutes in your groups to prepare either to interview (write questions) or to be interviewed (predict and prepare questions). C will use the presentation skills checklist in Activity 2 Unit 5 to assess and feedback when observing the interview.

Allow 10 minutes for the interview.

You may choose to do the interview face to face or virtually (arrange your chairs back to back).

- **What do you think could be the different pressures if the interview is done F2F or virtually. Put your ideas in the table below.**

F2F interview	Virtual interview (with or without video)

After each 10-minute interview allow 5–10 mins for feedback; both the interviewer and the observer provide feedback to the interviewee.

Change roles and repeat.

Task (ii). The project schedule

Now that you have your team complete, look at the Project Planning Template below and work in groups of 4–5 to complete it. Complete the project plan below using both the Himeno Media Project Plan modelled in the previous activity, and the GlobeNet proposal in Unit 3 Activity 3 to guide your decisions.

Start by discussing what your deliverables are, and what your success measures might be to evaluate these. Use the box below to jot down your ideas.

■ **Now complete the GlobeNet Project Plan below in groups.**

GLOBENET PROJECT PLAN TEMPLATE

Project Name:____________________ **Project Manager:**__________

Project Deliverables:____________________________________

Project Success Measures:________________________________

____

Start date:________ **End date:**_________ **% Complete:**__________

Task No.	Task Description	Task Owner	Start Date	End Date	Status

- **Form a 'gallery' of project plans around the training room and invite all groups to read each other's plans noting differences and improvements.**

Final discussion.

Activity 4. Reflection and further reading

Reflection

How did you do in this unit?

- **Look back at the original learning targets of this unit and evaluate your own strengths and weaknesses. Tick either + (positive) or – (negative) in the table below. Specify which tasks in each skills areas and activities you are evaluating. Then reflect on these and make notes in the final column.**

Tasks	+	–	Reflection notes
The reading tasks:			

Tasks	+	–	Reflection notes
The writing tasks:			
The speaking tasks:			
The listening tasks:			

Further reading

Lockwood, J. & Forey, G. (2016) Discursive control and power in virtual meetings. *Discourse and Communication*, 10(4).

Mayer, J. (2019) Managing culturally diverse teams. *Applied Information Management Program. University of Oregon. USA.*

Pullen, P. & Prokopi, E. (2016) Leading virtual teams: dos and don'ts. Presented at PMI® *Global Congress 2016–EMEA* Barcelona, Spain. Newtown Square, PA: Project Management Institute.

UNIT 7

Working on the project

The big ideas

The **learning targets** for this unit are to:

- Understand the language of, and practise, collaborative problem-solving in English
- Work in teams in English to come up with a range of project/campaign ideas
- Package your ideas creatively for GlobeNet through a virtual presentation
- Understand the structure of the monthly report and practise writing one
- Practise language modality choices for a range of CommunicAsian scenarios

Activity 1. Input: Readings and discussion

Creativity and an ability to 'think critically and problem solve' are highly valued in any business as these are where 'the next big ideas' come from for innovation and problem-solving. How would you define them and what sort of business environment encourages and nurtures these abilities?

■ **Jot your ideas down in the box below:**

■ **Look at the vocabulary and idiomatic expression items in bold. If you don't understand them, refer to the dictionary in Appendix 1 and/or try and guess the meaning from the context.**

Now read the text below:

Reading 1 COLLABORATIVE TEAMS AND CREATIVITY AT WORK

There is constantly a debate about the **merits** of staff only working from home because sitting down with your colleagues, or just having unplanned chats over the water cooler don't happen if you are not at work interacting with others. Where project teams are working together on creative and problem-solving tasks, it is essential to have regular contact with your colleagues, whether it be face-to-face or virtually. Being able to do collaborative project work in teams is viewed as a highly desirable skill in the twenty-first century workplace. Being able to have the kind of critical thinking skills that facilitate creativity and problem solving is also a highly desirable skill in business.

continued . . .

cont.

Many advertising and public relations groups get their best ideas out of collaborative project teams working on **branding ideas and messaging**. But there also needs to be individual inspiration and original thought.

For example, **tag lines** such as 'Go to work on an egg' (the UK Egg Board) or 'Put a tiger in your tank' (well-known petrol brand) show original and creative thinking, and an ability to 'play' with words and use **metaphor**. Using visuals and music also contribute to messaging as well. Memorable and successful branding and advertising lines tease the customer to think about what is being advertised from a number of angles.

The majority of good ideas come from inspiration and team work. One member might be **'the spark'** behind a good idea, other members then will craft that basic idea into something **tangible** and usable.

Hearing what team members say and suggest in creative collaborative work demands responses. In the very act of responding thoughtfully you are being creative. This activity often results in a **chain reaction** amongst members of a team who are expected to contribute. These thoughtful responses are the best form of creativity. Hearing other people's insights, or advice, makes you think of ways to respond, not just simply, but at a higher level than what just preceded your response. That is the power of people. Engaging in conversation with other team members sparks creativity. Not only does talking with people promote your own individual ideas, it can also **refine** your own ideas to make them better.

Irrespective of where the original idea came from, the way your individual mind interprets that idea is creative. The beauty is that it happened without you trying to be creative. Collaborative team work can be like magic!

- **Look at the vocabulary and idiomatic expression items in bold. If you don't understand them, refer to the dictionary in Appendix 1 and/or try and guess the meaning from the context.**

Now read the text below:

Reading 2 THE LANGUAGE OF PROBLEM-SOLVING IN THE WORKPLACE

Problem-solving and negotiating ways forward in the workplace, especially when difficulties hit, are critical English language communications skills. We are often **summoned to meetings** when problems hit, and the outcome has got be a way forward that has been **mutually arrived at**.

The language of such problem-solving is very **nuanced**. In the collaborative workplace where **ideas are floated**, discussed and worked through to some kind of resolution, the communication exchange requires good English communication skills. You need these to engage with the problem, show expertise and build trust with your colleagues. Culturally this can be difficult where conflict may be regarded as a bad thing and something to avoid, rather than a good thing to be confronted and leading to improvements. Conflict can provide businesses with the opportunity to do better if they choose to acknowledge problems and work on them. Workplaces where the **'elephant in the room'** is not discussed, ignore problems **at their peril**. This article promotes the idea of confronting and working through problems rather than **sweeping them under the carpet**, using excuses and **blame games**.

The business culture of problem-solving employs rich and nuanced language, and here we explore two examples.

First, we need to raise the key issues in a way that will not **put colleagues so much on the defensive** that they resist the process of acknowledging the problem and getting to a solution. In English, we use **MODALITY** to communicate our feelings and judgements to others **without intentionally offending** and **polarising** the situation. **Modal verbs** such as *may, might, would, should, can, could, ought to, have to* and *must* communicate obligation, possibility, evaluation and permission. These often serve to **soften** a difficult message.

continued . . .

cont.

For example look at the difference between: 'Tell him to do that immediately' as opposed to 'Perhaps you should suggest he do that immediately'. These modals can be further *modified* by using such markers as 'perhaps', 'maybe' or 'have you thought about...?' as seen above.

Secondly, where you are suggesting something different, you can **couch your idea** to make it sound **hypothetical**; or, if you want to warn your colleagues about the effect of doing or not doing something, we can use **CONDITIONAL** sentences, showing clear cause and effect. For example:

'If you spend all the budget in the first quarter, it's going to mean we can't fund the launch in the 2nd quarter'. This functions as a certainty and therefore a warning of **the cause and then the effect**.

However, where we were debating whether to ask the client for an increased budget, you may want to use the following conditional to make your suggestion sound hypothetical. For example:

If we were to ask GlobeNet for more money for translating the message to Chinese at this late stage, they may see us as incompetent. This functions as both a **hypothetical suggestion** but also a warning.

Remember there is no right and wrong way to use business English, it depends on the context (purpose, content and audience) and it depends on your ability to make the right, intended choices in the context. You can practice these in the CommunicAsian scenarios in Activity 3.

Remember: language is a system of choices not a list of rules.

The story so far ...

- **Look at the vocabulary and idiomatic expression items in bold. If you don't understand them, refer to the dictionary in Appendix 1 and/or try and guess the meaning from the context.**

Now read the story below:

PROJECT MANAGEMENT HAS SOME ISSUES

Celia hung up at the end of her weekly call with Trevor, her CEO based in UK. She had learned quickly that Trevor liked to focus on **hard numbers** with evidence to support them: if she said that some task was 50% complete, she had better have the facts. That suited Celia; she liked to work with **sales pipelines**, **conversion rates**, and other **quantitative measures**.

She thought about Tony Tanaka, who was **just the opposite**. She liked his confidence and enthusiasm, but she got frustrated when she felt she was not being listened to. Their meeting the day before was a good example. Celia asked what **metrics** were being proposed by CommunicAsian to **track sales** and how to change the campaign based on those metrics. Tony's response was typical.

"The point, Celia, is to make sure we have the right message before we worry about how to deliver it. What is going to make **prospects prick up their ears** and think 'this is for me'. We had a creatives meeting on Monday – you would have loved it – everyone had to come up with a **tag line** for the campaign, and then everyone got to vote on how effective they thought it would be. We've just hired this new market analyst, Peter Lee, who's been working in London, and he's **bringing something different to the table**. I'm not going to tell you anything now about his ideas for the tagline – they are all meeting this week to brainstorm some more; some great campaign ideas floating around, and I promise you that you'll be happy to drop the roam and home title."

Celia did not say that she was the person who thought up 'Roam like you're Home', and she was rather proud of it. More than that, she was concerned that her boss was not going to be happy with such **vague** project progress reports. The meeting **wrapped up** with her feeling very dissatisfied. She thought about making an **escalation call** as the **project charter** suggested, but that didn't feel right. It wasn't a complaint, more of a miscommunication.

She decided to call Dawn. They had only met briefly at the proposal presentation, but she thought they would probably **get along**: two young women building their careers.

"Dawn, I decided to call you so I could just talk about this project without it **being minuted and documented**. As you probably know, this is the biggest project I've ever been in charge of, and it's **make or break for my career** at GlobeNet."

"I feel the same for me," said Dawn. "My chairman is calling me almost every day. I've never been under such **scrutiny**. But do you have specific concerns that you wanted to talk to me about?"

"Well, I don't want to criticise your manager, and he's good in many ways, but I get really frustrated that I can't get a written report and we have long, **rambling meetings** when he comes to our office **unscheduled**."

"Oh," said Dawn, "I take it you are talking about Tony Tanaka."

"Yes. I get that he's good, but when we talk I feel like we're using two different languages."

Dawn nodded down the phone. "I fully understand, he can be frustrating. I have had to learn how to rein him in and focus on detail. Leave it with me, and I'll make some changes without mentioning you. He does good work in the end."

"Yes," said Celia, "and thank you." She paused. "Can I ask a favour? Could we do a call every week this time just to **touch base** and support each other without it being official?"

"Of course," said Dawn, "I'd enjoy that. I'll put it in the diary for the next four weeks." She set the invite with the subject **'Sisterhood Call'**.

■ **Think about the following questions and discuss:**

(i) How is Celia feeling in this story episode? Why?

....

....

(ii) How does she deal with these concerns? Do you agree? Comment.

....

....

Activity 2. Input: Understanding and modelling spoken and written texts

Task (i). Audio listening: Internal meeting at CommunicAsian to discuss project changes (Transcript – Appendix 2)

Peter, Prasad, Tony and Melinda are all meeting to discuss the possibility of some project changes. Peter and Prasad are physically in the same meeting room and then they dial in Tony and Melinda who are part of the Steering Committee.

- **Look at the table below and discuss the words and expressions. Once you have understood the main issues in the meeting, try and guess any unfamiliar words from the context.**

Words and expressions	Meaning
To go through	
Steering Committee	
Dropping it	
Current plans	
To switch	
It's tough	
I take your point	
Change our minds	
Decision makers	
Influencers	
Stay in touch	

Overruns	
Put your heads together	
Come up with	
Go the extra mile	
Folks	

■ **Now go back to the script and complete the functional use of modality and conditionality. The first one has been done for you.**

Modality – examples and functions	**Conditionality – examples and functions**
Example: *I'd like to suggest two things* Function: *A polite way for Peter to introduce his ideas*	Example: *If it (cost increase) does, we need to go through the Steering Committee* Function: *The first conditional communicates something that is not negotiable/factual*

Task (ii). Project status monthly report

■ **Before you read the report think about the question below:**

What do you think is important to communicate in a monthly update to the GlobeNet client? What do we know about Trevor and Celia?

....

....

....

■ **Now look at Tony's monthly report:**

- note how it is structured with the different headings; how does each heading function and what kind of language is used? Complete the table at the end of the report.
- guess the words/expressions **in bold**
- comment on its appropriateness

CommunicAsian

Project Status Report for
GlobeNet Communications
'Roam like you're Home' Project
June 6th

1. OVERVIEW OF PROGRESS

   - The project is **on track** after four weeks of the 12 week schedule.
   - Countries and market segments have been identified and agreed for the launching.
   - We have built up social media **usage profiles** for each segment.
   - Work has started on **consumer testing** the messaging.
   - Data requirements for tracking are being defined.

2. MILESTONES AND ACHIEVEMENTS

   Details of achievements to date:

   - Countries and Market Segments
     - Agreed China tertiary and secondary students
     - Agreed Hong Kong students
     - Agreed Filipino health and care workers
   - Social Media Profiles of Segments
     - Much similarity of usage across segments
     - While China-based students use local social media tools they also **tend to** use Western tools for communicating with Western people or where English language is used.

- Messaging
  - 'Roam like you're Home' did not **generate enthusiasm** or understanding of the product when we tested it with focus groups.
  - Survey data are giving us good feedback on how potential targets see the value of the product in order to communicate that effectively.

3. UPCOMING WORK

In the next two weeks we shall complete the **messaging work** and launch the campaign.

The measures and reporting and analysis approach will be given to GlobeNet for **sign-off** next week, giving the team time to set up the reporting applications.

4. ISSUES AND CHALLENGES

There are some challenges with the survey collection in terms of response rates, but these can be addressed either by **tweaking** the survey or by more in-depth focus group discussions.

5. OTHER MATTERS

There are no other matters at this time.

Tony Tanaka
Creative Director

On a scale of 1 (low)–10 (high) how would you rate this report that was sent last week to the client? Give reasons for your evaluation.

....
....
....

Now complete the table below focusing on the organisation of the monthly report, think about the heading functions and the language used. The first one has been done for you:

Monthly report headings and format	Function	Language used
1. Overview of progress Uses bullet points for easy and quick reading	Key summary points of achievements so far	Present and present perfect tenses to show things in progress and achievement Business vocabulary: on track; identified, user profile, etc
2.		
3.		
4.		
5.		
6.		

Activity 3. Output: Spoken and written skills development tasks

Task (i). Email exchange

Dawn has a difficult management task on her hands. Tony is great at what he does but is not producing the kind of monthly reports that GlobeNet wants to see. She decides to email Sam and get her views on possible personnel changes to ensure this is going to happen in the future.

To: Sam

From: Dawn

Subject: Tony's (lack of) monthly reporting

Hi Sam,

I've had a call from Celia and she's become increasingly frustrated by Tony's lack of specificity in the monthly reporting ... basically too much hot air and too few metrics. I really don't want this to become a bigger issue.

Without doing Tony down I've promised to solve this issue asap. I'll meet with Tony and Prasad as the project manager soon!

Any ideas?
Maybe coffee tomorrow?
Talk soon, Dawn.

- **You are Sam, what is your advice before you meet for coffee? Think about:**

• Changing responsibilities for existing personnel to ensure that the problem is solved
• Reporting line for this
• How best to communicate the changes without "doing anyone down"

- **Jot your ideas down in the box provided below:**

- **Now write the response to Dawn; think about the content, purpose and audience. How long should the email be and should Sam copy anybody else in? Why/why not?**

> To: Dawn
> Cc:
> From: Sam
> Subject:

Task (ii). Campaign meeting roleplay

Preparation for the roleplay

The day Tony has been looking forward to has finally arrived, he is having his first creative meeting with his team to come up with slogans/logos and ideas for building awareness in Asia for the 'Roam like you're Home' concept. There are a lot of good ideas floating around! Their ideas will need to be turned into a three-slide presentation to Dawn for feedback.

Look at Tony's **ground rules** at the start of the meeting.

Tony: Thanks everyone for getting here. This is Peter's first time, so I'll just go over our meeting rules. Anyone can come out with an idea, however crazy, and everyone else has to build on that idea using an 'AND' statement. After five 'ANDS' we decide if the idea goes on to the whiteboard for further discussion or is dropped. I'll start. I think we should get a famous rapper from the US to record 'Roam like You're Home' rap.

Peter: But they don't like rap in Asia.

Tony: No buts. Turn it into an AND that will advance the idea.

Peter: I don't get it. Oh, yes I do. AND we'll get him to perform it with a Cantopop star.

Tony: Yes, you've got it. And we'll get them to promote it to all their social media followers.

Sam: And we'll have a competition with their followers to write a better set of words.

Peter: And we'll have as a prize a chance to record it with the stars.

Vince: And every station will be playing the GlobeNet song. That'd be worth millions.

Tony: We've gone past five, and I think this is one we drop. For a start, we'd need a budget about a hundred times bigger than what we have, and we've got no idea if it would work, but it was a nice way to show Peter how we approach it. Somebody else kick off.

As well as incorporating AND into your discussion, think about the modality and conditionality choices that will help build collaboration in your discussion.

- **Look at the three creative idea suggestions below and write at least two modality/conditionality responses for each: they can communicate support or not.**

1. Sam: Let's make the Sim card packaging a collectible – pictures of local stars.

   ....
   ....
   ....
   ....

2. Vince: Let the first 500 sign-ups in each country go into a draw for a free iPhone.

   ....
   ....
   ....
   ....

3. Peter: Let's do an Instagram campaign showing some girl in London sending pictures of famous landmarks and the family receiving them back here, and then the tag: It's like having London in your living room.

   ....
   ....
   ....
   ....

The roleplay

- **Form groups of four and take one of the following roles.**

Role 1: Tony – Department Head
Role 2: Peter – recent new hire
Role 3: Graduate intern – Vince
Role 4: Graduate intern – Winnie

- **On the whiteboard below, explain your preferred campaign slogan. This should also include a logo design.**

- **Now design your three slides to present to Dawn.**

Present them to Dawn in 3–5 minute slot.

Discuss and feedback.

Task (iii). Writing a monthly report

The last monthly report, submitted by Tony to GlobeNet, was a disaster. This month Prasad will oversee the report and has been gathering key data to ensure it meets client expectations.

In a recent meeting with the project team, these are the notes he wrote:

- *I'm not sure about the Philippines. The numbers look good at 45,000 workers went to UK last year, but the UK government seems to be restricting immigration. Students are easier.*
- *So maybe we need to look a bit harder at Thailand. Only about 5,000 tertiary, but maybe 30,000 secondary if schools in UK meet their targets.*
- *90% of people we talked to use WhatsApp and almost as many use WeChat.*
- *55% were interested in voice roaming and 65% in data.*
- *We need to start getting and measuring sign-ups in the next week or so.*
- *Our surveys haven't worked yet. We need a better incentive to get more responses.*
- *We need to get some data on GlobeNet's profitability by customer so we can plan the numbers needed to make the project succeed.*

■ **Use these notes to write this month's report in the box below, showing more numbers and detail. Go back to the model monthly report organisation and ideas about language use in Activity 2 before you start writing this report.**

GlobeNet Monthly Report

Task (iv). Covering email

- You are Prasad and you send this monthly report to Dawn. Think about who you might cc in and how long the email should be and what it should say. Use the box below:

To: Dawn
Cc:
From: Prasad
Subject:

■ **Feedback and discuss.**

Activity 4. Reflection and further reading

Reflection

How did you do in this unit?

■ **Look back at the original learning targets of this unit and evaluate your own strengths and weaknesses. Tick either + (positive) or – (negative) in the table below. Specify which tasks in each skills areas and activities you are evaluating. Then reflect on these and make notes in the final column.**

Tasks	+	–	Reflection notes
The reading tasks:			
The writing tasks:			

Tasks	+	–	Reflection notes
The speaking tasks:			
The listening tasks:			

Further reading

Bremner, S. (2010) Collaborative writing: Bridging the gap between the textbook and the workplace. *English for Specific Purposes,* 29(2), 121–132.

Peirson-Smith, A., Bhatia, V.J., Bremner, S. & Jones, R. (2010) Creative English and public relations in Hong Kong. *World Englishes,* 29(4), 523–535.

UNIT

8 Problems, problems, problems

The **learning targets** for this unit are to:

- Understand and practise how to deal with external client and customer conflict
- Explore the nuance of business chat exchange
- Understand and practise texting/chatting in a business context
- Understand the written genre and language of business complaints

Activity 1. Input: Readings and discussion

■ **Look at the vocabulary and idiomatic expression items in bold. If you don't understand them, refer to the dictionary in Appendix 1 and/or try and guess the meaning from the context.**

Now read the text below:

Reading 1 DEALING WITH CONFLICT WITH YOUR CLIENTS AND CUSTOMERS

No business relationship operates **harmoniously** 100% of the time. When customer conflict arises, however, it needs to be dealt with in a professional and positive way. Here are a number of tips:

1. **Confront the issue immediately, with care and diplomatically**

   The first thing to do is to ensure that the problem is not ignored. In many Asian cultures, business conflict is regarded as a **negative disruptive force** and is therefore often avoided. However, if the problem is not dealt with swiftly it grows bigger and **potentially** can develop into something much more serious ultimately impacting your business. So dealing with problems immediately can save time and pain later on.

   Dealing with conflict on email can be particularly difficult as you do not have the **benefit** of seeing the client/customer face-to-face to **gauge** real emotions and feelings. Rather than send emails in the hope of resolving the issue, set up a face-to-face meeting, even if has to be virtual.

2. **Don't jump to assumptions and conclusions**

   It is **tempting** to make assumptions and **jump to conclusions** when conflict occurs, so outline your **perception** of the issues and say how it makes you feel. You may be totally wrong in your assumptions and conclusions. For example, look at this recent scenario by a CEO friend of mine.

   *I had recently seen two of my best employees speaking to Stella, the HRO manager of a firm in the coffee shop downstairs. I phoned Stella and accused her of **poaching** my staff. Bad move! My assumptions were wrong, Stella and my two employees were all at college together and regularly catch up.*

continued . . .

cont.

3. Follow up the resolution of the conflict with a clear message

Resolving the issue in an **open and transparent** way is very important. A follow-up message either spoken and/or written may be appropriate and provides an opportunity of closure. In the case above my friend wrote a short email apologising to Stella. This action of course will depend on the **severity** and nature of the conflict. If there has been just a minor misunderstanding, this may not be necessary. However, in this case my friend thought apologising in writing was important. She wanted to keep Stella as a friendly rival, not an unfriendly one.

In conclusion, the key issues are to **open up**, not **close down** conflict; don't jump to conclusions without asking questions, discuss the source of the conflict and get to some kind of resolution and understanding. Getting closure on the conflict is also important and this may require a final message to all **relevant** parties involved.

4. Customer service conflict

In customer service, whether it be face-to-face, on the phone or online, there is a **mantra** that 'the customer is always right'. Essentially this means that it is inadvisable to have a damaging confrontation with a customer; you don't want to lose business and you want to **keep the customer sweet**. This means that in business situations where a customer becomes angry or rude about something, you should try your best **to defuse** the situation by **empathising** with how they are feeling; probe the source of the frustration and apologise if there has been something that your business has done. You also will offer to rectify, or even compensate for, your mistake. This soft skill is highly valued!

■ **Look at the vocabulary and idiomatic expression items in bold. If you don't understand them, refer to the dictionary in Appendix 1 and/or try and guess the meaning from the context.**

What do you think are the advantages/disadvantages of using texting for business purposes?

....
....
....
....

Now read the text below:

Reading 2 TEXTING IN A BUSINESS CONTEXT

Social media chats have been the subject of a number of studies where they occur between friendship and family groups. These have helped us to understand new ways of meaning-making when using this **new media**. But how does chat work in businesses and workplaces? It has been found that texting (or webchat) can offer businesses both time efficiency and new **pragmatic strategies** to achieve transactions and exchanges both internally and externally. Business texting is extremely useful when we think of the speed of exchange that can be achieved amongst internal business colleagues, for example, in the **immediacy** of identifying and solving problems. This is also the case externally where online ordering and customer service can be **done synchronously**, using texting. This is good for business as they can operate efficiently and effectively around the clock! However, this new media can be hard to **navigate** for employees when businesses mandate **style guides** and policies about using this new media which conflict with either normal practice or the respondent's style. Some companies insist on writing formally when texting, insisting on perfectly formed grammatical sentences – the argument being that this approach projects a professional image. Another challenge is where customers typically have their own particular styles of meaning-making when texting; age, ethnicity, gender and socio-economic backgrounds may impact the text construction in the choice of words, punctuation and symbols. Reflecting these in business responses, if permitted, is difficult. These observations all add interesting challenges in achieving expertise in business communication when using English for business chatting/texting.

So how can we build effective business relationships using texting at work? Several studies have explored how the use of **emoticons**, **emojis**

continued . . .

cont.

and **punctuation** make meaning at work. For example, the use of ... (dot dot dot) can communicate uncertainty and even **banality** about a topic under discussion, whereas several question marks (???) or exclamation marks (!!!) may denote disbelief and/or either extreme annoyance, or even good news celebration when used by the texter. Look at this authentic exchange in a customer service exchange where a customer has been trying to make an appointment to get his internet connected.

Agent: So we can come between 10–5pm tomorrow.
Customer: But I work ...
Agent: That's OK as the technician will ring you 20 minutes before he arrives.
Customer: So I have 20 mins to get home on a normal 45 min commute??? ☹

By using punctuation for meaning making we can see that the customer is not happy with the arrangements that the agent is trying to make.

CAPITALISATION can also communicate anger, surprise and upset, and the use of this is not normally appropriate in business contexts, although customers use it to communicate frustration. It spells SHOUTING. This same webchat exchange ended with the customer texting:

Customer: What I'm saying is that I WORK between those times, I can't get home with only 20 mins notice.

The use of emojis and emoticons are often discouraged in business communication by companies particularly where the texting is directed to external clients and customers. The business argument is that the use of these also **erode** the professional image of their company/brand. One CEO was once heard saying *I don't want clients to think we are that informal ... and that we only hire teenagers.*

Studies have also found that **chronemic meaning** is embedded in texting where time gaps in the text exchange may indicate customer **disinterest** or even customer support inefficiency. What do you think when you, as a customer, are **put on hold** for long stretches of time?

continued . . .

cont. However, in some business contexts (e.g. customer service) text support through social media and web chat is rapidly emerging as a **preferred** customer option when trying to solve problems and getting answers to questions. Businesses also like it because it gives them a 'digital' **edge** in the market place, and **caters to** the needs of a younger customer base. This is why texting is a **channel** that we, as expert business communicators, need to understand and practise. Like all channels of communication the key issues to think about before you text are: what is the purpose of your text, who is the audience and how much content are you going to include. It is also important, just as in voice and email, to understand nuance in client and customer texts; i.e. what are the clues given beyond the actual words used?

The story so far ...

- **Look at the vocabulary and idiomatic expression items in bold. If you don't understand them, refer to the dictionary in Appendix 1 and/or try and guess the meaning from the context.**

Now read the story below:

Managing Cost and Scope

Melinda was happy with her performance to date. Her financial reports and **forecasts** had been praised at the Project Board for their clarity and analysis, and she had found some ways to save money when the budget looked like it might be exceeded. Also, she felt she worked well with Prasad, they made a good team. Last week Prasad wanted to add a fourth country to the project as Tony's team had identified it as high potential, and they reported that it could be done without impacting the budget, so the Board approved the change. Smooth. Melinda thought how much she had learned in her short time on the project: the constant balancing and rebalancing of scope, cost and time together with an unending focus on the results.

When Prasad's face appeared on the video call she smiled. "Hi," she said, "I hope your day is as good as mine."

"It's not," said Prasad. "I've **screwed up**." He was almost in tears. "When I said we could add the new country based on what we were already doing I got it wrong. I was thinking it was Taiwan but it's Thailand. That means more translation, more screen design, at least one more person. And we've told the client, we'll have to **wear it**. Could I run it through another budget – say IT support – so it doesn't impact our project?"

Melinda noted that it was now 'our' project but made no comment. "Prasad," she said, "these things happen. We can't hide it: if the Project Board knew we'd even considered that option we'd both be fired right away. Look, I can see you're upset. Why don't you send me an email outlining the impact and I'll update the numbers for tomorrow's meeting."

Prasad **mumbled** thanks and went off to **compose** the email. Melinda set herself up for a late night, and past eleven o'clock she completed her report and sent it to Prasad for checking. She was surprised that there was no acknowledgement, so she texted and then called on WhatsApp. There was no response. The Project Board had a strict rule that all papers must be sent the day before the meeting, so, at five to midnight Melinda distributed the financial report.

At the board the next day Vivek was chair in Dawn's absence, and he asked for the agenda to be changed to deal with finance as the first item. "What is this extra $6,000 in expenses? It's **come out of nowhere**. You say it's because of the extra market we approved, but you told us last week it was cost free. How can we trust your numbers? Are you **out of your depth**?"

"I think Prasad should comment on that," said Melinda.

"Prasad is sick today," said Vivek. "Did he even approve these changes?"

> Melinda thought hard. Was Prasad really sick or was he just avoiding a difficult meeting. She decided that she could not talk about his mistake without him being there: that would be unfair.
>
> "No," she said. "I sent them for his approval, but when he had not replied I decided I had better send them."
>
> Vivek sounded angry. "You produce new numbers without consulting the project manager and expect the Board to approve? I propose that this report is withdrawn and the meeting **adjourns** until we have a proper project authority to report."

As expected, the Board agreed with Vivek's motion. Now it was Melinda who was close to tears.

■ **Discuss:**

(i) Why is Melinda close to tears at the end of this meeting?

....

....

....

(ii) Do you think Prasad was really sick so he could not attend the meeting? Why/why not?

....

....

....

Activity 2. Input: Understanding and modelling spoken and written texts

■ **Look at the following scenario:**

Trevor is planning a trip to visit the Hong Kong office and talk through some of the CommunicAsian project issues with Celia. However, he is having some problems working out how to get to the hotel which he has booked on-line.

Task (i). Deconstructing webchat

- **Look at the authentic chat exchange below between Trevor and a customer service agent at the hotel he has booked into in Hong Kong. Trevor wanted a hotel address for a reservation he had already made.**

Hotel agent has joined the session 10:27

Agent: 10:28 Hello Trevor. Thank you for contacting the *GLOBAL RESERVATIONS* office for *GROUP* hotels. What is your reservation code and how may I help you today?

Trevor: 10:28 Hi – my reservation code is CN835725 can you send me the hotel details please for my taxi driver from airport?

Trevor: 10:29 Also please let the hotel know I'll arrive around 10.00pm on Wednesday.

Agent: 10:30 I see. I am sorry. I am not located at the hotel or in the area. I am at the Global Reservations office. Please contact the hotel directly.

Agent: 10:30 Would you like to have the contact details?

Trevor: 10:31 The email link does not work and how come you have no access to *GROUP* hotel information??

Agent: 10:32 Let me check if that is available on our system.

Agent: 10:34 May I have the specific hotel you are referring to?

Trevor: 10:34 Can you not check the reservation number?? Else why do you ask for it?

Agent: 10:35 Please hold.

Agent: 11:40 Please give me a few more minutes to check the address.

Agent: 11:42 Please navigate to the next link https://www.Group.com/hotellux/hotels/ hongkong/ctucc/hoteldetail#

Agent: 11:42 The link of the hotel is https://www.Group.com/hotellux/hotels/ hongkong/ctucc/hoteldetail#

Agent: 11:42 On the upper right corner of the page, you will see a drop down menu of the language you would want to use to see the page.

Agent: 11:44 The address of the hotel is on the bottom part of the page.

Agent: 11:44 Would there be anything else?

Trevor: 11:44 Thanks for putting all the onus back on me – that's what I call service ...

Trevor: 11:45 I hope the training improves ...

Agent: 11:45 You are welcome and thank you for contacting us. If you need further assistance, please chat us back again. Have a nice day!

Agent has left the session. 11:45

(i) Where did communication breakdown in this webchat? What caused this?

....
....
....

(ii) How would you improve the agent's service and responses to Trevor?

....
....
....

Task (ii). Email exchanges of complaint

When Trevor arrived in Hong Kong the taxi driver said he had never heard of Hotel Lux. Eventually they found it and Trevor was not impressed with its location, its cleanliness nor its facilities.

■ **Look at the complaint email he has written below to the hotel manager.**

To: Mr. Yeung (Manager Hotel Lux)
From: Trevor Lavender (CEO GlobeNet)
Subject: Complaint about your HK hotel

Dear Mr. Yeung

As an international business person with regular travel to Hong Kong, I rely on a hotel that is well located and is clean. I was disappointed when arriving in HK; Hotel Lux was hard to locate, and the cleanliness and access to facilities have been problematic. (Para 1)

I had problems too with your contact centre before I left London where I had tried to get assistance about where the hotel is located and I asked for an address, only to receive robotic responses and urls that didn't open. I therefore arrived in HK late at night not knowing the address and the taxi driver had great difficulty finding the location. (Para 2)

However, on arrival I have been allocated a room at the back of the hotel that is both dirty and noisy. It seems that the room has not been occupied for a number of weeks, it is dusty and it lacks good ventilation. Furthermore, the bathroom does not look as though it has been cleaned recently and there are water stains in the bath. Finally the facilities advertised i.e. the gym and the pool are both closed for renovation works. (Para 3)

Given that I have another 4 nights at your hotel I would like to be moved into a cleaner and brighter room in the front of the hotel. (Para 4)

Your swift response would be greatly appreciated and if you can't provide this, I will move to another hotel. (Para 5)

Yours sincerely,
Trevor Lavender.

- **In the table below note down the function/purpose of each paragraph in this complaint email, and also the kind of language that is being used (e.g. what tenses are being used and why). The first one has been done for you.**

Paragraph	Function/purpose	Language used
1.	*Setting the scene and summarising the complaint.*	*Present tense, introduction of self and expectations.* *Past tense of hotel problems experienced.* *Adjectives.*
2.		
3.		
4.		
5.		

Trevor also fires off an email to Dawn after meeting Celia in the HK office.

From: Trevor Lavender
Sent: Thursday, May 2, 11:13 AM
To: Dawn Chen; Celia Tang
Subject: Project Reporting for RLYH

Dawn

I am writing to you out of frustration with the project reports we receive every month. I expect reports to be detailed and supported with numbers. If a task is complete, then tell me what the outcomes and the findings are! What we receive is a 'good news' note saying basically 'trust us, everything's fine'. I have seen too many projects appear to be on track only because they are not measured properly, and the troubles only emerge when the deadline hits.

I have raised this before with Celia, and she tells me she has taken it up with your Mr. Tanaka, but clearly without any result. I reviewed last month's report which had been forwarded by Celia. Celia assures me this has been communicated to you and expects this to change in the next one I am expecting at the end of this week. I hope so.

I would expect an organisation of your experience to have solid project management processes and reports, but I am not seeing that at present.

Regards,
Trevor Lavender

How does Trevor feel in this email message? Give examples of his use of language.

....
....
....
....
....
....
....

Dawn has just received this month's report (see Unit 7 Activity 3 task (iii)) which the team say is ready to go out; she feels it is an improvement, but it is still a bit 'thin' from a data point of view. She is going to call an emergency meeting to ensure the need for comprehensive monthly reporting, including key numbers, is understood and achieved.

- **How do you think Dawn should reply to Trevor's email? Jot your ideas down in the box below:**

- **Now look at Dawn's response below:**

From: Dawn Chen
Sent: Thursday, May 2, 12:13 PM
To: Trevor Lavender; Celia Tang
Subject: Re: Project Reporting for RLYH

Dear Trevor,

I note your complaint and your concerns, and, as you say, this has been communicated to me by Celia. We have since taken action to ensure the monthly reports are more comprehensive and our next report will include the numerical details to support the solid progress of this project.

I have just received the report and am reviewing it before I sign off. This will be forwarded to you within this week.

I can assure you, from my regular meetings with the team, that the project is indeed on track and I am sure you will be pleased with the evidenced progress you will see in the next report.

Regards
Dawn Chen

Now Dawn sends the following email to the team to arrange to go through the report and to suggest enhancing the data evidence.

> **From:** Dawn
> **Sent:** Thursday, May 2, 12:20 PM
> **To:** Samantha; Tony; Prasad
> **Subject:** FW: Project Reporting for RLYH
>
> Hi all
>
> The email chain is self-explanatory. I received the complaint from GlobeNet CEO this morning, and replied saying that we are currently enhancing our reporting with more data. I have looked through a draft monthly report to go out this week and I still feel the numbers are flakey.
>
> Can we meet and can you, Prasad, bring along a detailed monthly data report? Tony I rely on you to bring details of activity.
>
> A client complaint on this project is something we do not need, so let's make sure they get a killer monthly report going forward.
>
> Talk soon,
> Dawn

Task (iii). Audio listening: Internal meeting at CommunicAsian: Project problems (Transcript – Appendix 2)

Dawn is chairing the internal meeting to address the concern about poor reporting from their client GlobeNet.

Present: Dawn, Samantha, Tony (on video in HK), Prasad.

- **Check you understand the meanings of the words/expressions below before you listen to the meeting.**

Words and expressions	Meaning
Get straight to the point	
Incompetent	
Sign off	
Ever occur to you	
Reassurance	
Over my head	
Getting our own house in order	
Appendices	
Productivity measures	
Put your heads together	
Costs overrun	
Withdrawn	
Pick up on it	
Cost us a fortune	
Cut-down version	
Priority	
Emergency	
Neglected	

As you listen to the meeting for the first time, jot down the problems Dawn brings up in this meeting and how she is feeling.

....

....

....

....

....

....

- **Now go back to the call and highlight the words/expressions in the script that show that Dawn is upset. Write them in box below:**

- **In pairs practice these terms of upset with your partner. Think about how you will use intonation and word stress to carry your meaning.**

Activity 3. Output: Spoken and written skills development tasks

Task (i). Texting and emailing

Vivek felt sorry for Melinda at the internal budget meeting that had happened earlier that week and wanted to know why Prasad wasn't present. He texted Prasad after he got out of that meeting on WhatsApp:

> What's the problem?? No budget increase approved. U **landed Melinda in it** today. Call me asap? ☹

- **How would you respond to Vivek's text? You have felt very stressed recently and you are finding Tony increasingly difficult to deal with. You feel awful for letting Melinda down ... as Prasad, respond to Vivek's text below:**

■ **As Prasad, text Melinda below:**

■ **Now look at how this chat exchange above might be done using email.**

Vivek writes to Prasad:

To: Prasad
From: Vivek
Subject: Missed meeting

Dear Prasad,

I hope you are feeling better.

As you may be aware, the proposed budget prepared by Melinda for the Board Meeting was withdrawn as you had not approved them, and you were not there to explain them. It was all rather embarrassing, Melinda was upset and I'd like an explanation asap.

Can you let me know what is going on?
Vivek

- **Write Prasad's response to Vivek below:**

To: Vivek
From: Prasad
Subject:

Prasad is also feeling very guilty about not contacting Melinda before the meeting.

- **Write Prasad's email below:**

To: Melinda
From: Prasad
Subject:

- **Discuss how constructing these text and email threads differ.**

....
....
....
....
....
....

Task (ii). Writing to complain

As project manager, Prasad has been overseeing the venue bookings for the GlobeNet launch. He has been negotiating with a large hotel to use their events room, but every time he talks to the coordinator she gives him different prices and conditions. He has just heard that there will be a 25% surcharge for technical support, which he told them last month they did not require.

- **Write an email to complain ... you need this sorted out as the Board will finalise the budget at next week's meeting.**

Task (iii). Roleplay: Confronting problems and expressing your concern

In Activity 2, we saw how Dawn confronted issues with colleagues and managed to clearly show her concern particularly about issues in the monthly reporting to GlobeNet.

- **Look at some of the other concerns with the GlobeNet project. How would you confront these?**

Discuss and roleplay the exchanges below:

(i) You are Vivek and you have noticed that the GlobeNet project has over-run its budget and the project is only half way through. You first bring this up at the reporting meeting with Prasad, what do you say?

……………………………………………………………………………
……………………………………………………………………………
……………………………………………………………………………
……………………………………………………………………………
……………………………………………………………………………
……………………………………………………………………………
……………………………………………………………………………

(ii) At the meeting, Prasad explains that they have made an upfront payment to an external provider Atlas IT which has taken some of the budget, but the main part has been CommunicAsian staff costs. You understand that Prasad's cousin owns Atlas IT, so you decide to inform the project manager Dawn of this situation. What do you say?

……………………………………………………………………………
……………………………………………………………………………
……………………………………………………………………………
……………………………………………………………………………
……………………………………………………………………………
……………………………………………………………………………
……………………………………………………………………………

(iii) What does Dawn now say to Prasad? Prasad explains that the amount paid to Atlas was very small and has not impacted the budget at all. In fact CommunicAsian got a heavy discount because it was his relative's company. Write the exchange between Dawn and Prasad below:

……………………………………………………………………………
……………………………………………………………………………
……………………………………………………………………………
……………………………………………………………………………
……………………………………………………………………………
……………………………………………………………………………
……………………………………………………………………………

Activity 4. Reflection and further reading

Reflection

How did you do in this unit?

- **Look back at the original learning targets of this unit and evaluate your own strengths and weaknesses. Tick either + (positive) or – (negative) in the table below. Specify which tasks in each skills areas and activities you are evaluating. Then reflect on these and make notes in the final column.**

Tasks	**+**	**–**	**Reflection notes**
The reading tasks:			
The writing tasks:			
The speaking tasks:			
The listening tasks:			

Further reading

Lacity, M. & Willcocks, L. (2017) Conflict resolution in business services outsourcing relationships. *The Journal of Strategic Information Systems*, 26(2), 80–100.

Lockwood, J. (2016) An analysis of web chat exchange in an outsourced service account in the Philippines. *English for Specific Purposes*, 47(July), 26–39.

UNIT 9

Solution and resolution

The **learning targets** for this unit are to:

- Understand the process of resolving problems in internal business contexts
- Explore and practise the principles and skills of 'active listening'
- Understand and develop skills in the language of responding to external and internal business complaint texts

Activity 1. Input: Readings and discussion

■ **Look at the vocabulary and idiomatic expression items in bold. If you don't understand them, refer to the dictionary in Appendix 1 and/or try and guess the meaning from the context.**

Now read the text below:

Reading 1 RESOLVING CONFLICT

As discussed in the previous unit, conflict is a part of every workplace and should not necessarily be viewed negatively; it often leads to improvements. Internal workplace conflict that is **out in the open**

continued . . .

cont.

should be **embraced**, understood and resolved rather than **swept under the carpet**. An ability to deal with conflict in an on-going way will ensure **subcultures** and **pockets of discontent** don't emerge and **fester** until they **blow up**; or worse still, **breed** a permanent unhealthy work culture. Here are the steps and some tips and techniques to deal openly and **transparently** with internal workplace conflict.

Step 1. Fix a time and location to talk about problems

Not only does fixing a time to listen to each other ensure the whole problem is understood, but it also acknowledges there is a problem that needs time and effort to resolve; so fixing a time and location to talk is the first positive step.

Let's imagine that the problem is that the IT team believes it is not adequately staffed and they are working significantly longer hours than anyone else at their workplace ... and then some, within the IT team, are working much harder than others. This has **come to a head** as one of the IT members accuses some of his colleagues of not **pulling their weight**, and has accused the workplace of underfunding and undervaluing the IT team's efforts. As a manager go through the following **protocol** with the whole team:

(i) Set the culture of the discussion as respectful – no blame, accusation or **personalisation**, just a statement of the facts.

(ii) Limit the time any individual has to speak; you don't want just one or two people, who may have particular **axes to grind**, to **monopolise** the discussion.

(iii) Keep to the facts and do not let emotions **creep into** the discussion; although if people do become emotional, acknowledge the upset and move on.

Step 2. Listen carefully and actively

Listening is so much harder than just hearing the words used. 'Active listening' is a skill that is promoted in conflict resolution and

continued . . .

cont. counselling. Essentially it relies on the individuals in the group/interview to listen and understand what is really being expressed. Frustratingly this may involve **'listening between the lines'** where there may be only **a hint** at the underlying issues causing resentment and conflict. It is important to probe and **unpack these issues**.

(i) *Move towards some positive agreements*

The early part of the discussion often highlights lots of disagreement and upset. Once these are sufficiently understood, it's important to move towards some kind of **positivity** and this will involve everyone making suggestions to resolve the situation. As supervisor/manager don't feel that the solution just needs to come from you; everyone needs to contribute to this in their own ways; **investing** their own ideas for resolution means that buy in will have the best possible chance of success.

Focus on what they all have in common, rather than the differences. For example with the IT team, in spite of their differences and upset, point out how well they are regarded as a team and department within the company; and also how well their clients regard them too! Make sure everyone feels their points of view have been respected and that the process is less of a win/lose scenario than a win/win scenario. Allowing time for apologies and empathetic responses is important here; it will **'clear the air'** and allow people to return to their normal working relationships.

(ii) *Document the outcomes and provide a timetable going forward*

Providing guidance and some kind of timetable for next steps is crucial, and this needs to be followed up by summarising the discussion, agreeing the way forward and providing a timeframe for action and for things to change.

Don't forget what has happened! Everyone learns from conflict and mistakes made in the workplace; use them to ensure similar problems do not arise again.

Imagine you have a friend who is supervising a small team, she phones to say: *I've just had a strong complaint from one of my team members reporting that some team members are abusing the sick leave rules.*

- **In your own words advise your friend by summarising the key the conflict resolution strategies provided in Reading 1. Make some notes in the box below.**

- **Look at the vocabulary and idiomatic expression items in bold. If you don't understand them, refer to the dictionary in Appendix 1 and/or try and guess the meaning from the context.**

Now read the text below:

Reading 2 THE LANGUAGE OF ACTIVE LISTENING

'Active listening' is a good strategy where problems and conflict require resolution. It is not just something that supervisors/managers need to practise, but every employee will find these skills useful.

What is **'active listening'**?

- **In the box below, jot down what you think are the difference(s) between 'hearing' and 'listening':**

Hearing	Listening

continued . . .

cont.

Active listening is the process of listening carefully and intentionally to the message(s) being delivered, and checking continuously that you have understood the message. It may involve skills in:

- Ensuring you give your **undivided attention** to the speaker
- Asking for repetition and clarification
- Asking for examples
- Listening for **literal** and hidden meanings
- Acknowledging emotional upset
- Remaining neutral in the discussion

Each of these requires effective English language skills in listening and speaking. Here are some tips and techniques on how to be a good 'active listener'.

1. Provide your speaker with **your undivided attention**. This may involve:
   - Avoiding distractions e.g. turn off your phone!
   - Limiting the time of the interaction as this allows you to hold your concentration.
   - Looking at your interlocutor directly; this is easy face-to-face but sometimes challenging when done virtually if you can't see him/her.
   - Putting yourself in the shoes of the speaker and resist lining up counter arguments as they are talking.
2. Think about how you are **non-verbally communicating**.

Physical and facial gestures carry meaning, so think about being appropriate. For example:

- Nod to show you are listening; if you can't see your interlocutor, use back-channeling such as 'uh huh'.
- Smile and show that you understand; keep your emotional responses in check.
- Sit up and use posture to your advantage.

3. Think about how you are **verbally communicating**.
   - Ask questions for clarification e.g. *What do you mean when you say you haven't received any payment? Do you mean this week, this month or ever?*

continued . . .

cont.

- Paraphrase and repeat back your message to the speaker to ensure you have completely understood e.g. *It sounds like you're saying you haven't been paid for 3 months, is that right?* Or *You haven't been paid for 3 months, is that right?*
- If you find yourself responding emotionally to something the speaker is saying, say so – but **keep your emotions in check and defer your judgement** e.g. *I may not be understanding you very well, but am I right in thinking that you believe I am responsible for this situation, is that correct? I am trying not to take this personally.* You may also want to acknowledge the upset of the speaker e.g. *I understand you must be feeling very angry about this situation, but let's be sure we have all the facts straight.*
- Give enough time to the situation and **don't jump to conclusions**. This is hard to do but allow the speaker to finish before you comment/ask questions. Try not to interrupt and don't start delivering counter arguments until you are satisfied that you have completely understood the situation e.g. *Now take your time, I want to be doubly sure I've understood your upset.*
- **Respond appropriately and encourage respect for each other**. This kind of common encounter at the workplace will provide information and perspective not only on this problem but also other underling issues. You want to establish trust with your speaker. This means being open and honest e.g. *To be completely honest with you, as you know the company is having financial difficulties right now, but as we said in our last message, we hope to have this resolved by the end of the month and you'll be paid. If there are any further problems, you will all the first to know.*

Assert your opinions respectfully e.g. *You may not like what I'm going to say, but I think you should know that there is a 50% chance of redundancies. We should know more by the end of the month.*

You will practise these skills in a roleplay, and evaluate them by using the Active Listening Checklist in Activity 3.

The story so far ...

- **Look at the vocabulary and idiomatic expression items in bold. If you don't understand them, refer to the dictionary in Appendix 1 and/or try and guess the meaning from the context.**

Now read the story below:

Back on Track

Melinda was **dreading** the next Project Board meeting, but on the morning she received an email from Prasad apologising for leaving her exposed, and a text from Samantha telling her not to worry. Dawn opened the meeting and said, "I think before we get down to business that Vivek has something to say."

Vivek took his cue. "I should say sorry to Melinda over my comments last time. Prasad has briefed me on what happened, and I see that she used her judgement appropriately. It was a difficult situation and she had to make a call."

"What did happen?" asked Tony. "How come Prasad missed the meeting?"

"Sickness, and stress" said Vivek, "and it's mainly because you pushed to include Thailand in the project launch."

Dawn intervened. "Can we stop **pointing fingers** and get on? We have only a week to complete. Can we start with the progress report please?"

Melinda and Prasad presented the progress and budget numbers, and this time there were no questions from the Board.

Samantha was relieved that the meeting went well, with no surprises and no major concerns. As she was packing up, Dawn asked for a quick word in her office.

"I think we're all back on track,' Dawn started, "but I have some concerns about Prasad. He's managed well when it's going smoothly, but, if there are problems, he ..." she trailed off.

"Yes," said Samantha, "I see that too. I think maybe we underestimated the difficulty he would have with the virtual team. First he doesn't have Vivek to talk to whenever something comes up, and second he's got Tony to deal with. It's been a challenge."

"I'd like you to have an appraisal interview with him," said Dawn. "I know Vivek's his manager, but I think Vivek gets too **defensive** when it comes to Prasad. I'd really like to know whether Prasad has learned from this project, and whether he wants to do this again. I want to be sure that, if we use him in this role again, he'll be stronger next time. Can you do that?"

"Sure. I'll call it a project performance review so that Vivek doesn't feel I'm interfering in his role. And I'll do a review with Peter as well so Prasad doesn't feel **picked on**."

"That sounds good," said Dawn. "I really want Prasad to succeed in this. We've got some big opportunities coming up and we'll need strong managers."

Back in her HR office Samantha began making notes to prepare for the appraisal. What he had done well: managing the schedule, reporting to the project board; and what not so well: facing up to problems and mistakes, and – maybe – going missing, leaving a colleague to take the blame. Then she tore up the paper and tossed it in the bin.

"That's not the way," she thought. "We want Prasad to trust himself and to feel trusted. He has to recognize what he's done well and not – if I make it about what I think, there's no ownership." She thought some more and began an email to Prasad.

> "Hi Prasad
>
> I want to meet to talk to everyone individually about the learning from this project and how we can use it in future. I also want to look at what you personally have learned that you can use. Can you send me your thoughts in an email so that can structure our discussion – I want to cover your thoughts on how we manage projects better. No formal document and nothing **off the table**."

She looked at it. It seemed about right, but she would leave it and review in the morning before she pressed SEND.

■ **Discuss.**

What do you think Prasad might say in his email to Samantha?

....
....
....
....
....
....

Activity 2. Input: Understanding and modelling spoken and written texts

Task (i). Audio of active listening on Prasad's performance on the project (Transcript – Appendix 2).

This is a face-to-face meeting organised by Samantha.

Present: Samantha, Prasad.

■ **Look at the words and expressions in the table below and check you understand them, or guess the meanings as you listen to the meeting between Prasad and Samantha.**

Words and expressions	Meaning
Struggle a bit	
Unresponsive	
Doubting	
Stress and pressure	
Just between ourselves	
Keep a close eye on me	
Get the blame	
Near completion	

Words and expressions	Meaning
The reporting line	
Exposed	
Relieved	
Be upfront	
Let you down	

- **Listen to the meeting and discuss the questions below reflecting on Samantha's active listening strategies.**

(i) How do you think both Samantha and Prasad felt at the end of their meeting?

....
....
....
....

(ii) Which questions do you think Samantha planned to ask, and which were spontaneous building on what Prasad was telling her?

....
....
....
....

(iii) Where in the exchange do you notice a change in Prasad's attitude? Why do you think this happened?

....
....
....
....

Task (ii). Deconstructing and responding to written business complaints

Client complaints are common in any business relationship. Last week Trevor Lavender complained to Dawn about the project timetable and the delays.

To: Dawn CEO CommunicAsian
From: Trevor Lavender CEO GlobeNet
Subject: Launch date
Date: November 5th

Dear Dawn,

At our monthly meeting last week, you informed us of yet another delay in completing the project.

Can I remind you that have booked all our venues in China and Hong Kong for an August launch, coinciding with the academic year. We are now coming close to missing that deadline, so I would like reassurances from you and your team that this date is fixed in your diaries and that the project will be finished.

I look forward to your response by the end of the week.

Regards, Trevor.

- **Look at the response below from Dawn. With a partner, identify the different moves in the overall structure of this response, identify the purpose of each paragraph, and note the kind of specific language she uses.**

To: Trevor Lavender CEO GlobeNet **From:** Dawn CEO CommunicAsian **Subject:** Launch date **Date:** November 6th Dear Trevor,	Paragraph #
Thank you for your message and I understand your concern about the deadline date. I am sorry and I hope I can reassure you on this point.	Paragraph 1

One major roadblock, as you may remember, was having to replace one of our team members, and also expand the specifications given to the team. As you know this set us back by almost two weeks. We do not anticipate any further problems in this regard and the team have done a great job in getting the project quickly back on track. I will continue to meet weekly with them and despite some challenges along the way, we are confident that we will meet the deadline agreed for the launch.	Paragraph 2
Do let me know if you have any concerns and I will most certainly keep you updated, and my apologies for the previous delays. Best regards, Dawn	Paragraph 3

- **Now complete the table below; Paragraph 1 has been completed for you.**

Organisation	Purpose and language features of each paragraph
Paragraph 1	**Purpose**: To acknowledge complaint and make an initial apology. **Language features**: Present tense used and modal 'can' to emphasise ability to reassure. Reference item 'this' refers to deadline.
Paragraph 2	
Paragraph 3	

Activity 3. Output: Spoken and written skills development tasks

Task (i). Active listening roleplays (1.5 hours)

- **Look at the three scenarios below. For each one, practise your active listening skills, changing roles for each one. Use the checklist provided below.**

Observers are to watch the exchange carefully and use the Active Listening Checklist to provide feedback. Feedback should take 5 minutes.

ACTIVE LISTENING CHECKLIST	COMMENTS
1. Did the supervisor give undivided attention to the employee? Did the supervisor acknowledge the emotional upset by showing empathy/apologising/backchannelling/facial and paralinguistic gestures? Did the supervisor remain neutral and show respect?	
2. Did the supervisor probe for further information? Did the supervisor ask for repetition, clarification, exemplification as required? Give examples. Did the supervisor manage to move forward in the active listening roleplay?	
3. How do think the 'active listener' handled the interaction? In the box write down your assessment from 1 (poor) to 10 (excellent). Provide reasons for your score.	

Allow 5–10 mins to prepare for each of the roleplays.

Scenario 1: Anger at being passed over for promotion (15 mins)

In groups of three, identify each member as A (the employee with the issue), B (the supervisor) and C (the observer). How far are A and B able to resolve the problem and move forward? C observes and jots down his/her feedback on both positive and problematic parts of the scenario encounters and feeds back at the end of the meeting.

The issue

You are A and are very upset because you were verbally promised a promotion by your line manager, but this has not eventuated. You think you may have been passed over because of an incident last month where you shouted at one of your colleagues because a deadline had not been met. B, the supervisor was concerned about that, and other more minor incidents where you displayed short-comings in being able to manage without anger.

The point of the meeting is for A to communicate the upset and for B to make clear the issue and then probe/actively listen. Finally, you need to find a way forward.

Observers are to watch the exchange carefully and use the active listening checklist to provide feedback. Feedback should take 5 minutes.

Scenario 2: Personal issues impacting work (15 mins)

In groups of three, identify each member as B (the employee with the issue), C (the supervisor), and A (the observer). How far are B and C able to resolve the problem and move forward? A observes and jots down feedback on both positive and problematic parts of the scenario encounters and feeds back at the end of the meeting.

The issue

You are B and are very upset because other members of your team have accused you of not pulling your weight in a recent project that has had a tight deadline. This is unusual for you as you have a track record of being reliable and doing your bit ... you are very ambitious and want to succeed but you have some significant personal issues that need addressing.

The point of the meeting is for B to communicate the upset and for C to make clear the issue and then probe/actively listen. Finally, you need to find a way forward.

Observers are to watch the exchange carefully and use the active listening checklist to provide feedback. Feedback should take 5 minutes.

Scenario 3: Disengaged and looking elsewhere (15 mins)

In groups of three, identify each member as C (the speaker with the problem), A (the supervisor) and B (the observer). How far are C and A able to resolve the problem and move forward? B observes and jots down his/her feedback on both positive and problematic parts of the scenario encounters.

The issue

You are C and you are thinking of leaving your new job because the job role has changed and is not challenging. You have scheduled a couple of job interviews next week. Your supervisor (A) has noticed your lack of engagement recently, and wants to find out what is going on.

The point of the meeting is for C to communicate his/her concerns and for B to make clear the issue and then probe/actively listen. Finally, you need to find a way forward.

Observers are to watch the exchange carefully and use the active listening checklist to provide feedback. Feedback should take 5 minutes.

Task (ii). Email exchange: Writing an adjustment email

You are Prasad, the Project Manager, and you have received the following email from Dawn complaining about the lack of regular information about the launch preparation for the GlobeNet project.

To: Prasad
Cc: Tony, Samantha
From: Dawn, CEO
Subject: Are we prepared for the GlobeNet launch?

Dear Prasad,

As you know there is a lot of concern in GlobeNet about our preparations for the launch of the project at Chinese New Year. Trevor has written again about this deadline, I think Celia is getting anxious. I think it is February 5th, right?

My problem is that I am not getting regular updates from your team. I have asked for this several times, but apart from a message on Dec 17th, I have heard nothing. This situation is embarrassing when I talk to the client ... .so please update me immediately and keep them coming weekly now.

Specifically I want an immediate update on what your preparations are and assurances that we are on track for the launch.

Please supply this information to me by Friday at the latest.

Regards, Dawn.

- **As Prasad, respond to Dawn's complaint by email. Look back to Activity 2 to see how to organise your response and choose appropriate language.**

To: Dawn, CEO
Cc: Tony, Samantha

- **Do you think you could text Dawn with a response? Why/why not? Have a go at texting in the box (screen) below:**

Activity 4. Reflection and further reading

Reflection

How did you do in this unit?

- **Look back at the original learning targets of this unit and evaluate your own strengths and weaknesses. Tick either + (positive) or – (negative) in the table below. Specify which tasks in each skills areas and activities you are evaluating. Then reflect on these and make notes in the final column.**

Tasks	+	–	Reflection notes
The reading tasks:			

Tasks	+	–	Reflection notes
The writing tasks:			
The speaking tasks:			
The listening tasks:			

Further reading

Koester, A. (2006) *Investigating Workplace Discourse*. Chapter 6: Negotiating consensus and conflict in workplace talk. Taylor & Francis.

Ruiz-Garrido, M.F. (2011) Complaining in the business world: Complaint and adjustment emails. Chapter 5. In Perez-Llantada, C. & Watson, M. (2011) *Specialised Languages in the Global Village – A Multi-Perspective Approach*. Cambridge Scholars Publishing, UK.

UNIT

10

Declare success

Project product launch and leadership

The **learning targets** for this unit are to:

- Understand the components of a successful product launch
- Explore the thinking behind the narrative of a successful project
- Produce a presentation from a business storyboard
- Understand the importance of leadership in global business contexts
- Explore intercultural and linguistic challenges when leading and mentoring teams and individuals

Activity 1. Input: Readings and discussion

- **Look at the vocabulary and idiomatic expression items in bold. If you don't understand them, refer to the dictionary in Appendix 1 and/or try and guess the meaning from the context.**

Now read the text below:

Reading 1 THE PRODUCT LAUNCH

The successful conclusion of a project is a time to celebrate and tell the world about the amazing product you have developed. This is usually done by organising an amazing event. There are number of things to think about so **leaving it to the last minute is not a clever idea**. Product launch things to think about include:

The venue and entertainment: You want to select a great venue and location that reflects your product and industry. For example, launching a **new fashion line** in a **prestigious upmarket hotel** in Paris or Shanghai would be the right thing to do! Remember too that you want to reach your target demographic e.g. new telecommunications software is always going to be targeting a young set of buyers. Organising great entertainment brings in the crowds. Celebrities are often booked as an **added attraction** to the product launch and again these need to be selected to attract the right kind of visitors to the event.

Select a **theme** for your product launch. For example, in advising GlobeNet on a theme for their overseas roaming deal, a theme of travel may be appropriate. This theme may also affect your choice of venue and entertainment.

Timing of your launch is also important. Depending on the demographic you want to attract, make sure they are not at work or at home looking after their young families. Obviously a late night event will not attract an ageing demographic.

Finally think about your advertising campaign to attract visitors to the event. Social media activity will target a **relatively** young group, but what about an ageing group? **Keep up** your advertising campaign after the event as well and make sure you keep the contact details of all your visitors.

Good luck!

■ **Make notes on your advertising campaign below**

....
....
....
....
....
....

Winding down the first phase of the project and transitioning

Much is written about the processes of winning and launching the first phase of a successful business project, but there are also important skills required in **winding down** the first phase of the project and transitioning to the next stage.

Here are the important steps in the process of winding down a project.

Step 1. Allocate specific time to winding down and transitioning the project

This requires thinking about the following key questions:

- Have we fulfilled all the requirements of this phase of the project contract?
- Are the financial statements/budget in order?
- Is the **paperwork** and administration complete?
- Have we evaluated the project, learnt lessons and celebrated success?

Step 2. Keep communicating with the client

When you are building a business such as CommunicAsian, good **testimonials** ensure you will win work **going forward**. Asking for evaluative comments and testimonials will **come in handy** for the next RfP!

Marking the end of a phase of a project may take place with some kind of celebration. Don't let this stage **drift away** before you move onto the next implementation phase.

Step 3. Get all the paperwork and budgets in order and signed off for Phase 1

Documenting the project and **archiving** it is important. When the next RfP **comes around**, you may want to access this as important information and/or use it as **exemplars** of the project management process. There may also need to be final financial reporting and account closure, and **disbursements**.

Don't forget these important internal and external tasks and communications.

■ **Look at the vocabulary and idiomatic expression items in bold. If you don't understand them, refer to the dictionary in Appendix 1 and/or try and guess the meaning from the context.**

Now read the text below:

Reading 2 INTERCULTURAL ISSUES IN CORPORATE LEADERSHIP

Corporate leadership is all about managing and motivating people to achieve results and leadership styles need to be aligned with the organisation's culture and structure. A government regulatory agency, based upon following rules and stability, is very different from a university department, where professors and lecturers are largely self-directing.

Leadership styles are essentially about the way:

- The leader manages and motivates the team
- The leader behaves as a role model

There has been a lot of research into the different leadership styles, and their effectiveness, but it is generally accepted that the different styles fall into four main categories.

Authoritarian	**Paternalistic**
Democratic	**Laissez-faire**

continued . . .

cont.

1. **Authoritarian leadership:** This is the strictest type. Authoritarian leaders tend to have complete control over the decision-making process. Communication is top down and one way. This leadership style can be effective when decision-making is urgent or work is routine and subordinates are unskilled.
2. **Paternalistic leadership:** This is softer form of authoritarian leadership, but still with very little delegation. It has been likened to a parent–child relationship in terms of the power dynamic. This leadership style can be effective in healthcare and safety environments.
3. **Democratic leadership:** Unlike with authoritarian leaders, the focus of power is more with the group as a whole, and leadership functions are shared within the group. However, the leader still has the final say. This category is most effective when used with a skilled and experienced team.
4. **Laissez-faire leadership:** Laissez-faire means to leave alone, to let it be. The leader has little input into day-to-day decisions, with a conscious policy to delegate power: the team is expected to be the best judge of what to do. This style is most effective when staff are able to take on responsibility and have the skills and experience to do their jobs.

Leadership styles may change over time or when corporate structures change. As a team gains experience, the leader may move from an authoritarian style to a more democratic style, based on the increased skills and confidence in the team. This ability to change styles is sometimes referred to as 'situational leadership' – an ability to adapt the style to suit the situation.

In most businesses there has been a shift away from the directive styles of leadership towards more participative ones. This stems from a number of factors: a better educated workforce, changes in workforce values and expectations of an employer, and changes in organisation structures often pioneered by the big and successful tech giants such as Google. These allow for independent and self-regulating teams where, if they have a leader, it is someone agreed upon by the team itself.

An example of this structural change is the growth of 'agile teams'. Agile management, in essence, focuses on meeting outcomes with a

cont. flexible, trial-and-error strategy that often groups colleagues in a start-up or start-up like structure to creatively address deliverables. It requires, as the most important issue in leadership, an ability to develop a risk-taking culture within the team.

This agile culture is characterised by exploration, expansiveness, and creativity. Work teams need to be inventive and open-minded places where people spark new ideas and explore alternatives. The team needs to communicate constantly as the situation changes. As teams are increasingly virtual across countries, this is seen as the biggest leadership challenge for organisations today.

The story so far ...

- **Look at the vocabulary and idiomatic expression items in bold. If you don't understand them, refer to the dictionary in Appendix 1 and/or try and guess the meaning from the context.**

Now read the story below:

PRASAD STEPS UP

Dawn and Tony were in Dawn's office preparing for a big presentation that afternoon. It was a **pitch** for a project that promised to be bigger than GlobeNet, and the whole senior team was **lined up** to show the strength of CommunicAsian.

"There's a lot of talk about us around the industry," said Tony, "a lot of interest in what we're doing. That interview I did with the magazine was really great coverage."

"Yes," said Dawn, "we've had more enquiries in the past two weeks than the whole of the year. If we can **convert** half of them **into contracts** we'll have a great year. This one today is the one I most want to win."

"Okay then," said Tony, "let's gather up Samantha and go. We don't want to be late."

On their way out the three of them called in on the project room. "Wish us luck," said Dawn, "and keep going with your work. The final week before we have the official launch with the client – a lot to do."

Prasad smiled and gave a **thumbs up sign**. "We'll get there. Good luck today." He turned back to his laptop. An hour later Peter Lee came over to his desk.

"Prasad, there's something I don't quite understand. I've been going through the statistics, and in most places we are getting a lot of people visiting the home page, and about 15% are signing up on the **landing screen** – that's pretty **consistent**, except for Philippines. There we seem to be getting only about 1% starting the sign up flow. I don't understand it."

"Let me talk with my development team," said Prasad. "We'll do a UX – **user experience test** – to see what is happening, and I'll come back to you."It was another hour before Prasad came back. "We have a problem," he said. "The screen navigation for Philippines is going into **a loop** instead of taking interested prospects to the **sign-up screen**. We had tested it, but it seems to have been **corrupted** when we added Thailand."

"Can you fix it?" asked Peter.

"Of course. We'll work over the weekend and deploy it Sunday. The problem is that we've got no record of the people who tried to sign up. They entered their email addresses, but we've lost them. We will have hundreds of unhappy people who will be annoyed with GlobeNet."

"Is there anything we can do?"

Prasad thought for a long time. "There might be," he said. "I'll need to talk to the partners in Manila who may be able to pull data from the archives. Give me ten minutes."

When he returned he looked a little more relieved. "Well, they can give us a list of the **email registrants**, but it's expensive, and they also want us to **indemnify** them in case it's in **breach** of the data privacy laws. I tried to call Samantha, but her phone's switched off for the presentation, and I don't want to ask Vivek."

"Can it wait until everyone gets back?"

"We need to get on to it right away. Their people don't work tomorrow and we need time to contact the **prospects** and tell them we've fixed the problem. Maybe I should call Vivek ..."

Suddenly he remembered Samantha's words at his review meeting. "So, for the rest of the project you need to lead 100 percent. It's your project, your success, your failure. Okay?"

"It's my project," he said, and called the Philippines development partners. "Send the agreement over and I'll approve it. We need the data by end of business today."

Do you think Prasad made the right decision? Discuss.

....
....
....

Activity 2. Input: Understanding and modelling spoken and written texts

Task (i). Audio listening: Meeting to prepare for client presentation (Transcript – Appendix2)

- **Look at the words/expressions in bold and discuss the meaning. If you don't understand, can you guess the meaning form the context?**

Prasad and Peter are in the boardroom.

(i) When Prasad said *I've never thought of it that way*, what was he referring to?

....
....
....

(ii) How do you think this idea can inform the product launch presentation?

....

....

....

Task (ii). Writing the storyboard outline

What is a business storyboard? When developing a business PowerPoint, use sequential illustrations and graphics as a starting point to enhance the narrative, explanation, description or instruction. It looks like a cartoon. It is simple to do, but clarity of the purpose, content and audience of your business presentation must be clear before you start.

Prasad decided to ditch his prepared slides and get back together with his team and follow Tony's advice of 'telling the story' and turning what could be viewed as negatives into positives. Prasad has sent around a storyboard template to plan the presentation and writes to his team:

To: Creatives Team
From: Prasad
Subject: Planning our final presentation
Attachment: Storyboard template

Dear all,

Just had a productive meeting with Tony which has given me **food for thought**! Our first attempt is too descriptive, let's make it more nuanced and show how our project has done something that no other agency could do!

Our final presentation for this phase of the project is really a sales exercise. What we are trying to do is **showcase** that we have done a good job and show that we have achieved that because we are different from other agencies. We don't want to tell the client that we are better, but we do want them to make that conclusion on their own.

Let's storyboard this to ensure the presentation flows ... i.e. outline the results and make the key points ... but presented as a story of our own successful management. About six slides? I want your input and then we'll meet with Tony tomorrow with our ideas.

See attached a storyboard template ... give it your best shot and our meeting is 2 p.m. tomorrow in the board room.

- **In groups of 4–5 now use the storyboard template below to get the narrative, the results and key points all lined up.**

Storyboard visuals	Message in text

You are going to turn this into a presentation in Activity 3.

Task (iii). Email exchange

Dawn has just received the following email from Trevor Lavender (GlobeNet UK) congratulating CommunicAsian on the great job they've done and wishing them a successful launch.

To: Dawn (and the CommunicAsian team)
Cc: Celia Tang
From: Trevor Lavender
Subject: All the best for your launch today

Dear Dawn,

Please pass on my congratulations to your whole team on the magnificent job your team has done over the past

12 weeks. Most importantly we've met the deadlines and we have a great campaign! The numbers are looking promising too.

I am pleased Celia will be there to celebrate and she has promised to make final presentations on the project to our board at the end of the month when she is in the UK. She mentioned you might be in the UK, is that the case?

We will be raising our glasses here too (even though it's breakfast time).

When you have time, let's do a virtual hook up with Celia ... maybe next week? I want details now of the implementation phase.

Best wishes,
Trevor.

- **Reply to this email. Unfortunately you can't meet virtually next week as you are going on a 2 week holiday: this conversation about the implementation phase however is critical. What do you say?**

To: Trevor Lavender
From: Dawn
Subject:

■ **Justify what you have written to Trevor. Discuss.**

....
....
....
....
....
....

Activity 3. Output: Spoken and written skills development tasks

Task (i). The launch presentation

■ **Now you have a good storyboard, turn this into a short presentation of about 15 minutes with about six slides.**

Once the slides are done, present to other groups in your class. Use the presentations checklist to help you assess the presentation.

Task (ii). Email exchanges

This phase of the contract has finished successfully and Dawn sends out a congratulatory email to the team quoting Trevor's message and talking about some of the benefits to CommunicAsian as a company.

To: CommunicAsian colleagues From: Dawn Subject: Well done team!

- **Your team members text back to you! Choose two members of the team and write their text back to Dawn.**

Compare you texts with others in your class. How do they compare?

....

....

....

....

....

....

Task (iii). And the final story ...

- **Look at the vocabulary and idiomatic expression items in bold. If you don't understand them, refer to the dictionary in Appendix 1 and/or try and guess the meaning from the context.**

Now read the final story below:

Looking Back and Looking Forward

The project launch celebration was being held in CommunicAsian's boardroom in Singapore. The whole team was there, and Celia was flying in from Hong Kong for the occasion. The room was decorated with the red and white colours of GlobeNet, and two large screens at each end of the room gave **real-time updates** on **sign-up** figures.

Dawn was doing final checks that all was complete and in order. Her boss, the Board Chairman would come later, so everything had to **be just so**. It had been a difficult ten weeks, but she had learned a lot about her team and how they responded to pressure. Everybody contributed, and the tension between the creatives and the techies had probably pushed both to do better. Around the room were pinned some of the ideas for **taglines** including Dawn's favourite: a picture of a smiling snail with its shell and the caption 'Don't leave home when you travel'. But as Vivek said, it rather clashed with the idea of fast broadband. The selected one was in the centre of the wall with three variations for social media usage: 'GlobeNet Shrinks the World', 'GlobeNet Links the World' and 'GlobeNet Thinks the World', and the campaign was built around those messages. That had been approved **unanimously**, and only Tony knew it had been created by Rory. He kept that quiet.

They held the last project board meeting the day before, and Dawn asked everybody what they felt was best about the project. Vivek said "working virtually. Using our technology," as if there could be no doubt. Tony, rather surprisingly, said that he learned a lot working with Prasad to get better analytics, and he thanked Vivek and Prasad. Samantha said that she loved that people had **grown with responsibility**. "I was talking to someone the other day about Melinda, and he said, 'oh, you're talking about Little Miss **Bossy**'. I was delighted."

"You made some very good decisions," said Dawn.

"Thank you," said Samantha, "I'll remind you of that when I have my appraisal."

"Forgive me again," said Dawn. "Next Monday, I promise."

The screens were showing sign-ups by country. Already there were several hundred after the **soft launch** a week ago, so initial signs were good. Even the Philippines had recovered a little, and the numbers showed that the decision to add Thailand was a good one.

Dawn's phone **beeped**. Celia was in reception, and Dawn went to greet her.

"Oh, it's great to see you. It's not the same when you only meet on video."

"I agree," said Celia. "You can't really get to know people that way."

They went through to the boardroom, and Celia closed the door carefully before examining the numbers updating on the screens.

"I've got something to tell you," she said. "Well, something to thank you for, really. My boss Trevor is so happy with this project that I'm moving to a global role. I'll be moving to London with a **promotion**."

"Congratulations," **beamed** Dawn. "I'm so pleased. Thank you for trusting us with this project. And because of this project, we've won three others with a UK focus, so I will be spending a fair bit of time in London probably. We can continue the sisterhood."

"That will be great," said Celia. "I've prepared a small speech for today. I'm going to say that this is not the end of a project, but the start of a **beautiful partnership**. We've proved we work well together, now **let's conquer the world**."

"That's my sort of language," said Dawn.

The launch **went off without a hitch** and the team adjourned to a local restaurant around the corner to celebrate. Dawn took the opportunity to wrap up this phase of the project with a short speech at dinner. She's asked you, as the Communications Interns recruited for the project, to write it. "Something short and motivational-we've got the implementation phase coming up next and I want them to know how well they've done ... but I don't want them to get **complacent**!"

- **Write Dawn's final speech in the box below:**

- **Present the speech and discuss.**

(i) Was the purpose, content and audience clear?
(ii) Did the speech balance the need to be upbeat and congratulatory, without inducing complacency?

- **Feedback.**

Activity 4. Reflection and further reading

Reflection

How did you do in this unit?

- **Look back at the original learning targets of this unit and evaluate your own strengths and weaknesses. Tick either + (positive) or – (negative) in the table below. Specify which tasks in each skills areas and activities you are evaluating. Then reflect on these and make notes in the final column.**

Tasks	**+**	**–**	**Reflection notes**
The reading tasks:			
The writing tasks:			
The speaking tasks:			
The listening tasks:			

Further reading

Groysberg, B., Lee, J., Price, J., & Cheng, J.Y.-J. (2018) The leader's guide to corporate culture *Harvard Business Review.* January–February.

Lockwood, J. (2019) What do we mean by workplace English? A syllabus framework for course design and assessment. Chapter 2. In Hyland, K. & Wong, L. (eds) *Specialised English: New Directions in ESP and EAP Research and Practice.* Routledge.

APPENDIX 1 The dictionary

Business words and expressions

This Global Business Matters dictionary of words uses the following keys:

- n – noun
- v – verb (including phrasal verbs)
- adj – adjective
- adv – adverb,
- i.e. – idiomatic expressions compiled from authentic usage in the case study.

A first cut (i.e.) – a first attempt
All show and no substance (i.e.) – making an impression is more important than depth of thinking/experience
Absenteeism (n) – staying away from work
Accommodation (adj) strategies (n) – ways of making yourself understood using different words, gestures or visuals
Accuser (n) – a person who says you have done something wrong
Actively (adv) engage (v) – to communicate about something (adv actively enhances meaning positively)
Adapt (v), adaptability (n) – to change in order to relate well to someone; the act of change to accommodate someone/something
Added (adj) attraction(n) – something that adds to an attraction
Adjourn (a meeting) (v) – to finish the meeting for a short time
Administrative (adj) issues (n) – things (maybe challenges) related to business administration
Affordance of – benefits of
Agile Teams (n) – specific business term meaning flexibility of teams collaborating and problem-solving across the totality of work issues

Amazing (adj) – very good, common in business
Ambiguous (adj) – could have a number of different/conflicting meanings
Analytical (adj) – ability/process of looking in detail, sometimes involving numbers, to understand a problem
Angles (n) – perspectives
Annoyance – angry/upset
Annualised (adj) amount (n) – an amount of money worked out on a yearly basis
Annualised (adj) revenue (n) – money received/earned on a yearly basis
Anticipate (v) – expect something in the future
Anti (adj) money laundering (n) – against illegal movement of money
Appendices (n) – lists/extra information provided at the end of a manuscript/report
Appraisal (n) – a performance feedback meeting
Archive (n) – a place (physical or virtual) where documents of past activity are filed
Assertiveness (n) – the act of standing up to/confronting something/someone
Asset (n) – something (people/personality/valuables) you have/own
Assimilationist (adj) – becoming similar
Asynchronous – outside real time
At their peril (i.e.) – at their risk/danger
Augment (v) the meaning (n) – add to the meaning
Authoritarian (adj) – one body/person centralised power
Awareness (adj) campaign (n) – planned process where people are introduced/become familiar with a product/process
Axes to grind (i.e.) – complaints

Back on track (i.e.) – return to the original plan
Backlash (n) – a negative response to something to be controlled
Balance these considerations (i.e.) – weigh up different things in an equitable way
Balanced (adj) solutions (n) – a well-judged solution
Balance (v) – weigh to be the same
Banality (n) – emptiness/stupidity
Be upfront (about it) (i.e.) – to be open/transparent
Beam (v) – smile a lot to show happiness/approval
Beamed (v) live (adv) (i.e.) – to transmit in real time
Beat (v) – to win
Beaten (as in beaten the forecasts) (v) – exceeded forecasts
Beaten (to be) (v) – to lose

Beautiful (adj) partnership (n) – an agreement between organisations, people, etc. to work together; (i.e.) – to cooperate with someone or with a group to accomplish something
Beep (v) – to make a short, loud sound
Benefit (n) – an advantage; (v) – to be helped by something, to help someone
Best practices (n) – a working method that is officially accepted as being the best to use in a business or industry
Bidders (n) – people or companies who offer to pay a particular amount of money to buy something and/or people who compete for work
Blacklisting (n) – putting someone's name on a list of people who are considered not acceptable
Blame games (i.e.) – a situation in which people attempt to blame others rather than to resolve a problem
Blow up (i.e.) – to become suddenly very angry
Bossy (adj) – tells people what to do/likes control. Pejorative/negative term
'Boo to a goose' (i.e.) – '*She doesn't say boo to a goose*' to be very shy and lacks assertiveness
Booted up (v) – to start a computer using its bootstrap procedure
Bottom up (adj) – starting at the lowest levels or from the smallest details of the organisation, system or plan
Brainstorming (n) – an activity or method in which people meet to suggest new ideas
Brand building (n) – the process by which a company creates or improves customer's knowledge or opinion of a brand
Brand taglines (n) – a slogan or motto, a phrase that accompanies your brand
Branding ideas (n) – thought or ideas that capture the essence of a brand
Brash (adj) – loud and rude
Breach (the law) (v) – to break or violate a law
Breed (v) – to cause something to happen; (n) – a type or class
Bring (something different) to the table (i.e.) – to contribute/present an idea/skill
Broadband provider (n) – telephone or cable companies that provide access to internet and other related services to its users
Broke it (silence) (i.e.) – ended a period of silence
Build (v) rapport (n) – the process of developing a relationship with someone else
Build (v) trust (n) – to develop trust
Bundle (n) – a group of channels offered together
Bureaucrat (perfect) (n) – an official in a government department who follows rules and procedures strictly

Business English as a Lingua Franca (BELF) – used as a substitute for Business English that covers both the teaching and researching of Business English with the purposes of facilitating both business communications between speakers of other languages and NS (native English speakers), and between NNS (nonnative speakers)

Call (n) – 'it's your call' – it is your decision
Campaigns (n) – organised public relations/advertising activity with a specific goal
Capitalisation (n) – the total liabilities of a business including both ownership capital and borrowed capital
Captured (v) – to captivate and hold the interest of
Casual conversation (n) – informal talk/chat in social interaction
Cater to (v) – to provide what is needed
Cause and effect (n) – a relationship between actions and consequences of those actions e.g. if you invest your savings in that stock, you may lose all your money
CEO (acronym) – Chief Executive Officer – the executive with the chief decision making authority in an organisation or business
Census data (n) – factual information about populations/demographics; often used to make decisions
Census date (n) – the last day when someone can withdraw from a course without incurring any liability for tuition fee
Chain or thread (n) – record of a series of email exchanges
Chain reaction (n) – a series of events, each caused by the previous one
Chalk and cheese (i.e.) – opposites, completely different from each other
Change minds (i.e.) – to rethink or reconsider
Channel (media) (n) – a means of communication, e.g. print, audio, video, etc.
Chronemic (adj) – present in time; the way time communicates e.g. lateness of response may communicate lack of interest
Clear agendas (n) – a well-defined list of matters to be discussed
Clear the air (i.e.) – to get rid of bad feelings between people or groups
Close down (i.e.) – the act of ending operations of a business, system or industry
Cloud based (adj) – refers to applications, services or resources made available to users on demand via the Internet from a cloud computing provider's servers; local servers (n) – the ones that provide a service by running an application which is on the same machine as the client application
Coined (v) – defined
Collaboratively (adv) – a way that involves two or more people working together for a special purpose

Collate (v) – to collect, compare carefully; findings (n) – the results of an inquiry or investigation
Come around (v) to be converted to another person's opinion
Come back (v) – to reply
Come in handy (i.e.) – to be useful
Come out of nowhere (i.e.) – to happen very surprisingly or unexpectedly
Come to a head (i.e.) – to reach a crisis point
Come up with (v) – to produce ideas/plans; suggesting or thinking of an idea or plan
Comes across as (v) – to give other people an impression of
Comes out ('if it comes out we know we're in trouble') (i.e.) – if it emerges, is revealed… (come out with ideas) suggest, out forward
Commitment (n) – an agreement or pledge to do something in the future
Common repository (n) – a place where things are gathered for all to see/access
Commonsense (n) – sound practical judgment concerning everyday matters
Commonplace (adj) – ordinary/everyday
Comms link (n) – communications channel that connects two or more communicating devices
Compensate (v) – to offset an error or a defect
Competitive advantage (n) – a condition or circumstance that puts a company in a favourable or superior business position
Complacent (adj) – inertia/inaction caused by sense of self-satisfaction
Complainant (n) – the party makes a complaint
Complex (adj) – hard to separate, analyse or solve
Compliance (n) – the act of obeying a rule, order or request
Complications (n) – things that make a situation very difficult
Compliment (n) – a remark that expresses approval/admiration
Compose (an email) (v) – write an email
Comprise (v) – to consist of/include
Compromise (n) – an agreement in an argument in which the people involved reduce their demands /change their opinion in order to reach agreement
Conceptualise (v) – plan the scope/content
Conditional (adj) – subject to, implying, or dependent upon a condition
Conform (v) – to behave/think according to a specified norm
Conglomerate (n) – a company that operates in different markets and perhaps in different countries
Consistent (adj) – always behaving or happening in a similar, especially positive, way
Constructive (adj) – to help /improve; criticism (n) – the act of criticising with the intent of improvement
Consultant (n) – an expert in a particular area who advises people

Consumer testing (n) – a process of measuring the properties or performance of products

Contact centre (n) – a business location from which all customer interactions across various channels (voice, email and webchat) are carried out and managed

Contingency (n) – something that might possibly happen in the future, usually causing problems, or necessitating further arrangements

Conversion rates (n) – percentage of applicants/users who take a desired action

Convert into (v) – to change from one thing to another

Corporate social responsibility (n) – a business model that helps a company be socially accountable

Correlate (v) – to show a causal relationship between variables

Corrupted (adj) – untrustworthy; corrupted computer relates to a problem where the data is not readable

Cost control (n) – the practice of identifying and reducing business expenses to ensure the health of the business

Cost efficient (adj) – minimise expenditure

Costs (fixed, variable, controlled):

(i) Fixed cost (n) – business costs, such as rent, that are fixed and constant whatever the quantity of goods or services produced
(ii) Variable cost (n) – a cost that is not fixed e.g. casual staff
(iii) Controllable cost (n) – costs that are managed

Costs overrun (n) – the spending more money on a project than was planned in the budget, or the actual extra amount that is spent

Cost us a fortune (i.e.) – to cost a lot of money

Couch your ideas (i.e.) – to express something in carefully chosen words

Craft (v) – making or producing with care, skill

Creative (adj) – producing or using original and unusual ideas ; branding (n) – the promotion of a particular product or company by means of advertising with a distinctive design

Creative campaign (n) – an original/unusual promotion/brief

Creep into (v) – to enter a place/space without being noticed; may result in change without anyone noticing

Critical thinking (n) – the ability to think 'outside the box' in an original way/evaluate an issue from many different perspectives

Criticism (n) – the act of negatively assessing something/someone

Cultural adaptability (n) – ability to recognise, adjust and work effectively within a range of different cultural norms and contexts

Current plans (n) – business plans of the moment

Customer experience (n) abbreviation CX – the customer satisfaction (journey) based on the service provided

Customer experience navigation (i.e.) – way a customer interacts with website and e-commerce applications
Customer service representatives (n) – people that help customers with complaints and questions
Cut him off (v) – to stop someone as they are talking
Cut in (v) – to interrupt what someone is saying by saying something yourself
Cut-down version (adj) – reduced in size or condensed of an original bigger version
Cutting corners (i.e.) – to do something in the easiest, cheapest, or fastest way without regard to quality

Dashboards (n) – computerised tool used for information management and business intelligence
Dated (adj) – 'dated approach'; old fashioned/out of date approach
Dead of night (i.e.) – middle of the night when it is very dark
Deal with (v) – to manage someone in an effective way
Decision makers (n) – people who make important decisions
Defensive (adj) – protective reaction to someone/something being negative
Defer (v) judgement (n) – to postpone or delay judgment
Defuse (v) – to make a difficult or dangerous situation less difficult/dangerous
Delegate (v) – to assign a particular job, duty, right, etc. to someone else to carry out
Deliverables (n) – something that is provided or achieved as a result of a process
Democratic (adj) – favouring equality and encouraging all voices/opinions
Demographic (n) – the statistical characteristics of human populations (such as age or income) used especially to identify markets
Demonstrate (v) – prove, display; market (n) – the business or trade in a particular product, including financial products
Derail (v) – to obstruct the progress of something
Desirable (highly) (adj) – having pleasing qualities or properties
Disapproval (n) – 'shows his disapproval'; shows he does not approve/like/agree
Disbursements (n) – the payment of money as outgoings from a business
Discipline (n) – a field of study e.g. business studies
Discount (v) – to reduce the original cost
Discriminate (v) against (prep) – to single out a type of person or thing for special negative treatment or denial of equal treatment
Disinterest (v) – lack of interest
Dispersed (v) – apart

Dispersed teams (n) – teams working apart
Diversity (n) – different nationalities, ages, genders etc represented e.g. in a business
Document (v) – provide with factual or substantial support for statements made
Dodge a bullet (i.e.) – to have a narrow escape; to avoid injury, disaster, or criticism
Doer (n) – one that takes an active part
Doesn't have to last that long (i.e.) – does not exist for a significant amount of time
Doesn't speak to (i.e.) – doesn't include/address
Don't push back (i.e.) – to accept
Dos and don'ts (i.e.) – rules of something
Double our size (i.e.) – twice the size or amount; to expand the business considerably
Doubt (v) – call into question the truth of
Drama (n) – a state, situation, or series of events involving extreme behaviours
Dread (v) – to feel extreme reluctance to meet or confront
Drift away (v) – lose personal contact over time
Drive business success (i.e.) – lead business success
Drop it (i.e.) – to stop talking about something

Ebb and flow (i.e.) – a flowing and changing situation
Economies of scale (i.e.) – higher the volume, the cheaper the product
Edge (have and edge on) (i.e.) – an advantage over people/situation
Elephant in the room (i.e.) – a major problem or controversial issue that is obviously present but avoided as a subject for discussion
Eliciting (v) the views (n) – asking for information/ideas
Eliminate (v) – to remove/get rid of something/someone
Email chain (n) – the entirety of the back and forth conversation in an *email* exchange
(An) email thread (n) – a series of email exchanges about a topic – see email chain
Embrace (v) – to take in or include as a part, item, or element of a more inclusive whole
Emergency (n) – something dangerous or serious needing immediate attention
Empathise (v) – to be able to understand how someone else feels
Engaging remote participants (i.e.) – interacting with participants who are apart
English is the lingua franca – use of the English language as a global means of inter-community communication with second language speakers

Enthusiasm (n) – a feeling of energetic interest in a particular subject or activity
Erode (v) – to slowly reduce or destroy something
Escalation (process/person) (n) – the process of becoming greater or more serious; refer it up to higher authority in the business
Ethnic (adj) markets (n) – markets comprising particular national group(s)
Ever occur to you (e.g. did it ever occur to you?) (i.e.) – Did you ever think that …?
Evolve (v) – to develop gradually
Exemplar (n) – a typical or good example of something
Expatriate (n) – foreigner who lives long term in another country e.g. British in Japan
Explicit (adj) – clear and exact
Expose (v) – open to view; reveal
Exposure (n) – the conditions that provide an opportunity to learn or experience new things
Expressions of interest (n) – a statement by a company or investor of their intention to compete for an opportunity to do a project or become involved in a business

Facilitate (v) – to make something possible or easier to happen
Fair (adj) point (n) – understandable point
Fester (v) – to undergo or exist in a state of progressive deterioration
Field descriptions (n) – a longer explanation for a single piece of data
Fill you in (i.e.) – to bring you up to date/give information
Fingers (tightly) crossed (i.e.) – a hand gesture commonly used to wish for luck
First cut (n) – draft or first attempt
First impression (n) – the event when one person *first* encounters another person and forms an immediate judgement
Fit in (v) – become part of
Fixed price (i.e.) – agreed price not to be changed during the contract
Flashes of brilliance (i.e.) – very good ideas that appear suddenly
Flexibility (n) – capability to adapt to new, different, or changing requirements
Float ideas (i.e., v) – to suggest something in order to gauge interest in it, or others' perception of it
Fluid (adj) – smooth and continuous without end in sight
Folks (n) – people, especially those of a particular group or type; can be used as a salutation
Food for thought (i.e.) – something significant to think about
Forecasts (n) – a statement of what is judged likely to happen in the future, especially in connection with a particular situation

Foreign investment (n) – involves capital flows from one country to another, granting the foreign investors extensive ownership/stake in domestic companies and assets
Foresee (v) – to know about something before it happens
Forethought (n) – the good judgment to consider the near future in your present actions
Formality (n) – the quality of being appropriate for an official occasion
Front runner (n) – favourite candidate
Functional specification (n) – a multi-page document that describes how the product or service will be provided
FYI (acronym) – For Your Information

Gaps (lengthy) (n) – a break (long)
Gauge (v) – to measure/judge
Generate (v) (income/interest) – to bring into existence; make money/develop interest
Geographically (adv) dispersed (v) teams (n) – a group of individuals who work together from different geographic locations and rely on communication technology in order to collaborate
Get across (v) – communicate
Get along with (v) – to be on congenial terms
Get (v) clarity on (n) – to develop a clear understanding of something
Get down to business (i.e.) – to start doing something that is required in a serious manner
Get(ting) off track (i.e.) – to lose direction
Get on with (v) – perform or make progress on something; to have a good relationship with someone
Get our own house in order (i.e.) – to make one's own affairs right, before or instead of criticising someone else
Get straight to the point (i.e.) – to reach the most important or crucial part of something immediately
Get the blame (i.e.) – to be the one responsible for some bad result or outcome
Globally (adv) comprehensible (adj) – to be intelligible to and understood by those from different language backgrounds
Go for it (i.e.) – to apply the necessary effort or energy to do or pursue something
Go(ing) forward (v) – in the future
Go off without a hitch (i.e.) – go smoothly and without problems
Go the extra mile (i.e.) – to make more effort than is expected of you
Go to work on an egg (i.e.) – to have sustenance for the working day (egg branding slogan in the UK)
Go through (v) (problem) – to experience a negative experience

Good mood (n) – a feeling of happiness/contentment
Gossip (v) – to speak about someone/something (usually negatively) without it necessarily being true
Grab a cup of coffee (i.e.) – to buy/drink coffee quickly
Grounds (n) – basis for belief, action, or argument
Ground rules (n) – agreed rules between everyone for the meeting
Grow with responsibility (i.e.) – learn from the responsibilities given/taken
Growth (n) – progressive development
Guests of honour (n) – the most important guests at an occasion

Hands on (adj) (i.e.) – to have direct, frontline and practical experience
Harmful (adj) – causing bad effect
Harmoniously (adv) – in a way that has a pleasant tune (music), applies to working relationship
Heads up (i.e.) – a warning that something is going to happen, usually so that you can prepare for it
High performing (adj) – better, faster, or more efficient than others
High strategic priority (n) – very important way of achieving goals; of great importance in your plan
Highlight (v) – to emphasise special importance
Highs and lows (i.e.) – referring to both the successful or happy times, and the unsuccessful or bad times
Hint (n) – a nuanced way of giving direction/opinion
Holds up (i.e.) – proves to be true
Hook (n) – 'use a hook to get the audience interested'; use a joke/question/anecdote to attract the attention of the audience
Host (n) – a person/organisation that is responsible for a special event
Hot air (i.e.) – a lot of talk without any substance
Huge (adj) asset (n) – a big advantage or resource
Humiliation (n) – the feeling of being ashamed
Humour (n) – the ability to be amused by something seen, heard, or thought about
Hypothesis (n) – a tentative assumption
Hypothetical (adj) suggestion (n) – something involving or being based on a suggested idea or theory

Identify (v) market segment (n) – to find, through research, a target groups of consumers
Idiomatic expressions (n) –words with particular meanings (not always intuitive); slang (n) a type of language that consists of words and phrases that are regarded as very informal, are more common in speech than writing, and are typically restricted to a particular context or group of people.

Idiomatic (adj) language (n) – informal language belonging to particular groups
Immediacy (n) – the fact that something seems real and important, so that you feel involved with it
Immigrants (n) – a person who has come to a different country in order to live there permanently
Impatience (n) – the feeling of wanting something to happen now
Impetuous (adj) – said or done suddenly, without fully considering the likely results
Implement (v) – carry out something that is planned
Implications (n) – the (unexpected) effect that an action or decision will have on something else in the future
Implicitly (adv) – in a way that is suggested but not communicated directly
In isolation (i.e.) – without relation to other people or things; separately
Inbound (adj) sales (n) – a sales process driven by the customer rather than the company
Incompetent (adj) – not having or showing the necessary skills to do something successfully
Indemnify (v) – to make compensation to individual/company for incurred hurt, loss, or damage
Influencers (n) – have specialised knowledge, authority or insight into a specific subject.
Informational (n) – relating to or characterised by facts about something; providing information
Inherent (adj) – existing in something as a permanent, essential, or characteristic attribute
In-house (adj) – done or existing within an organisation
Innovative (adj) product (n) – new and original product or service
Insights (n) – the power or act of seeing into a situation
Inspiration (n) – someone or something that provides uplifting ideas for doing something
Instant success (n) – an immediate success
Instinctive (adj) thing (n) – one that you have or do without thinking or reasoning; 'gut' reaction/feeling
Instrumental (adj) – instrumental motivation for language learning involves the learner wanting only to use the language in a pragmatic way to get something done
Integrate (v) – to combine two or more things in order to become more effective/tidier; incorporate into a larger unit
Integrative (adj) – integrative motivation for language learning involves the learner wanting to become part of the society and culture as a language user
Interdependence (n) – dependence between people e.g. in a team

Internal distribution (n) – distribution of documents within the company
Interrogate (v) – to question formally and systematically
Intertextuality (n) – the interrelationship between texts
Intimidating (adj) – feelings of fear/timidity
Invest (ideas, money, time) (v) – to put money, effort, time, ideas into something to make a profit or get an advantage
Invited (v) bidders (n) – specifically asked to bid
Irrespective (adv) – without considering; not needing to allow for
Irritating (adj) – causing displeasure, anger, or annoyance
Iterative (adj) – doing something again and again, usually to improve it

Jargonistic (adj) – specialised terminology and therefore difficult to understand by outsiders
Jeopardise (v) – put (someone/something) into a situation in which there is a danger of loss, harm, or failure
Jump to conclusions (i.e.) – to guess the facts about a situation without having enough information
Jumping to (or make) assumptions (i.e.) – telling yourself that something is true without actually having any evidence that it is
Just (adv) – common modifier that minimises what is being discussed/considered
Just between ourselves – (i.e.) – in confidence
Just like to point out (i.e.) – just like to highlight or focus on
Just the opposite (i.e.) – to say that something is completely different from what has just been said

Keep a close eye on (i.e.) – to observe carefully
Keep emotions in check (i.e.) – keep emotions under control
Keep strict control (i.e.) – keep tightly regulated
Keep the customer (someone) sweet (i.e.) – to be kind/friendly so that someone will continue to co-operate
Keep up with (v) – move or progress at the same rate as someone or something else
Key personnel (n) – refers to individuals who are specifically and uniquely important
Killer (adj) proposal/app (n) – a very very good proposal/app

Laissez faire (n) (French) – a policy or attitude of letting things take their own course, without interfering
Land someone in it (i.e.) – cause someone to be blamed for something
Landing screen (or page) (n) – standalone advertising web screen created specifically to market
Laudable (adj) – deserving praise and commendation

Layer of complexity (i.e.) – a level of difficulty/effort in addressing something
Leaving it to the last minute is not a clever idea (i.e.) – do it now
Let you down (i.e.) – fail to support or help someone as hoped/expected.
Let's conquer the world (i.e.) – let's go out and be very successful
Leverage (n) – power to influence people and get the results you want
Life cycle (n) – the length of time that something lasts or can be used e.g. stages of a business project
Lift (v) – to take hold of and raise something in order to remove, carry, or move it to a different position; Lift spirits/morale – to provide a positive feeling/encouragement
Like a dog gnawing a bone (i.e.) – giving something undivided attention in an almost obsessional way
Linear (adj) – sequential
Lined up (v) – organised, prepared
Listening between the lines (i.e.) – implicit understanding of someone's real feelings or intentions from what someone actually says
Literal (adj) – factual, exact
Lockstep process (n) – a situation in something is achieved only by systematically and strictly going through a process one step at a time and in order
Logistics (n) – the detailed coordination of a complex operation involving many people, facilities, or supplies
Logos (n) – a design or symbol displayed on a company's products, vehicles, signs
Loop (n) – a circle/'loop in' (i.e.) keep someone informed

Made out (v, i.e.) – performed/pretend
Mainstream (n) – a prevailing direction/the norm
Make or break (career) (i.e.) – be the factor which decides whether (something) will succeed or fail.
Makes sense (i.e.) – sensible
Malicious (adj) – intended to harm or upset other people
Manage (v) upward (adj) – to ensure your manager/supervisor are prioritised in your work management
Mandating (v) – ordering, requiring something that is non-negotiable
Mantra (n) – a statement or slogan repeated frequently
Market segments (n) – group of potential customers/consumers who share one or more common characteristics e.g. age
Marketing automation developer (n) – builder of a computer app to deliver marketing systems
Matrix management structure (n) – an organisational structure in which some individuals report to more than one manager

Maximise time (v) – to make the best of the time available
Measures (n) – a ways of achieving something, or a method for dealing with a situation
Media (n) – means/channel of communication
Mediation (n) – intervention between conflicting parties to promote reconciliation, settlement, or compromise
Memorable (adj) – likely to be remembered
Memorise (v) – to learn something verbatim
Menstruating (v) – to have a flow of blood from the uterus, usually for three to five days every four weeks, in women who are not pregnant
Merit (n) – proven capability to perform in a job
Message (v) – to communicate/send message e.g. text
Metaphor (n) – a thing regarded as representative or symbolic of something else
Metrics and processes (n) – standard (numerical) measurements that are used to evaluate and benchmark the performance of business processes
Milestones (n) – scheduled event that indicates the completion of a major deliverable event of a project
Mindset (n) – a way of looking at something e.g. a numerical mindset (i.e. numbers are key to understanding)
Minutes – permanent, formal, and detailed record of business meeting
Misled (v) – to take in a wrong direction deliberately
Mobile devices (n) – a portable computing device such as a smartphone or tablet computer
Mobile virtual network operator (MVNO) (n) – a reseller for wireless communications services
Modal (adj) verbs (n) – verbs in English communicating evaluation, obligation, probability and permission
Modality (n) – language choices that show opinion, possibility, evaluation, command e.g. should, might etc
Monitor (v) – keep track of; the act of conducting a systematic and repeated sequence of measurements, or observations
Monopolise (v) – have and control fully and exclusively
Mouthed (v) the words (n) – to use mouth, rather than voice to say something
Mumble (v) – to utter with a low inarticulate voice; say something softly
Mutually (adv) arrived at (i.e.) – to reach a particular decision or understanding in a shared manner/reciprocally

Narrow (it) down (i.e.) – to pare the number of people or things down on a list down to a more manageable or select number
Navigate (v) – to lead a company, activity, etc. in a particular direction in order to deal effectively with a difficult situation

Near completion (i.e.) – almost finished
Negative (adj) – characterised by or displaying a pessimistic attitude
Negative disruptive (adj) forces – hurdles or difficulties; circumstances around a situation that has destructive effects on it
Neglected (adj) – not well looked after; ignored
Network (n) effects (n) – increase in the number of participants adds value for each participant
New fashion line (n) – latest clothing a fashion designer produces for a specific category within her fashion company
New media (n) – electronic interactive media/channels of communication, such as the internet/laptops etc
No one size fits all (i.e.) – not any product/process fits in all instances
No way (i.e.) – expression emphasising 'no'
Normal (adj) social (adj) chit-chat (n) – usual light informal casual conversation
Norms (n) – existing/accepted ways of behaving
Notice period (i.e.) – the specific time required to inform of the end of contract
Nuances (n) – a subtle or slight degree of difference, not explicitly stated
Numbers (hard) – quantitative data; statistics

Objective (n) – aim or purpose
Objectify (v) – 'objectify young women' – looks at women as sexual objects
Obscure (adj) facts (n) – unusual/ partly hidden information
Offensive (adj) – aggressive movement or attack
Offshored (adj) contact centre (n) – contact centre owned and managed by the onshore company providing services in a different country
Off the table (i.e.) – withdrawn
On my behalf (i.e.) – for my benefit/convenience
On one end of the spectrum (n) – at one end of a continuum that may relate to opinions– a polarised viewpoint
On-shore to off-shore (i.e.) – transitioning work from home to a country abroad usually for economic gain
On the same page (i.e.) – to be in agreement
On top of (v) – 'to be on of the brief'/have full understanding/control of the brief
On track (i.e.) – on schedule; progressing or developing as planned
On trial (i.e.) – as a test of something; on probation
One-off (n) – a thing that is made or that happens only once
Open (adj) team culture (i.e.) – is made up of the values, beliefs, attitudes and behaviours shared transparently by a team.
Open up (i.e.) – to make available or accessible
Open up the discussion (i.e.) – to elicit discussion

Optimise (v) – to plan or carry out activity with maximum efficiency
Out in the open (i.e.) – in or into public view or knowledge
Out of the box (i.e.) – outside of, or beyond what is considered usual and conventional thinking
Out of your depth (i.e.) – in a field or situation that exceeds one's knowledge or ability
Outburst (n) – a surge of anger
Outlier (n) – statistical data which is extremely different from the others in the same sample, unexpected
Outsourced (adj) – business work sent overseas to cut costs
Over my head (i.e.) – confusing or difficult to understand; bypassing one's authority
Overlapping (n) – covering part of another
Overrun (n) – (budget) spending more than allocated in the budget; (Items) produced or printed more than the amount ordered
Oversee (v) – to watch over and direct; supervise
Overtight budget (i.e.) – not having enough money to spend

Pace (v) – rate of speed at which activity or movement proceeds
Paperwork (n) fulfill (v) requirements (n) – completed written documents needed
Participative (adj) – relating to or involving participation of colleagues participate in decision making
Paternalistic (adj) (Latin – father) – people in authority making decisions for others
Peak (adj) – top of
People (n) from (prep) their (pron) side (n) – people supporting one's opinion, position
Persevere (v) – keep trying
Personalisation (n) – the process of making something suitable for the needs of a particular person
Perspective (n) – a particular point of view
Persuasive (adj) – convincing
Phenomenon (n) – an interesting/unusual occurrence, circumstance
Pick on (i.e.) – unkind treatment; to criticise
Pick up on it (i.e.) – to detect or notice something; to become alert to or aware of something
Pilot (v) – to guide or lead; to control the course of; to try for the first time
Pin down to details – to force someone to give firm opinions or precise information
Pitch (n) – a persuasive presentation e.g. sales presentation
Plain English (i.e.) – a style of communication that uses easy to understand English that is clear and precise

Play with words (i.e.) – to use words that sound similar or that have several different meanings in a clever or funny way
Poach (v) – to attract an employee or customer away from a competitor
Pockets of discontent – particular groups feeling dissatisfied towards something
Point fingers (i.e.) – to blame or accuse someone
Polarise (v) – move to opposing factions
Portfolio (n) – pool of investments; collection of documents as evidence for employment; or group of complementary or supplementary products marketed together
Positive (adj) disposition (n) – pleasant manner
Potential(ly) (adj) – possible
Potential hold-ups (i.e.) – possible delays
Practical jokes (n) – pranks or tricks played on a person
Pragmatic (adj) strategies (n) – strategies guided by practical experience and observation rather than theory
Praise (v) – to express favourable judgement; commend
Preceded (v) – to go before as in place, order, rank, importance or time
Precise (adj) instructions (n) – clear and accurate directions
Preferred (customer) (adj) – having special status or receiving special treatment or benefits
Preferred (adj) option (n) – liked better or best; used or wanted in preference to others
Premature (adj) – occurring, growing, or existing before the customary, correct, or assigned time
Prestigious (adj) upmarket (adj) hotel (n) – appealing to or designed for high-income consumers hotel; prominent or renowned hotel
Prevalent (adj) – commonly found
Prick up their ears (i.e.) – to suddenly pay close attention to something
Priority (n) – the state or quality of being earlier in time/importance/preference
Probationary period (n) – a process or period in which a person's fitness, as for work or membership in a social group, is tested for a period of time
Probe (v) – to try to discover information about a situation by asking questions and examining facts
Productivity (n) measure (n) – the ratio of a measure of total outputs to a measure of inputs used in the production of goods and services
Project charter (n) – a document that is agreed by all parties on how a project should proceed/be managed
Project management training (PMT) (n) – a course that teaches knowledge and skills in managing the lifecycle of a project
Promotion (n) – the act or fact of being raised in position or rank
Prospect (n) – a potential client/customer; the possibility that something might happen in the future, especially something good

Protocol (n) – an agreed procedure for doing something
Public Relations (PR) (n) – the messaging/communicating activities of keeping institutions and businesses in touch with the public
Publicity launch (n) – an initial event to attract public attention to people or products as by use of mass media
Publicly (adv) accused (v) – to formally and openly accuse a person or corporation of a wrongful action
Pull your weight (i.e.) – to do your fair share of the work
Pumped her fist (i.e.) – a celebratory gesture in which a fist is raised up in the air communicating success
Punctuation (n) – the practice or system of using certain conventional marks or characters in writing to mark meaning e.g. ! denotes surprise
Punctuation deviations (n) – violation of the system of using punctuation devices for intended communicative effect
Push back – to disagree openly, confront or challenge
Put a tiger in your tank (i.e.) – put a lot of vigour, determination and motivation into something; UK advertising tagline in 1960s for petrol
Put on hold (i.e.) – request to wait, pause or delay
Put on the defensive (i.e.) – prepare to withstand, or a counter aggression or attack
Put up with (i.e.) – to endure without complaint, tolerate
Put your heads together (i.e.) – to work together to come up with an idea or resolution

Qualified (adj) – confirmed/shown to have the right skills, experience etc
Quantitative (adj) – numerical and statistical information
Quarter (n) – 3 month block
Quit (v) – to stop, cease or discontinue

Rain on your parade (i.e.) – to ruin one's plan or optimism
Raise your profile (i.e.) – increased attention paid to a company or an individual usually due to advertising/media
Rambling (meeting/person) (adj) – talking without a specific goal, purpose or direction
Real time (adj) updates (n) – updates of information as they happen
Reassurance (n) – the action of removing someone's doubts or fears
Rebate (v) – pay back
Redesigned (adj) – made a revision in the appearance or function of something
Reference checks (n) – employer contacts previous workplaces of candidate to check work record and seek recommendation of candidate
Reference (n) – written document from previous employers appraising the candidate

Refine (v) – to improve an idea, a method, a system, etc. by making small changes
Reflected in (i.e.) – attribute displayed in the results or outcome of something
Registrants (n) – a person who is registering
Regulatory (adj) agency (n) – an agency that is authorised by the legislature to establish and enforce rules in a particular department/section of the government.
Rehearsed (adj) responses (n) – answers which are practised from anticipated questions or topics
Rein him (it) in (i.e.) – to limit or control someone or something
Relatively (young group) (adv) – compared to other (groups)
Relevant (adj) – related well to a subject or to something happening or being discussed
Relieved (adj) – happy that something unpleasant has not happened or has ended
Remote global teams (n) – virtual global teams
Remote teams (n) – people in a project with the same boss but physically in different offices, countries or cities
Repetitive (adj) – happens in the same way all the time
Reporting lines (n) – used to refer to who you are managed by and you are accountable to; this may be more than one person (see matrix reporting)
Reprimand (v) – to scold, chastise, tell off
Request for Proposal (RfP) (n) – a business document that provides details about a project sent to prospective bidders
Research-based advertising and messaging – marketing materials that meet the researched needs of the target audience
Reserved (adj) – shy, quiet, not very communicative
Resolve fairly painlessly (i.e.) – to find a solution without difficulty
Resolved (v) – agreed
Reusable (adj) – able to be used more than once
Revenues (n) – the income that a business or government receives regularly
Right team at the right time (i.e.) – alignment of a good team at the perfect moment
Rigid (adj) – not permitting any change; unreasonably strict
Robotic (adj) – a person who works/behaves/speaks like a robot
Robust (adj) – strongly formed or constructed; sturdy
Roll call (n) – calling off a list of names (as for checking attendance)
Roll out (i.e.) – introduce, present, reveal
Rules of engagement (n) – agreed practices followed by the participants in situations of opposing interests (conflicts), such as negotiations.
Run me through (i.e.) – explain to me

Safeguard (n) – precautionary or counter measure available to an entity that enables it to protect itself
Sales exercise (n) – an activity that helps delegates to practise selling or improve selling skills
Sales pipeline (n) – a snapshot of where prospects are in the sales process; this shows you how many deals salespeople are expected to close in a given time
Sarcasm (n) – the use of remarks that clearly mean the opposite of what they say, made in order to hurt someone's feelings or to criticise something by making it appear humorous
Sarcastic (adj) – having character of sarcasm
Save time and pain (i.e.) – to avoid wasting effort on something
Save up (v) – keep (information/money) to share/spend until later; save money towards a particular expense
Say so (n) – permission
Scaffolding (n) – a metaphor for assisting/mentoring the development of a skill and providing feedback
Scope milestone (n) – a marker that shows progress in a project timeline/set of agreed tasks
Screw up (i.e.) – to make a mistake
Scrutiny (n) – the careful and detailed examination of something in order to get full information
Second guessing (v) – criticising or judging another person before you know the facts
Segments (n) – each of the parts into which something is or may be divided e.g. a market
Segmentation (n) – division of the market into target groups e.g. market segmentation
Self-regulating (adj) – governing itself without outside involvement/interference
Send a shock through (i.e.) – to cause distress/surprise
Set (the direction) (v) – lead the direction
Severe (ity) (n) – high degree of harshness or sternness
Sexual harassment (n) – unwanted or offensive sexual attention, suggestions, or talk, especially from an employer or other person
Sexual orientation (n) – a person's sexual identity in relation to the gender; lesbian, gay etc
Shared vision (n) – in an organisation (n) – a group whose members have the same view of what they are working towards
Shift away (i.e.) – to move or cause to move from one place or idea to another
Short list (n) – a list of preferable items or candidates that have been selected for final consideration, as in filling an employment position

Shortlisted (adj) – to be on one of a small list of people who have been chosen from a larger group
Showcase (v) – to exhibit or display
Sign off (i.e.) – (a deal) agree to/authorise; to announce the end of a communication
Sign up (i.e.) – to agree to be a participant or recipient by signing one's name; enlist
Sign up screen (n) – an app interface to login or sign up
Signals (n) – an action, movement, or sound that gives information, a message, a warning, or an order
Sisterhood (n) – a feeling of shared interests and solidarity among women
Sizeable (adj) – notably above average in amount, size, or scope
Slip a bit (i.e.) – be delayed
Slogan (n) – a phrase used repeatedly, as in advertising or promotion
Smart (adj) analytics (n) – systematic quantitative analysis of data or statistics to obtain meaningful information for better decision-making
Social media strategies (n) – emoticons, emojis, use of abbreviations etc for meaning making when texting; may relate to marketing strategies using social media
Soft launch (n) – an occasion when a product, service, or business is made available or opened for the first time, but only to a limited number of people at first
Soften (the message) (v) – make less direct
Solid (adj) – (idea) well-considered idea
Some concern – some worry
Source (v) – to obtain (materials or parts) from another business/country for your business/personal use
Spark(v) – to be very enthusiastic/passionate; set alight
Speak to (v) – to give evidence of or comments on (a subject)
Spearhead (v) – lead on a project/idea
Specifications (n) – a detailed description of how something should be done/made
Specifics (n) – exact details
Spell out (i.e.) – to explain something in a very clear way with details
Spend a fortune (i.e.) – to pay a great amount of money
Spirit, distilled (n) – process to make strong alcoholic drink
Staid (adj) – unchanging, stable
Stand up for (i.e.) – to support or defend
Standalone (adj) service (n) – assistance or service that is self-contained and usually independently operating
Standard/specific/tailored (adj) questions (n) – types of questions specially made for a particular purpose
Stay in touch (i.e.) – to maintain contact with another person

Steady (adj) work flow (n) – constant work
Steering committee (n) – a committee that decides on the priorities or order of business of an organisation and manages the general course of its operations/projects
Storyboard (n) – visuals and graphs that accompany a narrative text as preparation for e.g. a presentation with powerpoint
Strategic plan (n) – plan for business direction
Stress and pressure (n) – emotional or mental strain resulting from demanding (work/personal) circumstances
Stress (v) – to emphasise
Structure (n) – plan/organise well for something
Struggle (a bit) (v) – to experience difficulty and make a very great effort in order to get something done
Style guide (n) – a book or set of documents that provides a set of rules for writing in an organisation
Subculture (n) – the way of life, customs and ideas of a particular group of people within a society that are different from the mainstream
Subject Matter Expert (SME) (n) – someone who has deep and particular expertise in something, often used to advise
Subscription (n) – amount paid to receive a service
Subscription base (n) – recurring payment
Substance underneath the sizzle (i.e.) – depth beyond the superficial impression
Suggestive remarks (adj) – comments causing people to think about sex, often in a way that makes them feel uncomfortable
Summon (v) – authoritatively or urgently call on (someone) to be present
Supplementary (adj) question (n) – follow-up question
Suppliers (n) – a company, person, etc. that provides things that people want or need, usually having a long term business relationship
Supply chain (n) – the movement of goods from one location to another
Support people (n) – workers who provide extra assistance for specific jobs
Suspended (adj) from work (n) – employee is asked not to come into work because of an incident that requires investigation
Sweep under the carpet (i.e.) – to ignore, deny or conceal from public view or knowledge
Switch (v) – to exchange or trade
Synchronous (adj) – occurring at the same time
Synchronously (adv) communicating (n) – two or more parties are exchanging information in real time
Systematically (adv) applied (adj) – methodically put into practice

Tackle (v) – to attack (someone or something)
Tagline (n) – an often repeated phrase associated with an individual, organisation or commercial product; a slogan

Tailoring your approach (i.e.) – to adapt so as to make suitable for something specific
Takeaway (n) – 'the takeaway from the meeting was…' the most important piece of knowledge/advice.
Take it out…travel budget (i.e.) – to withdraw money from travel budget
Take off (i.e.) – to increase in activity very rapidly
Take over (v) – to dominate or control
Takes off (i.e.) – succeed
Take the point (i.e.) – to grasp the essential meaning of what a person is saying, to understand a person's argument
Talent Acquisition (n) – refers to the process of identifying and acquiring skilled workers to meet your organisational needs
Talker (n) – a person who speaks a lot
Tangible (adj) – capable of being clearly grasped; substantial rather than imaginary
Targeted (adj) behaviour (n) – deliberate behaviour towards a particular group
Tease (v) – to make fun of or provoke playfully
Teaser campaign (n) – an advertisement that aims to get people interested in a new product by giving only a little, but interesting/persuasive information about it
Telecoms (n) – telecommunication companies; refers to all types of voice, data and video transmissions
Templates (n) – anything that serves as a model
Tempting (adj) – having strong appeal; enticing
Tend to (v) – to be inclined or have a tendency to do something
Terminate (v) – 'terminate employment' – to sack an employee
Testimonials (n) – a statement in support of a particular truth, fact, or claim
Theme (n) – a main idea or topic
Thin (adj) – (argument) superficial/shallow
Think on his/her feet (i.e.) – to be able to think clearly in times of stress, especially when addressing people
Threats (n) – negative event that can cause a risk to become a loss
Thumbs up sign (i.e.) – a sign or indication of approval
Tight (adj) deadlines (n) – strict schedule by which something must be done
Timelines (n) – written representation of a period of time, usually a line, that shows the order in which related events happen
Timing (n) – the ability to choose the right moment to do or say something, or the time when something happens
To be just so (i.e.) – to keep things very neat and organised
Tools (n) to communicate (v) – useful ways/devices to communicate

Top down (i.e.) – approach in which high levels of management make decisions and pass down for implementation
Top-selling (v) – best selling
Touch base (i.e.) – to contact someone to update them or receive an update from them.
Tough (adj) – difficult to deal with; demanding or troubling
Track sales (n) – trace the revenue of a product
Track (v) success (n) – to monitor achievement
Traditional (adj) notions (n) – old-fashioned concept or idea
Transparent (adj) – decisions/procedures that are open; not secret
Trapped (adj) – in a tight corner; cannot escape
Tricky (adj) – risky; complicated
Troubleshoot (v) – deal with problems
Try them out (i.e.) – to test or use something experimentally
Turn up (v) – happens unexpectedly or in a way that was not planned
Tweaking (adj) – to change something slightly, especially in order to make it more correct, effective, or suitable
Twists and turns (i.e.) – things that are unexpected
Two-way and two-pronged (i.e.) – two-sided; bilateral

Ubiquitous (adj) – existing or being everywhere at the same time/popular
Unanimous (adj) – with the agreement of all people involved
Undivided (adj) attention (n) – to focus intently on one thing
Unfamiliar (adj) – not known to you
Unique (adj) – only one that exists
Universal norms (i.e.) – the normal beliefs of people in most cultures
Universal (adj) truths (n) – a truth that is discernible in any context
Unpack (issues) (v) – to explain (a question, issue, etc) by analysing its component parts
Unprofessional (adj) image (n) – not showing the standard of behavior or skills that are expected in business
Unreasonable (adj) denial (n) – unacceptable refusal to agree
Unresponsive (adj) – appears dead/lacks reaction
Unscheduled (adj) – not arranged; not planned
Unsurprisingly (adv) – not expected
Upsales (n) – selling products/services to existing customers
Usage profile (i.e.) – a summary of the communications patterns and technology requirements for a group of users
User experience test (n) – pilot run with customer
User (n) journey (n) – demonstration of the way users currently interact with the service/website/product end to end
Usual pleasantries (i.e.) – polite social utterance; a civility

Vague (adj) – not clear in meaning or expression
Valid (adj) – offer term remains fixed
Value (v) – to regard highly
Verbal (adj) abuse (n) – very negative statements made to a victim
Verbal, non-verbal communication (i.e.) – verbal communication involves the use of words or speech. Non-verbal communication involves the use of visual or cues such as facial expressions, eye or body movements, gestures to make meaning
Viable (adj) – possible, feasible
Victimising (n) – singling out for cruel or unjust treatment
Video capability (n) – ability to process a sequence of images electronically into an analog or digital format and displayed on a screen
VIPs (n) – very important persons

Wear it (v) – to tolerate something
Website (n) navigation (n) – refers to the process of navigating a network of information resources in the World Wide Web
Wind down/up (v) – to go slowly towards the finish
Withdraw (v) the complaint (n) – to take back the complaint
Withdrawn (adj) – not wanting to communicate with other people
Without intentionally (adv) offending (adj) – to insult or displease someone without meaning to
Wonder (v) – think about
Work from home (WFH) – to do your job from your home
Wrap up (v) – to complete something, such as a task; to put the finishing touches on something or finish meeting

Your call (i.e.) – your decision

APPENDIX 2

The audio transcripts

UNIT 1

Activity 2

Task (iii) Audio listening: The CommunicAsian welcome speech

Hi everyone,

It is my pleasure to welcome you to CommunicAsian . . . we have so many new employees starting with us this ***quarter*** *and I'd like them to stand up so everyone can recognise you in the corridors! (Pause)*

CommunicAsian is positioning itself to be the most creative and the most dependable communications campaign partner in Asia, and this last year has seen out client base grow by 50% ... and that is why we are welcoming more people into our company today. You are all selected because of your creativity and demonstrated ability to ***persevere*** *with challenges . . . our briefs are always challenging, but that's the excitement of working at CommunicAsian. We are looking forward to your* ***flashes of brilliance*** *in helping our clients* ***conceptualise*** *their products and services in a way they thought wasn't possible! And meet their deadlines!*

I want to tell you a little success story from this last month. We were asked by a large USA based drinks manufacturer (Scotts) to promote their new ***spirit*** *they called NightCap . . .so it was called Scotts Nightcap. The way* *it was being promoted in the USA was to an older* ***demographic*** *as a comforting, warm drink consumed at home, in front of the fire at the end of a cold day. What about promoting such a product in Asia they asked? Their sales targets were ambitious, growing up to US 5 million in exports over a 3 year period from the start of this campaign . . . and we were chosen to* ***come up*** *with the ideas to make that happen. We only had a month before they wanted to launch this campaign; this meant researching the potential target group and coming up with a* ***tagline*** *for a newly defined demographic.*

Our team came up with the concept of Scotts on the Rocks for a younger demographic. Put ice in it and turn it into a 'night out'. You know what? Scotts on the Rocks has become an ***instant success*** *in Singapore, Hong Kong, Japan, Seoul, Shanghai and even Vietnam . . . you can find it in most Asian nightclubs.*

So this is what we do and who we are . . .

We're now over 5 years old and employ 80 people in Asia; we're hoping to at least double our team in the next 2 years and expand into other countries and diversify our work . . .

And who are we? The thing that distinguishes our senior team is not only our experience, but also our diversity – please meet our senior management team:

Talent manager – Samantha Greenwood – who most of you will have met during your recruitment;
Creative Director – Tony Tanaka, usually based in Hong Kong

And then on the screen, meet our:

Finance manager-Melinda Rodriguez – She's a Filipina based in Manila
IT Development and Operations Director – Vivek Sengupta in Bangalore
(each person says hi)

Well that's us! So welcome and mingle. I'd like you to help yourselves to drinks and food at the back and get to know us! Vivek and Melinda for obvious reasons won't be joining us, but you'll meet them sometime soon.

UNIT 2

Activity 2

Task (ii). Audio listening: Internal meeting between Dawn, Samantha and Melinda about the GlobeNet RfP.

Samantha: You wanted to meet at two o'clock? Is this still a good time?

Dawn: Yes. Let me just get Melinda on Skype.

Samantha: Oh, I thought this was about my appraisal.

Dawn: No, we've got an urgent opportunity. We've been invited to respond to a Request for Proposal to do a big campaign across Asia and UK. I'll **fill you in** a bit more when Melinda joins so I don't have to **go through** it twice. Sorry, but your annual **appraisal** will need to **slip a bit**.

Samantha: No problem. I guess if it is not urgent you're not desperate to tell me all the things I'm doing wrong.

Dawn: (laughs) No, I'll **save that up** for a couple of days. Ah, hi Melinda.

Melinda: Hi Dawn. How are you?

Dawn: Good. I've got Samantha with me.

Samantha: Hi Melinda.

Dawn: I wanted to talk to you support people about an RfP we received this morning from GlobeNet – they're a big UK based telco with a presence **in** Hong Kong and they want to expand their Asian business. They want someone to put together a campaign for them and develop some **smart analytics** to track its success. I've spoken to Tony Tanaka and we're going to **go for it**. It could be our biggest project ever, it's pretty exciting.

Melinda: Oh, that's great.

Samantha: So what do you want from us **support people**?

Dawn: I'm going to need both of you really involved. We've got four weeks to respond, and we're going to need our response project team here in Singapore. Melinda, I need you to put a budget together for the response costs and to **track** our spending. You'll need to find the money from some other saving, and we'll need at least a **first cut** by tomorrow.

Melinda: I'll need a lot more information about the team and where they are coming from.

Dawn: Sure. I'll be sending you both the RfP after this meeting, and then we'll have a con call with Tony and Vivek at four. They will be joint project owners.

Samantha: (after a pause) Oh. Joint project owners. But if one of them says black the other says white. They're like **chalk and cheese**.

Dawn: This is where you come in. We need them both: Tony is our smartest creative guy and Vivek is our top analytical developer. This is the first time we have had a project with both of these things equally important. You, Sam, need to make sure they work effectively together.

Samantha: That won't be easy, but I'll try.

Dawn: I don't want you to try. I want you to do it. And Melinda, I want you to own the budget for the bid and for the project. You are going to have to protect it and stand up to Vivek and Tony if they try and change it without your **say so**.

Melinda: I'll try.

Dawn: Once again, this is not about trying. Look, you are both managers in this company. Now is the time to manage. Vivek and Tony are not big bad wolves. They are part of this company too.

Samantha: Yes, Dawn, you're right. Melinda and I will talk about how we achieve that.

Dawn: Good. Sam, you'll need to talk to them both about the project team make up, and Melinda, you'll have to get their inputs on the costs. Can you both think about these before our four o'clock call?

Samantha: Sure.

Melinda: Yes Dawn.

Dawn: Good. We'll reconvene then.

UNIT 3

Activity 2

Task (ii).

Meeting 1

Present (all by telephone conference call): Dawn, Vivek, Tony, Melinda, Prasad and Rory.

Dawn: Is everybody here? (*Lots of voices saying 'yep'*)

Good, thank you all for making time this evening. We need to prepare for Wednesday's meeting with GlobeNet and think of any questions we need to ask. Tony, do we know who else will be at the meeting?

Tony: GlobeNet changed their minds. They have decided to hold separate meetings with each of their **invited bidders**, so it'll just be me. They want us to let them know what **people from their side** we want to have there for discussion and clarification.

Vivek: It shouldn't just be Tony. Prasad should be there to cover reporting and such.

Tony: No need. I can ask questions.

Dawn: I think Vivek is right. We don't want just one person, and if there are technical issues someone like Prasad would be able to ask follow up questions. Besides, it will be good experience for him.

Melinda: This is Melinda. I'd just like to point out that there is no provision in the travel budget to take Prasad to Hong Kong for the GlobeNet meeting.

Vivek: **Take it out** of my **travel budget.** I'll just cancel one of my trips to Singapore.

Dawn: We are **getting off track**. What are the things we need to know? Tony, you cover the market side, Vivek, the systems and analytics, then we **open up the discussion** if anyone thinks we have missed anything. Tony [silence]. Tony, I think you may be on mute.

Tony: Sorry, I was on mute. Yes, the RfP talks of marketing in three Asian countries to be identified. Who identifies them, them or us? And secondly, what's more important to them: the **message or the measures**.

Dawn: I'm pretty sure they would say equally important. You can't –

Vivek (interrupts): Of course they're equally important. You can't manage what you don't measure. And the measures are most important. Do they want us to collect and track them? Do they want **dashboards** or regular reporting? Will it be **cloud based or local server?**

Prasad: We've only got four weeks. This is Prasad. I think we need to know when they want the project fully delivered.

Tony: The point about the message is that it's not just delivered and done. It **evolves** as it strengthens.

Rory: I think we should ask about **market segments**. Do they want to restrict to the ones they mention or consider others?

Dawn: These are all good ideas, but we need to get more specific. I think GlobeNet want questions sent in advance. Can I suggest that Tony and Rory work together to build a set of marketing questions, and Vivek and Prasad do the same for the systems side. Melinda, you write down any finance or budget questions you've got. If everyone can send their list through to Prasad by lunchtime tomorrow, we can finalise by end of day. Is that okay? Good.

Meeting 2

Dawn: Hi everyone, I hope you have all received the agenda and RfP I sent out last night . . . and Vivek . . . what time is it there right now in Bangalore?

Vivek: 7.30am Dawn . . .

Dawn: and Tony and Melinda? You guys are on the same time zone as Singapore in Manila and HK . . . so we're here at 10am. Thanks Vivek for getting up early to join the meeting. So here in the Singapore I have Sam.

Sam: Hi everyone!

Dawn: So that's everyone. Sorry we haven't got visual support yet . . . Vivek when is that new platform coming?

Vivek: It's almost ready . . . should have it up and running for the monthly project meetings in about 2 weeks . . .

Dawn: OK be nice to have asap . . . So the main aim of today is to get your feedback on the RfP that I hope you all read last night, and particularly your prepared thoughts about who should be on the call to GlobeNet and any clarifications/questions we should pose, I mean ask them. We can send these questions in before we meet. . .

Tony: Hi everyone, Tony here . . . just to say I really think I should be on the call as I'd like to showcase some of our recent campaign projects. . .

Dawn: Can I **cut in,** I mean, can I interrupt here Tony? . . . I don't think this is the right forum for that as we're not presenting our credentials as much as finding out what they want . . . any ideas?

Tony: Oh OK . . . but someone from the Creative Department should be there . . . maybe a question around their own ideas of the demographics . . . I mean what about other professionals like all the Asian bankers in London?

Dawn: Good point and perhaps you could do some homework on that one before the meeting . . . that will show our commitment, Vivek?

Vivek: I have a question about tracking the success measures for this project . . . I mean I'd like to know something about their timeframe . . . are we talking 3,6, 9 months ... maybe a year?

Melinda: Good point Vivek as this will impact our budget and resources for the analytics . . .

Dawn: Ok great points so far, so in summary we're saying timeframes and budgets. . . . and yes we could do a bit of research on the demographics . . . so Tony can you get onto that? I'm thinking maybe delegate that to Prasad and he could be at the meeting?

Tony: Fine with me.

Melinda: Let's see if they have an indicative budget? Maybe . . .

Dawn: I think that may be **premature** . . . I mean a bit soon to ask . . . but Vivek I think the tracking timeframe question is good.

Tony: They seem to want a group with a creative flair . . . that's us! I'm thinking a tag line like . . .

Dawn: Hang on Tony . . . we haven't even won the bid yet! Questions/comments everyone? I'll send something to GlobeNet tonight . . . so can you get any further thoughts down and email me by 6pm Singapore time . . . so 3.30 the latest Vivek? Is there anything else at this stage?

Tony: Yes, when we write the proposal . . . remember our Himeno one, we can model it on that!

Dawn: Good one Tony, yes! Thanks to everyone on the call and I'll look forward to getting your final thoughts. I'll copy you all into my email to GlobeNet. Have a good day/evening.

UNIT 4

Activity 2

Task (iii). PowerPoint – CommunicAsian presentation

Slide 1: Sumo into Europe

Dawn: Good morning. I am Dawn Chen, and I am the head of CommunicAsian, and with me I have our Head of Creative, Tony Tanaka, who will be talking through the main findings and recommendations on your project to establish a Sumo sports channel in Europe. We'll keep the presentation short to give us more time for questions and discussion. Tony actually managed this project directly, so he is **on top of** all the details. Tony, over to you.

Tony: Thank you, Dawn, and thank you Himeno for giving us such an interesting project. I even got my parents involved in reading the Japanese magazines about Sumo. My Japanese is very basic but my parents still use it every day to speak to my grandmother, so they've kept it up. So, let's remind ourselves of what you asked us to do.

Slide 2: The Brief

Tony: Essentially, Himeno was looking to see if you could **leverage** the rights to televise Sumo into a new market in Europe. You said there were only two criteria: the revenue had to be an **annualised amount** of US$ one million within six months, and the channel is to be a **standalone service**, not part of a **bundle** like ESPN or Sky.

If we found there was potential business, then we looked at the **brand building** that would support its development. We did a **pilot** using social media to build awareness – I'll come on to the results of that later, but it was really good. Before that, I'll show you what we did

Slide 3: What we did

Tony: The first thing was obviously to identify target market segments, and we set criteria that they had to be a minimum size – say 50,000 people at least – and residents. For the business model we assumed that customers would need to sign a 1-year contract at a minimum, so that ruled out short-term students or tourists.

The first group was easy to identify: Japanese residents. The second group, European students of Asian subjects, we identified by analyzing Google searches and **correlating** them. We found that very many of these students would Google something specific about their study, and then follow links into related information. So something on Buddhism would lead to Zen, would lead to Japanese culture, would lead to Sumo.

The third group self-selected. We set up a Sumo page and invited people to register interest, and we received about 25,000 registrations – too small to be a focus area in the first six months, but we tracked them anyway for the longer term.

For each of these groups we conducted surveys which unfortunately had a pretty low response rate, so we held extra focus groups to compensate.

Finally, we ran a fun 4-week teaser campaign on social media to see if we could build an interested audience for the future. The whole project took about 6 weeks. Let's look at what we found.

Slide 4: Findings

Tony: When we focused on the Japanese resident numbers, it was clear that UK should be our market, and the student numbers were similar – over 100,000 each. We estimated, based on **census data**, that there are about 40,000 Japanese households, with half of them interested in Sumo.

With the student groups, quite a small number were interested in a pure television channel, but that number grew to over 40% if it was available on mobile devices. It obviously will be available on mobiles, but we hadn't made that clear.

There is a lot more detailed analysis in the report, but the price point of about $10 – eight British pounds – was fairly consistent. That would mean just 10,000 subscribers for Himeno to meet your initial target.

We think $10 is very reasonable: the Badminton Channel, another minority sport in Britain with its own dedicated channel, charges $15 – twelve pounds – and has 22,000 subscribers. It's been going for about 2 years.

Slide 5: Our Campaign

Tony: Our campaign. This was the fun part of the project. We wanted to see how well we could generate a buzz for Sumo to build an audience for the long term. We used social media with a new question each week. The first question was 'where do people train every day for a contest which lasts two seconds?' I had no idea that the average Sumo bout was only two seconds.

At the end of the week, we posted the answer and some videos of two second bouts, together with a new question, 'What contest starts with a handful of salt?' We ran it for 4 weeks, and then pulled it together under the tag 'Who knows Sumo?' We had our whole team searching for the most obscure facts about Sumo – they loved it. And, it got results.

Slide 6: Results

Tony: As I hope you have heard consistently in my presentation, there is a viable market for Sumo in the UK in the short term, and there seems to be a significant potential in the longer term based on our pilot awareness campaign. We had over 200,000 likes and visits in just 4 weeks.

Let me quickly hand back to Dawn and then we can answer any questions you may have.

Slide 7: Thank you

Dawn: Before we open up to questions, I'd like to thank you all for your time, and also to say that, after doing this feasibility project, CommunicAsian would love to work with you on the implementation.

UNIT 5

Activity 2

Task (iii). Internal meeting at CommunicAsian to prepare for interviews

This is a telephone meeting organised by Samantha.

Present: Samantha, Tony, Vivek, Prasad.

Samantha: Good morning all, and thanks for being on time. I don't think this will take very long. Have you all had a chance to review the resumes and cover letters I sent out? And are you all okay with the interview schedule? Good. So today I wanted to plan for the interviews: any **specific questions** or **standard questions** we want to ask, and how we'll conduct them. At least two will have to be by video, so I suggest we do all three that way to **be consistent**.

Vivek: I have Prasad with me as I want him to be doing the interviews **on my behalf**.

Tony: Asthe person will report to you, I think you should do it. I will do it from my side.

Vivek: No, I want Prasad to do it, the person will be working most closely with him anyway, and Prasad knows what I look for – he's been working for me over 2 years.

Samantha: Sure. Given Prasad's role on the project it **makes sense**. Let me just explain why I shortlisted those three. We had 27 applications, but very few had both marketing and analytic experience. Most were business analysts. Vivek and Tony then narrowed it down to five, and I talked to them all, mostly covering **administrative issues**: expected salary, references, notice period and such, and that eliminated two. So these three are worth interviewing, I think. I haven't probed skills and experience, and that's what you guys will do in the interview. All clear? Let's go through them one by one. Peter Lee?

Vivek: If he spends as much time doing proper work as he did in formatting his resume, he would be outstanding.

Tony: Be fair. You only get one chance to make a **first impression**, so that document is crucial.

Vivek: It's **all show and no substance**.

Tony: There's lots of content if you look for it.

Samantha: So what in that content do you want **to probe**?

Vivek: There's lots of words like 'led' and **'spearheaded'**. What was he actually doing, what was the team structure, and let's pin him down to details. And you should get him to spend a few minutes with Dawn to see if his Chinese language is what he claims.

Tony: Maybe we should make it a general question like 'what is your best achievement' to get more detail, so they don't feel they are being **interrogated**.

Samantha: You can't do that. It's in all the interview 'prep notes' circulating on the internet nowadays so all the candidates have a little speech prepared. It's like asking the one about 'where do you see yourself in 5 years' time?'

Tony: The last time I asked that one the woman pointed at me and said 'in your chair'.

Samantha: Okay, so with Peter we want to find out what is the substance **underneath the sizzle**. How about Asmitha?

Vivek: She has worked for some very fine companies in Bangalore.

Tony: She seems very **thin** on marketing and branding experience.

Vivek: Maybe, but she went to a very good college, so she must be bright.

Tony: We need to know more about her customer knowledge. Did she do customer needs or just build to a specification from another department?

Samantha: Okay. More probing here on how much her work has been directly with customers and how much just delivering internally. Finally Rayyan.

Vivek: He seems very **solid**. PMI qualified, a lot of work experience.

Tony: That's what worries me a little. 15 years, and he's applying for an analyst position. And you talked about Peter's resume: Rayyan's resume and covering letter read as if they have been especially tailored to fit the role description. I'm not sure if that's good or bad: he's made an effort, but again, we need to see whether there is substance underneath.

Samantha: I think we can ask him more about his hobbies and interests, since they are on the resume. We can see if they are just there to impress or they're real. Same issue as Peter's language skills.

Tony: Good idea.

Samantha: Okay, so we've got an approach for each candidate. I'll summarise this in an email and send it out today. For the interview itself, I plan to introduce you all and then just listen: you two, Tony and Prasad, will be doing the questions. I'll get Tony to start. Since the technology may not be great, please use names a lot "hi, this is now Prasad' type of thing so the candidates know who they are dealing with, especially if you are coming in with a **supplementary question**.

I've scheduled an hour for each, but it doesn't have to last that long. I'll set up a chat group so we can text between the three of us privately while the interviews are on. Any other concerns or questions for now?

Prasad: None from me.

Vivek: Nor me.

Tony: Nor me. Thanks for organising this, Sam.

Samantha: You are welcome. Bye.

UNIT 6

Activity 2

Section 1 CommunicAsian Interviews

Now listen to the interview snippets in Section 1 and note down what each candidate was asked. Also give your rating out of 10 (1 being poor and 10 being excellent) on how they answered the questions. Use the table at the end of Section 1.

Check you understand the words and expressions in bold.

Section 1- Questions

Samantha (voice over, focus on candidate): What was the biggest problem you faced at work and how did you deal with it Rayyan?

Rayyan Shukor: I think when you are in banking, the biggest problems are always in **compliance**. That's why I make sure my team is always on top of it. I persuaded the Learning and Development Group to develop an e-learning module, and my team has to complete it every year.

Samantha: Did you have a specific problem you dealt with?

Rayyan: There are always problems. Ensuring that processes are kept up to date. **Anti-money laundering,** for example, with a new **blacklisting**. How do I make sure that the team understands and applies it? I manage it.

Samantha (voice over, focus on candidate): What was the biggest problem you faced at work and how did you deal with it Asmitha? *Asmitha Murthy*: Probably when I was running a testing team. We spent three weeks designing a test plan based on the **functional specification** and then discovered the development team had made changes in the actual system. Database layouts, even **field descriptions** were changed. So I put half the team to identify which bits of our plan could still be used and work with that, while the other half rewrote the changes plan. We got it done with only a week's **overrun**.

Samantha: That was a while ago. Have you had problems in your recent projects?

Asmitha: No, fortunately, no.

Samantha (voice over, focus on candidate): What was the biggest problem you faced at work and how did you deal with it Peter?

Peter Lee: Today's problem is always the biggest problem, isn't it? If there weren't any problems they wouldn't need me. The biggest problems are when your perfect plan suddenly gets **derailed**, which happens a lot in our business. My biggest? Probably when I was working on the **publicity launch** for the reopening of the Suez Canal and I had three **VIPs** flying out of London to Cairo to do the speeches. Two days before – airline strike. No way they could get there. What to do? You can't just replace your **guests of honour**. I got a team organized in Egypt to set up **comms links** and big screens, and organized a studio in London so the speeches could be **beamed live** to the event. For the people attending the big screens were probably better than having the speakers there, but I can tell you, I had my **fingers tightly crossed** all the way through. It all worked, though.

Section 2 CommunicAsian Interview Team Discussion: Tony, Samantha, Prasad

Tony: To be honest, Sam, I thought your question about the biggest problem would just get **rehearsed responses**, but actually it worked well.

Samantha: You think so? What did you think, Prasad?

Prasad: I agree. I thought what came across was that Rayyan sees himself as a manager, Asmitha likes a **steady work flow** with no problems, and Peter likes the **drama** of new problems for him to solve at the last minute.

Tony: Yes, that's a good summary, I think. Let's review some of the other responses.

Section 3 CommunicAsian Interviews:

More questions.

Prasad: How much do you use your project management institute (PMI) training in your job?

Rayyan: A lot. The PMI qualification is about planning and tracking projects, and this is **vital** in banking. Banking is probably the industry where planning and tracking is most important, and my team needs to appreciate that. My PMI gives me the **tools to communicate** the needs and plans to the team.

Tony: Rayyan, you left the banking industry to join Forward Outsourcing, but you left after a year. What were the issues there?

Rayyan: I was disappointed. They were a consultancy with most of their clients in the financial service industry, so they hired me for my banking experience. But I found they always wanted solutions in quick time, even if that meant **cutting corners** on analysis. They wanted a plan to roll out a mobile banking app to be done in three months – I thought it should take a year, given the risks.

Prasad: Asmitha, tell us about your lead tracking system and why it was such a success.

Asmitha: This was a company selling outdoor furniture. It had a website and Facebook page, but did not really track visitors or landing pages for people to commit to buy. We **redesigned** the website and built a tracker to **monitor** visits. For **inbound sales**, it takes an average of seven visits before customers buy your product. We also put in automated email and messaging to **prospects** after visit number five with reminder or **discount** offer.

Tony: How involved were you in the content – the discount offers, for example?

Asmitha: I wasn't involved in the detail of the content, but I was, for example, in the **website navigation**. The client was responsible for the messages and offers, but I and my team had the responsibility of making them work and ensuring that system response times were satisfactory.

Tony: How did you deal with last minute changes from the client?

Asmitha: I try and avoid last minute changes as they interrupt progress. Every day, I check messages and emails between 8.30 and 9.30 to see if there is anything urgent for the day, and then I switch them off for the rest of the day. My team and my client know this, so it works well.

Prasad: Peter, tell us about a campaign you have developed and how you measured its success.

Peter: In our company, the account managers like me generally get parts of projects to own. Like the Suez Canal I talked about, I was in charge of **logistics** – there was an account director **overseeing** all the different bits. But I did a branding campaign for a chocolate group that wanted a refresh. I worked with design on **logos** and then launched it with **influencers** on social media – measuring awareness by likes and such. I don't believe you can measure the success of advertising through sales. There are too many other factors: product quality, availability, service, but advertising and branding should be measured by awareness.

Tony: What **brand tag line** or **slogan** do you think is the best you've come across?

Peter: I thought 'Just cut it out' was really good, but my favourite is probably the space travel one, 'The sky's the limit' with the words 'no longer' scrawled in the middle. I thought it **captured** how the company was challenging us on what we thought we knew and opening up new possibility.

Section 4 Interview Panel Discussion and decision: Tony, Samantha, Prasad

Samantha: So how do you feel about our candidates?

Tony: A bit disappointed. None of them said to me 'you must hire me'.

Samantha: Well, we do need to hire somebody quickly for this project, and recruitment decisions are always a bit of **a compromise** between what you ideally want and what is available.

Tony: Yes, that's true, so let's **narrow it down**. I think we can **eliminate** Mr. 'Banking'. I think he sounded like a **perfect bureaucrat** – he wouldn't buy a lottery ticket without reading all the regulations, and even then he would have to get 'his team' to actually carry out the transaction.

Prasad: I agree. We knew he might be a **concern** given that he has worked for fifteen years and is just a team lead. I think he showed us why. I thought Asmitha was pretty **solid** and had **discipline** without being **rigid**.

Tony: You don't think it's rigid to only deal with the world for an hour each morning? Also, she doesn't seem actually to have had any input to creative stuff or market planning.

Prasad: But she delivers smoothly. Employee of the month and all that.

Samantha: Do you think she would **fit in** with the culture here? We tend to **value** flexibility, if something needs doing, whoever's available gets to do it, even if it's not their area.

Prasad: That's a **fair point**. Peter fits that, but I'm not sure if he's a **doer** or just a **talker**. He is certainly a talker.

Tony: I agree, but he also showed he can **think on his feet**, and he clearly doesn't lack confidence. I think he's a risk, but I'd vote to hire him from this bunch.

Prasad: I'll go along with your decision, since we need somebody, but I'd make sure there's a **probationary period** in case he doesn't work out.

Samantha: I agree with both of you. I'll go and brief Dawn.

UNIT 7

Activity 2

Task (i). Audio listening: Internal meeting at CommunicAsian to discuss project changes

Peter: Prasad, I've been going through the marketing data and I'd like to suggest two things. Firstly, we should run the China campaign in Mandarin – China is by far the biggest potential, and second, we should also run the campaign in UK – there're a lot of people from our countries already over there. I think –

Prasad: (interrupts) Hold on. Does this affect time or cost? If it does, we need **to go through** the **Steering Committee**.

Peter: Well we said after the needs analysis we would not do Chinese, but it was in the original proposal. **Dropping it** was a bad idea.

Prasad: OK, but it's not me you have to persuade. Let me message Tony and Melinda to see if they can do a quick conference, and if they agree we'll take it to the full committee.
It's OK, they can both dial in now.
Hi both, I've got Peter with me and he thinks we should change our project plan. I'll let him explain.

Peter: Thanks. I think two things. We need to run the campaign in UK. There are 20,000 Filipinos working in the health service already over there. We'll miss them if we only promote in the Philippines. And a lot of Chinese. . .

Tony: When we looked at this before, we decided that the people already there would also ready have phone plans. Why do you think differently?

Peter: You could be right, but their **current plans** won't include their own country in free minutes. A lot may choose **to switch**.

Melinda: When we looked at doing a full campaign in UK with the different groups and data fees it was going to cost about $10,000. Can you justify that? We'd have to convince GlobeNet.

Peter: It's **tough**. I think it would work, but we can't prove it without making the investment. But if it does work, it would make us almost certain to win the next contract from GlobeNet.

Tony: I **take your point**, but I think I'm going to say no for now. We only told them a few weeks ago that it was not a good idea. We may have got that wrong, but we'll look stupid if we **change our minds** so soon. What was your other thing?

Peter: I think we need to run the China campaign in Mandarin. It's the biggest market: why did we drop it when it was in the proposal?

Prasad: The people who are going to UK will all speak English.

Peter: Yes, but a lot of the **decision makers**, **influencers** don't. Parents and tourists for instance. We want to make sure as many people as possible know about the product. Friends staying in China who want to make sure they **stay in touch**.

Prasad: We have removed it from our project budget.

Tony: I think Peter's got a good point. I think we had about $5,000 in the original proposal for translation and different platforms. And we couldn't ask GlobeNet to change the budget now. Melinda, what's our profit on this project?

Melinda: Assuming no **overruns,** about $6,000.

Tony: Okay, let's look to spend a maximum of $1,000 on Peter's idea to promote in China. Maybe we just need a basic message, no analytics. It can refer them to the English website for details, maybe.

Prasad: I have a friend who might do us a translation. She's here in Singapore.

Tony: Great. Can I ask the three of you to **put your heads together** and **come up with** a plan and a costing – not more than $1,000. I think we can convince Dawn and Vivek with Peter's point about winning the next contract. We show we can **go the extra mile**.

Peter: Thanks for that. **Folks,** can we do the plan by tomorrow so we can get agreement and start to implement? We don't want to add to the delivery time.

Prasad: Fine. If you can stay on the line, Melinda, we'll work out what we need to do, and we'll get back to you, Tony, tomorrow.

Tony: Thanks, and good luck with it.

UNIT 8

Activity 2

Task (iii). Audio: Internal Meeting at CommunicAsian: Project Problems

Dawn is chairing the internal meeting to address the concern about poor reporting from their client GlobeNet.

Present: Dawn, Samantha, Tony (on video in HK), Prasad

Dawn: Let's **get straight to the point**. I'm made to look **incompetent** by our key client because of that report that you sent out and that I have never seen.

Prasad: I had never seen it either.

Dawn: You're the project manager . . . and as discussed, nothing should be going out without your **sign-off**. Tony, this monthly reporting has got to change to reflect evidence and numbers.

Tony: Yes, I do a summary report rather than all the detail in Prasad's reports that clients don't need to know. It's a one-minute status update.

Dawn: Did you ever stop to think that the client may want the detail? Did you think of asking them? Did it ever occur to you to tell Prasad or Sam as the escalation manager? Did you think at all?

Tony: I have always done this with our clients. What they want is just **reassurance**, not something like 'we sent out 103 surveys and had 74 responses with an average of 16 comments' – what are they supposed to do with that?

Dawn: Read Trevor's email. He wants those sorts of things to give him confidence that work is progressing as planned, and he gets that from the numbers. And he says that Celia tried to get you to change it, but you ignored her.

Tony: That's not true. She's never told me to change it. If she asked for more detail I tell her. I thought we got on. And now she complains **over my head** . . .

Samantha: I think it was Trevor who did that, but we're not here to solve problems at GlobeNet; we're solving problems and **getting our own house in order**.

Dawn: So what do we do? And I don't want the answer to be that I have to review everything that goes to a client.

Samantha: Of course not. But I think we need an agreed process and format for internal and external status reports. If Tony is right that most clients prefer the one-minute overview, then let's use that as a basis with more hard numbers, and maybe more detail in the **appendices**. Would that work?

Tony: Only if the numbers are relevant. I don't want stuff like the list of focus groups with the number of minutes from each participant.

Prasad: We use that for **productivity measures**. I need that for budgeting.

Samantha: So how about if you and Tony **put your heads together** after this meeting and decide what numbers we put into the client report. If you cannot agree, involve me and I will decide. When you have the structure, present it to me, and then the three of us can present it to Dawn.

Dawn: Then I have to present it to Trevor . . .

Samantha: No, I'll do that. You're the CEO, not the reporting manager. I'll send the revised version with explanation, and Tony can do that face to face with Celia when he is in Hong Kong next week.

Dawn: Right. I want this done before we finish for the day. And I don't want another email like this one ever again.

Tony: Understood.

Dawn: One more thing while we're here. Melinda said something about an extra **cost overrun** because we are adding Thailand to our set of countries. I wasn't at the Project Board meeting, but she said the cost overrun was presented and then **withdrawn**. What's going on? [silence.] Prasad, you're the project manager, what's going on? I thought we were adding Thailand with no extra cost.

Prasad: It was a mistake. I said it would not be extra cost because I thought it was Taiwan . . . so Chinese, and we already have that covered with our mainland China work. Tony must have known it was another language, and he didn't **pick up on it**.

Tony: I don't do your budgets. I assumed it was no extra cost because once you had done Chinese you could do everything else with some translate program. When I asked if we could add Thailand I was expecting you to come back and say what extra time and cost might be needed, so when you said none, I was delighted and went to tell the client the good news.

Dawn: So now they are expecting it and it will **cost us a fortune**. We can't go back to them and say we got it wrong, not after today's email.

Prasad: Tony, could we do a **cut-down version** like we do for China where we have the language just for the message and all the detail in English? That could cut down the cost.

Tony: I think so. Let me go back through the notes from the Thai analysis and I'll confirm back to you after that.

Dawn: Right, but **priority** today is the reporting. It seems to me that you people don't spend enough time talking to each other. We shouldn't have to have **emergency** meetings to resolve every issue.

Samantha: Yes, I'm sorry, Dawn. With all the work we've rather **neglected** learning and development, but I found a great workshop on 'Building Collaborative Teams' – I'll plan to roll it out.

Dawn: Good. It would make me very happy if today was our last crisis meeting.

UNIT 9

Activity 2

Task (i). Audio of active listening on Prasad's performance on the project.

This is a face-to-face meeting organised by Samantha.

Samantha: Hi Prasad, do sit down. As I said in my invitation, I want to meet with the key people in the project team to discuss how we have done and what we have learned, so you're the first. I don't think it should take long, but I've booked this room for an hour, so we have as much time as you want. Is that okay with you?

Prasad: Fine.

Samantha: So I don't want to talk about the project itself, we do that enough at the board meetings. I want to focus on how it has been for you: what has worked well and what not so well. It must have been hard being away from home and here in Singapore for so long.

Prasad: Oh, no, I've really enjoyed that.

Samantha: Don't you miss your home?

Prasad: Not really. I share the flat in Bangalore with three other engineers. My family is in Kerala, so I don't see them a lot. I've loved being here having a place of my own.

Samantha: I was talking with Dawn about the project and she commented that you do a great job when things are going well, but maybe you **struggle a bit** when there are things going wrong. Do you think she's right?

Prasad: What do you mean? When have I struggled?

Samantha: Well, you were very **unresponsive** over the Thailand problem, and you missed the management board meeting –

Prasad: (interrupts) I was sick.

Samantha: No-one's **doubting** you. But sometimes **stress or pressure** can make us ill. Did you feel lot of stress?

Prasad: Maybe some. But I was sick. My stomach, my head.

Samantha: That's okay, we're not doubting you. Do you feel more stressed without Vivek to talk to about issues?

Prasad: No, Vivek calls me every day, twice a day sometimes. He calls it my 'daily board report'.

Samantha: I didn't know that. I don't think he told Dawn, and he certainly didn't tell me.

Prasad: He said it was **just between ourselves**. He said that since he recommended me to lead the project, he needed to **keep a close eye on me**, because any mistake by me would reflect badly on him.

Samantha: You say it was like a daily board report. Tell me about it; what did you discuss?

Prasad: It wasn't much discussion. I report progress and any decisions or ideas we've had in the team, and he tells me if it's okay or I need to do something different.

Samantha: And this is every day?

Prasad: Yes.

Samantha: So did you call him on the day you talked to Melinda about the extra costs due to the Thailand misunderstanding?

Prasad: Yes.

Samantha: So Vivek knew about it before the board meeting? Knew about the extra cost overrun?

Prasad: Yes. He told me he would deal with it at the meeting. I said I probably would not attend because I was feeling so bad, and he said he would see that I wouldn't **get the blame**. Melinda was in charge of finances.

Samantha: Oh, Prasad, how did you feel about that?

Prasad: I felt bad. I felt bad about Melinda, but what could I do? Vivek is my boss.

Samantha: Okay, Prasad, here's what I suggest. Since the project is **near completion**, we keep this discussion between ourselves, but I will change the **reporting line** today so that you report to me directly. I will send out an announcement. And your daily calls with Vivek stop now. Vivek will probably realise why I've done it, but he can't say anything without being **exposed**. What do you think?

Prasad: Thank you, thank you, that would be great.

Samantha: It sounds like you're **relieved**.

Prasad: Yes. I thought I was doing a good job as team leader, and I wanted to **be upfront** with the Thailand mistake, but. . .

Samantha: So, for the rest of the project you need to lead 100 percent. It's your project, your success, your failure. Okay?

Prasad: Yes, Samantha. Thank you, I won't **let you down**.

UNIT 10

Activity 2

Task (i). Audio listening: Meeting to prepare for client presentation

Prasad and Peter are in the boardroom.

Prasad: Tony's just texted. He'll be another ten minutes. Traffic is pretty heavy from the airport.

Peter: Okay. I've done a few slides for the client presentation. Do you want to have a look at them while we are waiting?

Prasad: No, Tony said he doesn't want a slide presentation yet. He wants more of a discussion. He says that if you do the slides before you've really worked out what your story is, you get **trapped** into a way of thinking too early.

Peter: Well I think my slides are pretty good. I'll **try them out** on Tony anyway. I've got some good statistics. Adding Thailand and Taiwan cost us a bit but didn't cost the client, and Thailand's student numbers are very strong, almost as much as Hong Kong. Surprisingly, they really like having access to Laos as well as Thailand. Philippines, we've had over 10,000 **expressions of interest** and over 2,000 registrations – the best response so far. And China is almost exactly on forecast.

Prasad: How about the pricing?

Peter: The early sign-ups are above budget. We're hoping that **holds up** as the volumes increase. Let me show you.

Prasad: Sorry, no time. Tony's just texted to say he's here.

Tony: Hi guys, sorry I'm late. Let me just **grab a cup of coffee** and we can start. Prasad, why don't you just **run me through** what in your view have been the **highs and lows**, the **milestones** and decisions in this project.

Prasad: For me, Thailand, but I'm not sure if that's a high or a low.

Tony: That's right. It depends on the story you want to present to the client. Maybe it was poor project management because we expanded the scope without proper control, but on the other hand maybe it was demonstrating our **flexibility** and commitment to get the best result. Both of these fit the 'facts', but which way do we explain it to the client?

Peter: Well, a definite low was the trouble with Rory.

Tony: Not necessarily. When we started off, we needed to focus on the message and creative thinking, and that was Rory's strength. As the project moved on, we needed to **integrate** the message with the measures, and that's where you came in, Peter. We get the **right team at the right time**.

Prasad: But isn't that a bit dishonest?

Tony: Not at all. You don't hide the facts but you focus on how we responded to the facts, used them as opportunities to do things better. Take another problem, Vivek's **outburst** to Melinda at the meeting you missed. How would you present that as positive?

Prasad: Um, well they say that what doesn't kill you makes you stronger. I think that both Melinda and me are better managers after that.

Tony: Right. So, if you were presenting it, you wouldn't say the **specifics** of what happened, but you might say that we have a **robust** management committee process that ensures that our leaders are challenged and have to learn to defend their ideas and decisions, making for a better outcome. You get the idea?

Peter: That's good. So what we should do is to go back over the history of the project and see how different things contributed. Is that right?

Tony: Maybe, but that could get a bit **repetitive**. How about if we start off with the results and then identify three or four things that most contribute. Remember, a presentation is really **a sales exercise**. What we are trying to do is **showcase** that we have done a good job, and show that we've done it because we are different from other agencies. We don't want to tell the client that we are better, but we do want them to make that conclusion on their own.

Prasad: I've never thought about it that way.

Tony: Good. Peter, think about it this evening and tomorrow we'll finalise a plan outline and flow, and then we'll think about slides. You might want to 'storyboard' the presentation to get the message and flow right. . . . If we aim at a twenty minute presentation that will give us about five minutes on results, and three or four key points. Agreed?

APPENDIX 3

Reading list

The following list of references may be of interest to teachers and students alike as they provide the linguistic and pedagogical frameworks drawn on for this coursebook as well as outcomes of research that impact the teaching of business English.

Relevant ones are cited at the end of each of the units.

Beamer, L. (1994) Teaching English business writing to Chinese-speaking business students. *The Bulletin of the Association of Business Communication*, 57(1), 12–18.

Bremner, S. (2008) Intertextuality and business communication text books: Why students need more textual support. *English for Specific Purposes*, 27(3), 306–321.

Bremner, S. (2010) Collaborative writing: Bridging the gap between the textbook and the workplace. *English for Specific Purposes*, 29(2), 121–132.

Choy, W.K.W. (2007) Globalisation and workforce diversity: HRM implications for multinational corporations in Singapore. *Singapore Management Review*.

Groysberg, B., Lee, J., Price, J. & Cheng, J. Y.-J. (2018) The leader's guide to corporate culture. *Harvard Business Review*. January–February.

Halliday, M.A.K. & Matthiessen, C. (2014) *Halliday's Introduction to Functional Grammar* (4th edition). Hodder Education, UK.

Kameda, N. (2009) *Contrastive rhetoric in business writing across cultures.* 8th ABC Asia Pacific Conference at Nanyang Business School, Nanyang Technological University. March 2008.

Kankaanranta, A. & Louhaila Salminen, L. (2010) 'English? Oh it's just work' – A study of BELF user's perceptions. *English for Specific Purposes*, 29(3), 204–209.

Koester, A. (2006) *Investigating Workplace Discourse.* Chapter 6: Negotiating consensus and conflict in workplace talk. Taylor & Francis.

Lacity, M. & Willcocks, L. (2017) Conflict resolution in business services outsourcing relationships. *The Journal of Strategic Information Systems*, 26(2), 80–100.

Lockwood, J. (2013) International communication in a technology services call centre in India. *World Englishes*, 32(4), 586–600.

Lockwood, J. (2015) Virtual team management: What is causing communication breakdown? *Language and Intercultural Communication*, 15(1), 125–140.

Lockwood, J. (2016) An analysis of web chat exchange in an outsourced service account in the Philippines. *English for Specific Purposes*, 47(July), 26–39.

Lockwood, J. & Forey, G. (2016) Discursive control and power in virtual meetings. *Discourse and Communication*, 10(4).

Lockwood, J. & Song, F. (2016) Understanding each other. Strategies for accommodation in a virtual business project based in China. *Journal of Business Communication*. https://doi.org/10.1177/2329488416675841

Lockwood, J. (2019) What do we mean by workplace English? A syllabus framework for course design and assessment. Chapter 2. In Hyland, K. & Wong, L. (eds) *Specialised English: New Directions in ESP and EAP Research and Practice*. Routledge.

Mayer, J. (2019) Managing culturally diverse teams. Applied Information Management Program. University of Oregon. USA.

Peirson-Smith, A., Bhatia, V.J., Bremner, S. & Jones, R. (2010) Creative English and public relations in Hong Kong. *World Englishes*, 29(4), 523–535.

Pullen, P. & Prokopi, E. (2016) Leading virtual teams: Dos and don'ts. Presented at PMI® *Global Congress 2016 – EMEA* Barcelona, Spain. Newtown Square, PA: Project Management Institute.

Rose, D.& Martin, J.R. (2012) *Learning to Write, Reading to Learn: Genre, Knowledge and Pedagogy in the Sydney School*. Sheffield: Equinox.

Ruiz-Garrido, M.F. (2011) Complaining in the business world: Complaint and adjustment emails. Chapter 5. In Perez-Llantada, C. & Watson, M. (eds) *Specialised Languages in the Global Village – A Multi-Perspective Approach*. Cambridge Scholars Publishing, UK.Salem, Ashraf Atta M.S. (2009) A sage on the stage, to express and impress: TED talks for improving oral presentation skills, vocabulary retention and its impact on reducing speaking anxiety in ESP settings. *English Language Teaching*, 12(6), 146–160.

Sheldon, P., Kim, S., Li, Y. & Warner, M. (2010) *China's Changing Workplace*. Routledge.

Wong, I.F.H. & Phooi-Ching, L. (2000) Chinese cultural values and performance at job interviews: A Singapore perspective. *Business Communication Quarterly*, 63(1), 9–22.

Zhang, Z. (2007) Towards an integrated approach to teaching business English: A Chinese experience. *English for Specific Purposes*, 26(4), 199–210.

www.ingramcontent.com/pod-product-compliance
Lightning Source LLC
LaVergne TN
LVHW080807011026
849160LV00015B/1562
9780367356538